D0583691

Critical Essays on

THE ADVENTURES OF TOM SAWYER

CRITICAL ESSAYS
ON
AMERICAN LITERATURE

James Nagel, General Editor
University of Georgia, Athens

Critical Essays on

THE ADVENTURES OF TOM SAWYER

edited by

GARY SCHARNHORST

G. K. Hall & Co. / New York
Maxwell Macmillan Canada / Toronto
Maxwell Macmillan International / New York Oxford Singapore Sydney

G. K. Hall & Company
Macmillan Publishing Company
866 Third Avenue
New York, New York 10022

Maxwell Macmillan Canada, Inc.
1200 Eglinton Avenue East
Suite 200
Don Mills, Ontario M3C 3N1

Library of Congress Cataloging-in-Publication Data

Critical essays on the adventures of Tom Sawyer / edited by Gary
    Scharnhorst.
        p.   cm. — (Critical essays on American literature)
    Includes bibliographical references and index.
    ISBN 0-8161-7320-6
    1. Twain, Mark, 1835–1910.   Adventures of Tom Sawyer.
I. Scharnhorst, Gary.   II. Series.
PS1306.C74   1993   92-43993
813'.4—dc20   CIP

The paper used in this publication meets the minimum requirements of American National Standard for Information Sciences—Permanence of Paper for Printed Library Materials. ANSI Z3948-1984.⊗™

10   9   8   7   6   5   4   3   2   1

Printed in the United States of America

To my father,
whose acts of courage never made the papers.

Contents

◆

General Editor's Note

♦

This series seeks to anthologize the most important criticism on a wide variety of topics and writers in American literature. Our readers will find in various volumes not only a generous selection of reprinted articles and reviews but original essays, bibliographies, manuscript sections, and other materials brought to public attention for the first time. This volume, *Critical Essays on The Adventures of Tom Sawyer*, is the most comprehensive collection of essays ever published on Mark Twain's celebrated novel. It contains both a sizable gathering of early reviews and a broad selection of more modern scholarship as well. Among the authors of reprinted articles and reviews are William Dean Howells, Hamlin Hill, Judith Fetterley, Henry Nash Smith, and Cynthia Griffin Wolff. There is also a substantial introduction by Gary Scharnhorst, Professor of English at the University of New Mexico. We are confident that this book will make a permanent and significant contribution to the study of American literature, and we are delighted to have it as part of the *Critical Essays on American Literature* series.

JAMES NAGEL

University of Georgia, Athens

Publisher's Note

◆

Producing a volume that contains both newly commissioned and reprinted material presents the publisher with the challenge of balancing the desire to achieve stylistic consistency with the need to preserve the integrity of works first published elsewhere. In the Critical Essays series, essays commissioned especially for a particular volume are edited to be consistent with G. K. Hall's house style; reprinted essays appear in the style in which they were first published, with only typographical errors corrected. Consequently, shifts in style from one essay to another are the result of our efforts to be faithful to each text as it was originally published.

Introduction

GARY SCHARNHORST

Tom Sawyer . . . isn't your property any more. He belongs to us.
                                    —Rudyard Kipling to Mark Twain[1]

Tom Sawyer is surely unique among all characters in American fiction. His portrait, by Norman Rockwell, has graced a postage stamp. The guardian angel in Frank Capra's *It's a Wonderful Life* reads the story of his adventures. Walt Disney even named an island after him. Only in recent decades, however, has he seemed to epitomize a popular-mythic type, the Good Bad Boy of bucolic small-town America. In fact, *The Adventures of Tom Sawyer* appeared in 1876 to mixed reviews, earned Mark Twain almost no money, and over the years has enjoyed a decidedly checkered critical reception.

The problems originated in the very manner of its publication. Twain placed the manuscript of his novel with the American Publishing Company, a subscription firm in Hartford, soon after completing it in July 1875. "Give me a hint when it's to be out and I'll start the sheep jumping in the right places," his friend William Dean Howells promised in late November.[2] After some minor revisions, the book was typeset early in 1876 and Howells, the editor of the *Atlantic Monthly*, received a set of galley proofs on 20 March (*Twain–Howells*, I, 127). Twain urged Elisha Bliss, the company president, to issue the novel in time to tap "the early spring market," to "do your canvassing" and publish it no later than "the middle of May."[3] As good as his word, Howells puffed the book in the May number of his magazine. But its formal publication, apparently complicated in part by Twain's reservations about the size of the illustrations, would be delayed for over half a year. According to the *Boston Transcript* in late April 1876, it had been "withheld by the Hartford publishers" so that "it may be issued simultaneously in England and America."[4] Yet in late June, even after the book had appeared in England, the *Transcript* reported that *Tom Sawyer* would probably not "be published here for some months."[5] Privately, Charles Dudley Warner blamed

1

Elisha Bliss: "In a flush time Bliss is more difficult to open than an Egyptian tomb," he complained. Like two of Bliss's other forthcoming books—Warner's own *Moslems and Mummies* and Bret Harte's *Gabriel Conroy*—"Mark's Tom Sawyer is also waiting for the fall rise. I fear we shall none of us get rich out of it."[6]

Meanwhile, Mark Twain had asked Moncure Conway, an American minister residing in London, to arrange for the English publication of the novel. "Mark Twain has written a remarkable book called 'Tom Sawyer,' " Conway wrote his wife during a visit to Hartford in January 1876 (*Publishers*, 93n.). After several weeks of negotiations, Twain accepted an offer from Chatto & Windus to issue the novel and pay him a standard royalty. Thus the English edition of *Tom Sawyer*—or the "cheap edition," as the author derisively called it—appeared without illustrations in early June (*Publishers*, 102). Much as Howells had started the sheep jumping, albeit several months prematurely, with his plug in the *Atlantic*, Conway wrote one of the first English reviews of the novel for the London *Examiner*. This notice was followed by no less than ten additional English reviews, all of them appreciative if not glowing, in such magazines and newspapers as the *Athenaeum*, *Spectator*, *Illustrated London News*, *British Quarterly Review*, and the *Pall Mall Gazette*. The *Athenaeum* review, in particular, was sometimes cited with approval back in the States.[7]

As a regular columnist for the Cincinnati *Commercial*, Conway also devoted an entire "London Letter" to the novel. Like Howells, he touted *Tom Sawyer* without reservation or apology in this piece, printed in the *Commercial* for 26 June. Unlike Howells's review in the *Atlantic*, however, Conway's two notices included several long excerpts from the novel—the episodes about whitewashing the fence in chapter 2 and Tom and the pinchbug in chapter 5, the descriptions of Huckleberry Finn in chapter 6 and the death of Injun Joe in chapter 33. These four passages were, in fact, the first parts of the novel to appear in America, and as a result they were widely copied throughout July and August in such papers as the Philadelphia *Sunday Republic*,[8] New York *Evening Post*,[9] *Boston Transcript*, *Springfield Republican*, *Portland Transcript* and *Daily Argus*, *Cincinnati Daily Enquirer*, San Francisco *Call* and *Bulletin*, and *Hartford Courant*.[10] Conway even found one of the excerpts from the novel in a Paris paper,[11] and most or all of his "London Letter" was reprinted in the St. Louis *Globe-Democrat*, *Chicago Tribune*, and *Hartford Times*.[12] Twain, who was puzzled by the source of the extracts until he saw Conway's essay in the Hartford paper, soon expressed his gratitude for the "shrewdness" of his agent's plan (Welland, 103).[13]

Ironically, all of this advance publicity for the American edition of the novel—months in advance, as it were—served mostly to promote the sale of a pirated Canadian edition. "Belford Bros., Canadian thieves, are flooding America with a cheap pirated edition of Tom Sawyer," Twain groused to

Conway in early November. "We cannot issue for 6 weeks yet, and by that time Belford will have sold 100,000 over the frontier and killed my book dead" (*Publishers*, 105–106). Though the novel had been copyrighted in both England and the United States, the author had no legal recourse in the absence of international copyright. On 13 December, five days after Bliss finally received the first hundred copies of the American edition from the printer, Twain confirmed the worst in a letter to Conway: "Belford has taken the profits all out of 'Tom Sawyer.' . . . [The Canadian edition] has actually taken the market away from us in every village in the Union" (*Publishers*, 106–107). As a result, as Hamlin Hill has concluded, *Tom Sawyer* "was the least successful of all Twain's first six major books." Though Bliss would claim that he had sold some thirty thousand copies by March 1877, in fact he had sold only about thirteen thousand (Hill, 120).[14] Not only did the pirates steal his property, moreover, Twain was ridiculed for ostensibly profiting from the scheme. The reviewer of the American edition for the New York *World* added insult to injury: "If 'Mark' had not proved himself unpatriotic enough to sell his wares first to a 'Kanuck,' " he sniffed, "we should possibly have dwelt longer upon this book."[15]

The review in the *World* is symptomatic of the restrained welcome *Tom Sawyer* was given by several American magazines and newspapers when Bliss finally issued it. Because it was a subscription book, the novel was easily ignored. (Though John C. Gerber has claimed that the "appearance of the American edition of *Tom Sawyer* went almost unnoticed,"[16] the first section of the present volume reprints more than twice the total number of notices it hitherto is known to have received.) More to the point, the American critics who chose to review it paid more grudging respect to the book than had their English counterparts. Indeed, some of their reservations anticipate the charge of blood-and-thunder sensationalism leveled against *The Adventures of Huckleberry Finn* nine years later. "We should have liked *Tom Sawyer* better," opined the *New York Times*, with less "of Injun Joe and 'revenge,' and 'slitting women's ears,' and the shadow of the gallows."[17] The New York *Evening Post* echoed the complaint: "Certainly it will be in the last degree unsafe to put the book into the hands of imitative youth."[18] Though virtually all of the Connecticut and California papers that deigned to notice the novel warmly praised it, the critic for the Hartford *Christian Secretary* allowed he "almost wish[ed]" Tom's "grave faults"—that is, that he "lies and smokes"—"had been omitted" from the story.[19] Like *Huck Finn*, *Tom Sawyer* was sometimes attacked by the custodians of culture—by public librarians especially—though in the end it was defended as a lesser evil than the wildcat literature of Oliver Optic, Horatio Alger, and Harry Castlemon.[20] Even in 1913, William J. Long disparaged the "dime-novel sensationalism" of the novel, with its emphasis on "the lawless, barbarous side of boy-life";[21] and as late as 1940, Robert M. Gay opined in the venerable *Atlantic* that both

Tom Sawyer and *Huck Finn* "were far too rowdy for nice little boys and girls."[22] The former novel, like the latter, earned its popularity, it seems, over the objections of genteel reviewers.

And popular it became, at least among juvenile readers. New printings of *Tom Sawyer*, marketed as a book for boys, were issued every two or three years during the 1880s and 1890s. Theodore Dreiser remembered that *Tom Sawyer* was one of the few American books he had liked as a Hoosier school-boy,[23] and Owen Wister thought it was a "better portrait" of its era "than any history."[24] H. L. Mencken was shocked to learn later that James Thurber had never "got around to reading it all the way through."[25] Published in German, French, Swedish, and Danish versions within months of its first publication, it has been translated to date into at least thirty-three languages—more than *Huck Finn* (Norton, 94). In Germany alone it sold an estimated 240,000 copies between 1876 and 1937.[26] Twain considered a dramatic adaptation of the novel as early as 1874, approached Howells about working on a play based on the story in 1875, and actually completed a four-act version of it, since published, in 1884 (*Twain–Howells*, I, 95).[27] The next year, he sold "the right to dramatize & play Tom Sawyer on a royalty" (*Twain–Howells*, 520–21), and over the years more than a dozen dramatic versions of the story have been published, most of them for children. To be sure, none succeeded on stage because, as Twain explained in 1887, *Tom Sawyer* was a book "which cannot be dramatized. One might as well try to dramatize any other hymn. Tom Sawyer is simply a hymn, put into prose form to give it a worldly air."[28] In 1892, a San Francisco barkeeper caused a stir with a bizarre claim that he was the model for the hero and that the novel simply recorded boyhood adventures he had recounted to Twain in the 1860s.[29] "That story lacks a good deal in the way of facts," Twain told an interviewer who asked about the report three years later.[30]

Such impostures notwithstanding, *Tom Sawyer* was, in a sense, the victim of its own success. The novel seemed to two generations of readers to be little more than a minor classic for juveniles. Yet Twain had insisted in 1875, after finishing the manuscript, that it was "*not* a boy's book, at all. It will only be read by adults. It is only written for adults" (*Twain–Howells*, I, 91). For better or worse, however, Howells persuaded Twain to "treat it explicitly *as* a boy's story. Grown-ups will enjoy it just as much if you do" (*Twain–Howells*, I, 110–11). As a result, the author averred in his preface that "my book is intended mainly for the entertainment of boys and girls," though he hoped it would "not be shunned by men and women on that account."[31] Such a disclaimer was in reality a marketing gambit, not an authorial statement of purpose: Twain readily agreed to permit Conway to "leave out the preface" from the English edition "or alter it so that it will not profess to be a book for youth," for example (*Publishers*, 97). Nevertheless, the author's comment in the preface has both conditioned the audience response to the novel and, as Robert Tracy notes, "frightened off critics far more effectively than the *No Trespassing* sign posted in front of *Huckleberry Finn*."[32] William Lyon Phelps suggested in 1907 that "nearly all healthy boys enjoy reading *Tom Sawyer*, because the intrinsic interest of the story is so great, and the various adventures of the hero are portrayed with such gusto."[33] Though it has never lapsed from print, the novel received almost no critical (that is, adult) attention before its copyright expired in the early 1930s. Yet even at the nadir of Twain's reputation in the 1920s, *Tom Sawyer* continued to command a juvenile audience. Percy Boynton declared in 1920 that it "represents [Twain's] fresh and definite contribution to fiction for boys and girls,"[34] and Bertha Evans Ward described it in 1931 as "the foremost American story of boy life."[35] Two members of the Teachers' College at Columbia University even prepared a classroom edition of the novel, complete with suggestions for student activities ("study map of Missouri") and a list of discussion topics, in 1932. "To the great majority of boys and girls of junior high school age Tom Sawyer and his friends need no introduction," they asserted, and in "communities and classrooms where they are not known it is the fault of the grown-ups."[36] In 1950, no less a luminary than T. S. Eliot declared that *"Tom Sawyer* seems to me a boy's book," admittedly "a very good one."[37]

The culture-myth that has accreted around the character of Tom is, in fact, largely a product of the middle third of the twentieth century. The novel was adapted to film twice during the 1930s, implicit testimony to the appeal of its pre-industrial pieties, as seen through the soft lens of Hollywood, at the height of the Great Depression. The 1938 *Tom Sawyer*, produced by David O. Selznick, was virtually a rehearsal for *Gone With the Wind*, released by Selznick's studio the following year. Both movies were filmed in Technicolor; both valorized the antebellum South; and the roles of Tom and Becky were cast only after a nationwide talent hunt, much as Vivien Leigh was selected to play Scarlett O'Hara after a well-publicized search. The 1938 adaptation of Twain's novel, with its prettified tableaux and sentimentalized plot, was extremely nostalgic. In his review of the movie for the *New York Times*, similarly, Bosley Crowther allowed that *Tom Sawyer* had "entered so deep into the world's heart" that it was "proof not only against time but against Technicolor."[38]

Such prominent American artists as N. C. Wyeth and Norman Rockwell also illustrated editions of the novel during the 1930s, at the height of its popularity. Wyeth drew the obligatory whitewashing scene for the dust jacket of the 1931 Winston edition (which also featured an introduction by Christopher Morley), and Rockwell prepared eight full-page color illustrations and several dozen black-and-white sketches for a special Heritage Press edition of the novel issued in 1936. Significantly, Rockwell's first three color illustrations for this volume depict the very scenes that Moncure Conway had excerpted to promote the book sixty years before—Tom and Ben Rogers at the whitewashed fence, Tom and the pinch-bug in church, Huck Finn swinging a dead cat. The depiction of Tom and Ben at the fence, published as the frontispiece to the edition, was reproduced on a first-class postage stamp in 1972 in formal recognition of the novel's importance as cultural icon. Another of Rockwell's pictures, in which Aunt Polly administers the spoonful of "Pain-Killer" to Tom, appeared on the cover of the *Saturday Evening Post* in May 1936. In effect, as Allison R. Ensor explains, Rockwell "smoothed over the harsher, darker pages of the novel" with his "humorous and light hearted" paintings. He assiduously avoided "anything frightening or horrible" mentioned in the novel, particularly the character of Injun Joe, who nowhere appears in these color illustrations. "With the exception of Tom and Becky in the cave," Ensor concludes, "the terrifying, frightening experiences of the novel are all left out, just as they have disappeared from the memories of many Americans, who recall from the book only a playful summer's day outing on Cardiff Hill."[39] The artist's success in appropriating only the pleasant scenes in the story is implicit in the advertised claim of his publishers: "After you have looked upon Norman Rockwell's illustrations for *Tom Sawyer*, you will never again think of Mark Twain's book without thinking of these illustrations" (quoted in Ensor, 36). Rockwell's original paintings are now on permanent display in the Mark Twain Museum in Hannibal.

This nostalgic reinvention of the novel, often for crass commercial purposes, is no less evident in more recent years. The angel in *It's a Wonderful Life* (1946) not only carries a copy of the novel on his heavenly mission, he passes it, like a talisman, to the born-again hero in the final scene. In 1947, a "cheap and vulgar" dramatization of the story was broadcast on radio.[40] That same year, Frank Luther Mott estimated total sales of the novel at two million or more, most of them after door-to-door canvassing was abandoned by its publishers in 1904. It had become by mid-century by far the most popular of all Mark Twain's books.[41] The cultural (mis)appropriation of its iconography climaxed in 1955, when Disneyland first opened its gates. In the ersatz-West of Frontierland, a steamboat named the "Mark Twain" forever sails like a captive soul in Dante's hell around "Tom Sawyer Island." Passengers are ferried across the lake on motor-powered rafts named the "Injun Joe," "Becky Thatcher," and "Tom Sawyer" to this impeccably land-scaped islet, which features trash cans disguised as tree stumps and an "Injun Joe Cave" wired with the sound of howling wind. The novel, or more properly the culture-text distilled from it, has become so valuable a commercial property in recent years it has inspired a television cartoon series; a musical film produced by *Reader's Digest* and starring Johnny Whitaker, Jodie Foster, Celeste Holm, and Warren Oates; at least three teleplays, one of them starring Buddy Ebsen and Jane Wyatt; and a low-budget movie for teenagers that purports to modernize the story by setting it in southern California in 1978. ("Tom and Fin spend most of their time checking out the babes on the beach, coping with a cocky young lifeguard and planning for the end-of-summer surfing competition," *Variety* reported. "Onscreen drug use is limited to a comic-relief sequence in which Tom and Fin get high on Aunt Sunny's marijuana."[42] So much for Aunt Polly's patent medicines.)

Not surprisingly, the fair citizens of Hannibal have also tried to cash in on the notoriety of their favorite son, albeit with mixed success. The former McDowell's or McDougal's cave, where Tom and Becky were ostensibly lost, has been designated a United States Natural Landmark and reopened under the name "Mark Twain Cave." The brochure for this tourist trap "one mile south on Hwy. 79" shamelessly touts its appeal: "You will have the same exciting experience exploring this remarkable cave as Tom Sawyer and Becky Thatcher did many years ago." Lest someone actually remember how exciting such an experience might be, the brochure then reassures the visitor: "An experienced guide will escort you on the 55-minute circular tour." As recently as 1985, the rapacious promoters of the Mark Twain Sesquicentennial in Hannibal laid plans for a "Good Golly Aunt Polly" stage show, a play about "the cantankerous Becky Thatcher in her golden years," and a theme park with fast-food restaurants to be called "Tom's Ship Shop" and "Judge Thatcher's Barbecue." "We've got something to sell," explained one local planner. "We're talking jobs and total area economic development."[43] Mercifully, most of these plans fell through.

The evolution of Tom and the other characters in the novel—excepting only the vagabond Huck, significantly enough—into vehicles for mass-merchandizing has predictably inspired a sort of scholarly backlash, a demythologizing of the text. In the 1930s and 1940s, even as *Tom Sawyer* was reinvented in American popular culture, Walter Blair and Bernard De Voto were laying the groundwork for modern scholarly criticism of the novel. In his *Native American Humor* (1937), Blair traced some of the sources for Aunt Polly and Tom to Twain's life and reading, particularly to such literary antecedents as Ruth and Ike Partington in B. P. Shillaber's *The Life and Savings of Mrs. Partington* and Tom Bailey in T. B. Aldrich's *The Story of a Bad Boy*; and in his essay "On the Structure of *Tom Sawyer*" (1939) he corrected the prevailing notion that, as a boy-idyll, the story was but a random collection of anecdotes without clear order or coherence. Rather, according to Blair, Mark Twain travestied in the novel the traditional—that is, didactic—juvenile formula by writing a more realistic or "normal history of boyhood" and maturation.[44] So thorough was his analysis that Blair excerpted this essay in his book *Mark Twain & Huck Finn* over twenty years later. Meanwhile, in *Mark Twain at Work* (1942), De Voto broadly sketched the composition history of the novel and published for the first time the early "Boy's Manuscript," which, he argued, contained the germ of the later novel in the childish love affair of its hero.[45]

For the most part, however, *Tom Sawyer* was predictably scorned by scholars in the 1940s and 1950s, the heyday of the New Criticism, for whom it seemed to represent all that was wrong about American fiction. DeLancey

Ferguson maintained in 1943 that, with such superfluous ancillary characters as Alfred Temple and Cousin Mary, its episodic plot, and its notoriously loose construction, the text "violated every rule, past, present or future, of the 'art novel,' " that it quite simply "was not art at all."[46] Similarly, Gladys Bellamy allowed in 1950 that the tale was "melodramatic" and "inartistic in its minor effects,"[47] and Roger Asselineau carped in 1954 that the novel was "desultorily composed."[48] George P. Elliott, in the 1959 afterword to the most popular modern paperback edition of the story, insisted rather presumptuously that Mark Twain "was not serious in this book," that "there is no plot, there are no real themes," that "not even the author's style is completely consistent." Only if the reader "doesn't ask too much of it," according to Elliott, does the book "hold together."[49]

Such claims seemed exaggerated to a number of scholars who rallied to Mark Twain's defense in the late 1950s and 1960s. In "The Composition and Structure of *The Adventures of Tom Sawyer*" (1961), Hamlin Hill, Blair's former student at the University of Chicago, examined the manuscript of the novel in painstaking detail in order to prove that Twain carefully executed his "intention of showing Tom's maturation" by revising and reordering episodes as he wrote it. The manuscript "provides convincing evidence to corroborate Blair's interpretation of the book," Hill concluded.[50] Other defenders of the novel, including Louis Rubin, Jr., Leslie Fiedler, and Albert E. Stone, Jr., analyzed the novel from an interdisciplinary or American Studies perspective. Rubin considered *Tom Sawyer* a quintessentially American success story, for example;[51] Fiedler argued the novel was an "alternative" or polite version of the story Mark Twain would retell in *Huck Finn*;[52] and Stone averred that in it Twain weighed "the relation of the individual to the community, to social class, and to money."[53]

This contextual approach, eschewing the nice distinctions of academic formalism, dominated the discussion of the novel throughout the 1960s and 1970s. In the section of *Mark Twain: The Development of a Writer* (1962) that he devoted to *Tom Sawyer*, Henry Nash Smith pondered its theme of the "natural man beleaguered by society." Like Fiedler, Smith considered the novel something of a dress rehearsal for *Huck Finn*, one of several early attempts at embodying "vernacular values" in his fiction. If it is not quite a failure, it nevertheless betrays the slips and false starts of a literary apprentice whose "attitudes toward his material" were more often than not uncertain and confused. In the most superficial sense, Tom appears to rebel against social strictures and such repressive institutions as school and church, yet after each of his adventures he rejoins the flawed community of St. Petersburg. Though Twain paid lip service to the values of freedom and individuality, the novel as a whole celebrates conformity and bourgeois respectability. Lacking "a basic conflict between Tom and the society of the village," Twain evaded the contradiction at the crux of the novel and invoked the specter of evil incarnate in Injun Joe simply to sustain the story. He "would ultimately need a hero more hostile toward the dominant culture than Tom Sawyer was," Smith allowed.[54]

In the sixth chapter of his *Mark Twain: The Fate of Humor* (1966), James M. Cox neatly complemented Smith's analysis by applying the notion of play and the pleasure principle to the activities of Mark Twain's happy burghers. Whereas Smith thought *Tom Sawyer* pointed forward to *Huck Finn*, Cox considered it of a piece with the nostalgia of "Old Times on the Mississippi." As Cox read it, the novel succeeds in large part because of the gently ironic stance of its indulgent narrator, who subtly condescends to the world he evokes. This device enabled the author to portray Tom as a performer; that is, Cox contended, "what Mark Twain did was to treat his fiction as a performance rather than a story." Instead of a character hopelessly compromised by the demands of the conformative community, as Smith had suggested, Tom combines heroism "on the St. Petersburg stage" with victory "in the world of make-believe." He "succeeds in playing out his fantasies for the entertainment and salvation of the town." The whitewashing scene proves, if nothing else, that Tom may convert what adults consider an arduous chore into a form of play. "What every episode of *Tom Sawyer* enacts," according to Cox, in fact, "is the conversion of all 'serious' community activity—all duty, pain, grief, and work—into pleasure and play."[55] If, as Smith had argued, Injun Joe drives the narrative as a figure of evil incarnate, then in Cox's analysis Tom is the boy-genius who, as the pleasure principle incarnate, transcends the conventions of a jerry-rigged plot.

While he readily conceded, like the New Critics of the 1940s and 1950s, the "failure" of the novel "as a work of art" and its lack of "absolute literary merit," Robert Tracy in effect mediated between Smith's and Cox's views in "Myth and Reality in *The Adventures of Tom Sawyer*" (1968). The worlds of "reality" and "melodramatic romance"—what Cox had termed "the St. Petersburg stage" and "the world of make-believe"—are "continually interpenetrating" in the story, Tracy contended, and to control its "diametrically disparate elements" Twain tapped the dimension of "archetypal myth," particularly the folklore and legends that circulated among the children and slaves of the village. From this perspective, Injun Joe is obviously a demonic figure, a dark satan haunting the mythic landscape, even as, on a more realistic plane, he is the victim of "white injustice and mistreatment." In all, Tracy concluded that Twain expressed in the novel "an ambiguous attitude to both American civilization and the savage American wilderness" (Tracy, 531, 540, 541).

Read against the backdrop of the consumer-and counter-cultures of these years, moreover, *Tom Sawyer* also seemed a surprisingly polemical novel. On the one hand, Harry A. Jaffa made the case for Mark Twain as a nascent political economist, teaching the secrets of "American democratic capitalism" and laissez-faire through the medium of Tom in the whitewashing chapter and illustrating the tedium of "a communist society in which there is perfect freedom" in the pirating scenes on Jackson's Island.[56] On the other hand, L. Moffitt Cecil contended that Tom, by resisting or ignoring adult authority, rebelled against the civil hypocrisy that rules St. Petersburg. *"Tom Sawyer* could well serve as a primer" for "young activists and hippies," Cecil asserted.[57] Judith Fetterley qualified Cecil's conclusion in "The Sanctioned Rebel" (1971): Tom's actions in the first half of the novel, Fetterley conceded, comprise "a series of exposures which reveal the absurdity and hypocrisy of his world." But she related Tom's (mis)behavior in these chapters to the Bad Boy literary tradition and compared the story of his adventures to "a stage which has respectability at its other end." What Blair, Hill, and others had described as Tom's mature actions in the second half of an initiation story are, in Fetterley's view, simply expressions of his gradual domestication, his adoption of conventional values.[58]

Whatever their differences, these critics generally agreed on at least this one point: *Tom Sawyer* was a genial novel, a paean to innocent boyhood, a nostalgic celebration of such village virtues as honesty, loyalty, and filial piety. To be sure, as Helen L. Harris lamented in 1975, Twain attributed stereotypical racial traits to the "murderin' half-breed" Injun Joe.[59] But such a complaint was a decidedly minor chord in the crescendo of praise the novel enjoyed in the late 1960s and 1970s. Cecil pronounced it "Mark Twain's happiest and most hopeful novel" (Cecil, 131), for example, and Robert Regan thought it "the most amiable of all Mark Twain's novels."[60] Even critics who thought *Tom Sawyer* too lightweight to be taken seriously shared this consensus view: Leo Marx damned it as a "comic idyll of boyhood."[61] In "A Hannibal Summer: The Framework of *The Adventures of Tom Sawyer*," John R. Byers, Jr., meticulously established the time-frame of events in "the nostalgic record of [Twain's] relived Hannibal summer." By parsing out the "slow but steady progression of the days of the weeks and the weeks of the months," as Byers explained, Twain savored the memories evoked by his summertime idyll.[62]

By 1980, however, Louis J. Budd had noted a disturbing new trend in *Tom Sawyer* scholarship: "the readings of Twain's Hannibal novel" were "getting gloomier, if possible." Four years later, Budd reiterated the point: "the tide of taking *Huckleberry Finn* with the highest seriousness has overlapped *Tom Sawyer*."[63] De Voto had hinted at the shape this scholarship would assume as early as 1932, when he noted that the "pastoral landscape" of this "supreme American idyll" erupts repeatedly into "violence and terror."[64] Tom H. Towers pioneered this brand of critical revisionism in 1975 in " 'I Never Thought We Might Want to Come Back': Strategies of Transcendence in *Tom Sawyer*." Despite the book's "popular reputation," Towers averred, "horror is very real in *Tom Sawyer*, and it is the horror and Tom's reaction to it that lie at the core of meaning in the novel and connect it to the dark unity of Twain's later work." Like Moncure Conway in his "London Letter" a century earlier, Towers compared the village to the capital of czarist

Russia which shared its name: life in St. Petersburg "is charged with cruelty and violence" that result from "ubiquitous repression." More than a mere rebel against adult inhibitions, Tom "seeks freedom" and tries "to transcend the stultification" enforced in the town by escaping into the "spiritually vital world" of nature. Yet "nothing really works" to alleviate the "evil and violence" that prevail in the village, so that each thread of narrative—the murder of Dr. Robinson and trial of Muff Potter, the adventures on Jackson's Island, the treasure hunt, the love story of Tom and Becky—ends in "unexpected terror and loneliness." Lost in the utter darkness of the cave in chapter 31, Tom renounces his vain ambition to escape from the regulations imposed by adults. Thus the story has a more sinister ending than the idyllic one "so often imputed" to it. As Towers noted, "Tom sacrifices freedom to gain community, even though it is the deeply flawed community of St. Petersburg, the desperate community of the 'damned human race.' "[65]

Similarly, Cynthia Griffin Wolff described the terrors that stalk Tom's world in "*The Adventures of Tom Sawyer*: A Nightmare Vision of American Boyhood" (1980). The village is a cruel matriarchy "that holds small boys in bondage," as Wolff explained. Twain's models of adult masculinity, schoolmaster Dobbins and Injun Joe, are vicious and aggrieved sadists. Even as De Voto and Towers had observed, moreover, violence is endemic to the novel, with Tom by turns both victim and perpetrator. The overweening threat to women and children represented by Joe, "Tom's shadow self," is finally repressed, not resolved, when he is accidentally locked in the cave. "Taken seriously as a psychological recommendation," Wolff concluded, "the ultimate disposition of the problem of Injun Joe offers no solution but that of denial. Lock away the small boy's anger; lock away his anti-social impulses; shut up his resentments at this totally feminine world; stifle rebellion; ignore adult male hostility: they are all too dangerous to traffic with." Tom's unenviable fate is to conform to the rules of "a world that will always be run by its women."[66]

This somber tone typifies much of the discussion of the novel in the 1980s. Reading against the grain, several critics have detected more subversive implications in *Tom Sawyer* than had hitherto been recognized. John Seelye sounded the depths of the "darkening melodrama" in 1982, insisting, like Wolff, that it is set in "a nightmare world" haunted by "the specter of Injun Joe," the "avatar of satanic malevolence" who is "mostly a psychological presence, not a physical being." Much as the treasure-hunt sequence undermines the "dominant myth of success" celebrated in Alger's formulaic fiction, according to Seelye, in the end Twain abandoned the genteel courtship of Tom and Becky in favor of the male bonding of Tom and Huck, thus "certifying to the essential subversiveness of the story."[67] The recent revaluation of the novel is epitomized by Forrest Robinson's "Social Play and Bad Faith in *The Adventures of Tom Sawyer*" (1984). Revising Cox's notions about the function of play in the novel, Robinson insisted that Tom's performances are of a piece with adult histrionics on the St. Petersburg stage: "Tom shows off like everyone else in town, and he does so for the same reasons, according to the same rules, and with the usual amount of zest and pleasure." Tom is unique among the characters in the book, not because he inhabits a world of make-believe, but because he is an intuitive and "prodigious master of deception and the strategies of self-interest," as the whitewashing episode demonstrates. The "ruling characteristic in the social dynamics of the village," in fact, is tacitly approved deception, what Robinson termed "bad faith." "St. Petersburg society is a complex fabric of lies," he contended, and "Tom is exceptional only in the sheer quantity of his showing off." He is quite simply "St. Petersburg's preeminent gamesman."[68]

Rather than a happy aberration early in the career of an author destined to slip into the Slough of Despond, *Tom Sawyer* seems increasingly to have anticipated the thematics, if not the dark mood, of Mark Twain's mature works. As one more sign of the formal canonization of the novel, a facsimile of the holograph manuscript in Riggs Memorial Library at Georgetown University appeared in 1982,[69] and on the basis of this edition Edgar J. Burde has pointed to the precise moment in writing *Tom Sawyer*—a revision of text in chapter 28—when Mark Twain "seems to have unknowingly discovered the subject of *Huck Finn*."[70] Thomas A. Maik emphasized the gloomy view of the town in "The Village in *Tom Sawyer*: Myth and Reality" (1986). The people of St. Petersburg are guilty of "smugness, hypocrisy, cruelty, and lies," Maik asserted. That is, they are "infected with the same kinds of vices that plague the citizens" of Bricksville, Dawson's Landing, and Hadleyburg, all recreations of Hannibal in Twain's later and more savagely satirical fiction.[71] And according to Elizabeth G. Peck in "Tom Sawyer: Character in Search of an Audience" (1988), Twain's depiction of the prankster figure in his first novel foreshadowed "not only the thoughtless hedonism Tom displays in *Huckleberry Finn*, but Hank Morgan's overpowering narcissism of *A Connecticut Yankee in King Arthur's Court* and the environmental determinism of *The Tragedy of Pudd'nhead Wilson*." Tom evolves from a Good Bad Boy in the opening chapters of the novel that bears his name into a respectable member of a hypocritical community and "a mirror of its shifting expectations and designs," a precursor as such of the morally ambiguous Yankee and the contemptible Tom Driscoll.[72]

The Adventures of Tom Sawyer continues to inspire—or at least provoke— more critical commentary than any of Mark Twain's other works excepting only *Huck Finn*, *Pudd'nhead Wilson*, and perhaps *Connecticut Yankee* (Budd, "Introduction," 7). Much of this recent criticism is theoretically sophisticated, as might be expected given present trends in literary studies. In "Tom Sawyer and Children's Literature" (1985), for example, Fred G. See read the novel and the issues of order and authority it raises through a Lacanian lens. *Tom Sawyer* is, in See's analysis, an "especially interesting children's book" because it negotiates the borders between fantasy and brute fact, between the "power of play" and the "power of logic," between "ideas that [can] never be represented" and "isolated facts beyond our comprehension," between the "order of the child" and the "order of the adult." It is a text *about* borders— from the line in the dust Tom draws with his toe in chapter 1 and the fence he is told to whitewash in chapter 2 to his descent into the unmapped cave, "the place of underived discovery, of instinct free of time, rule, and sequence," in chapters 29 and 31. "The cave becomes not a limit but a dimension of testing," See explained. There "Tom discovers and evades an absolute entrapment, the fullest and most grotesque aspect of adult law; and then he turns back toward a middle ground." Having mastered "the border where law and chaos turn toward one another," Tom exists, as the text ends, at the very nexus or "site of negotiation." He has learned to balance "the option of logical rule against the temptation of pure fantasy."[73] Even more recently, Sanford Pinsker has discussed the novel in light of Johan Huizinga's theoretical musings about the play element of culture in "*The Adventures of Tom Sawyer*, Play Theory, and the Critic's Job of Work" (1988). Pinsker's essay in effect refers back to the earlier tradition of *Tom Sawyer* scholarship, which explicitly contrasted the juvenile and grown-up worlds silhouetted in the novel. By organizing his play "by the book," according to Pinsker, Tom behaves in a way fundamentally unlike "the getting-and-spending" adults.[74]

Finally, in "Undoing Romance: The Contest for Narrative Authority in *The Adventures of Tom Sawyer*," Henry B. Wonham applies some of the insights of narratology to the text in order to rationalize its apparent flaws. As Wonham notes, the narrator of the novel "seems trapped between two attitudes toward his material, one detached and ironic, the other engaged and romantic." These two distinct voices are "in a subtle competition for narrative authority," and the reader must read the text against a background of romantic indulgence and/or self-parody. As Wonham suggests, moreover, "Tom Sawyer's love of play is inseparably linked to his gift for narration" or yarnspinning, so that his tall tales join the cacophony of voices that complicate the text. "Even the most romantically inclined reader is aware," Wonham adds, "that Tom mercilessly exploits precisely the kind of voluntary credulity that the narrator expects from *his* audience." Yet Twain managed "to coordinate an ingenious compromise" to the interplay between "literary romance and the tall tale" by placing quite different demands upon "the narrator's readers and Tom's listeners."

An allegedly sub-literary tale that was readily dismissed in scholarly circles as recently as thirty years ago, *The Adventures of Tom Sawyer* has gradually been reclaimed from the margins of critical discourse and implicated in theoretical debate until it no longer seems merely a story of childhood in the old southwest or the nostalgic "prequel" to Mark Twain's greatest novel but a remarkably complex text in its own right.

* * *

The only book my father still owned as an adult that he had owned as a child was an old green cloth-covered Grosset & Dunlap edition of *The Adventures of Tom Sawyer*. His mother, a former schoolteacher who died when he was thirteen, had inscribed it on the flyleaf "to Bobby." (These words are, in fact, the only specimen of my grandmother's handwriting I have ever seen.) Dad wanted me to become a lawyer—one of the professions Judge Thatcher urges Tom to pursue, significantly enough. When I left for college, he acquiesced in my decision to major in English only because I told him I wanted to become a teacher like his mother. He had kept her gift-copy of *Tom Sawyer* for nearly thirty years, as I reminded him. He smiled and told me I was old enough to make my own mistakes. Twenty years later, literally on our way to the adoption agency, my wife and I chose a name for our new daughter: Rebecca, Becky for short. It was my suggestion. I have no doubt that my father, who had died two years earlier, would have approved.

Notes

1. "Twain on Kipling—Kipling on Twain," *Pall Mall Gazette*, 10 September 1890, 3.
2. *Mark Twain–Howells Letters*, ed. Henry Nash Smith and William M. Gibson (Cambridge: Belknap Press of Harvard University Press, 1960), I, 111; hereafter cited as *Twain–Howells*.
3. *Mark Twain's Letters to His Publishers 1867–1894*, ed. Hamlin Hill (Berkeley and Los Angeles: University of California Press, 1967), 92, 95; hereafter cited as *Publishers*.
4. "Items," *Boston Transcript*, 28 April 1876, 6:2.
5. "Items," *Boston Transcript*, 30 June 1876, 6:2.
6. Quoted in Hamlin Hill, *Mark Twain and Elisha Bliss* (Columbia: University of Missouri Press, 1964), 118; hereafter cited as Hill.
7. "Literary Notes," *Chicago Tribune*, 8 July 1876, 9:3; "Personal," *Chicago Tribune*, 13 July 1876, 5:1; "Notes," *Independent*, 27 July 1876, 12; and "Literary Notes," *San Francisco Chronicle*, 24 September 1876, 6:2. I am indebted to my friend and colleague David McPherson for tracking down two reviews of the novel, in the Edinburgh *Scotsman* and London *Standard*, in the British Library.
8. Merle Johnson, *A Bibliography of the Works of Mark Twain* (New York and London: Harper & Bros., 1935), 30.
9. Mary Elizabeth Burtis, *Moncure Conway* (New Brunswick: Rutgers University Press, 1952), 158.
10. "How Tom Sawyer Sub-Let a Contract," *Boston Transcript*, 29 June 1876, 7:2; "Huckleberry Finn," *Boston Transcript*, 30 June 1876, 6:2; "Injun Joe's Cup," *Boston Transcript*, 6 July 1876, 4:6; "The Boy, the Beetle and the Dog," *Boston Transcript*, 8 July 1876, 6:4; "Huckleberry Finn," *Cincinnati Daily Enquirer*, 5 July 1876, 2:6; "Whitewash/Tom Sawyer's Discovery in Human Nature," *Springfield Republican*, 7 July 1876, 3:1; "Tom's Happy Hot Sunday," *Springfield Republican*, 12 July 1876, 3:1; "How Tom Sawyer Got His Fence Whitewashed," *San Francisco Bulletin*, 8 July 1876, 1:8; "The Boy, the Beetle and the Dog," *San Francisco Bulletin*, 15 July 1876, 1:9; "Tom Sawyer/How He Whitewashed Aunt Polly's New Fence," San Francisco *Call*, 9 July 1876, 6:3; "The Boy, the Beetle and the

Dog," San Francisco *Call*, 13 July 1876, 4:3; "A Happy Boy," San Francisco *Call*, 16 July 1876, 8:2; "Huckleberry Hen" [*sic*], *New-York Commercial Advertiser*, 15 July 1876, 1:3; "How Tom Sawyer Sub-Let a Contract," *Portland Transcript*, 15 July 1876, 124; "A Happy Boy," *Portland Transcript*, 26 August 1876, 176; "The Boy, the Beetle and the Dog," *Hartford Courant*, 26 July 1876, 1:8; "How Tom Sawyer Sub-Let a Contract," *Portland Daily Eastern Argus*, 31 July 1876, 1:8; and "The Boy, the Beetle and the Dog," San Francisco *Alta California*, 28 August 1876, 1:6.

11.   Dennis Welland, "A Note on Some Early Reviews of *Tom Sawyer*," *Journal of American Studies* 1 (April 1967): 102; hereafter cited as Welland.

12.   St. Louis *Daily Globe-Democrat*, 2 July 1876, 10:4–6; *Chicago Tribune*, 3 July 1876, 7:5–6; and *Hartford Times*, 8 July 1876, 4:1–3. The essay was also excerpted in the *Cincinnati Daily Enquirer*, 1 July 1876, 2:1.

13.   Charles A. Norton, *Writing Tom Sawyer* (Jefferson, N.C., and London: McFarland, 1983), 101; hereafter cited as Norton.

14.   See also "Literary News," *Independent*, 15 February 1877, 10: "Sixteen thousand copies of Mark Twain's 'Adventures of Tom Sawyer' have been sold."

15.   "Literary Notes," New York *World*, 1 January 1877, 2:5.

16.   John C. Gerber, "Introduction" to *The Adventures of Tom Sawyer* (Berkeley, Los Angeles, London: University of California Press, 1982), 27.

17.   "New Publications," *New York Times*, 13 January 1877, 3:3.

18.   "New Books," New York *Evening Post*, 1 February 1877, 1:1.

19.   "Books and Authors," *Christian Secretary*, 17 May 1877, 2.

20.   E. L. Pearson, "The Children's Librarian *Versus* Huckleberry Finn: A Brief for the Defense," *Library Journal* 32 (July 1907): 312–14.

21.   William J. Long, *American Literature* (Boston and New York: Ginn & Co., 1913), 466–67.

22.   Robert M. Gay, "The Two Mark Twains," *Atlantic Monthly*, 166 (December 1940); rpt. in *Critical Essays on Mark Twain, 1910–1980*, ed. Louis J. Budd (Boston: G. K. Hall & Co., 1983), 118; hereafter cited as Budd.

23.   *Letters of Theodore Dreiser: A Selection*, ed. Robert H. Elias (Philadelphia: University of Pennsylvania Press, 1959), I, 121.

24.   Owen Wister, "In Homage to Mark Twain," *Harper's Monthly*, 171 (November 1935); rpt. in Budd, 100.

25.   *Conversations with James Thurber*, ed. Thomas Fensch (Jackson and London: University Press of Mississippi, 1989), 59.

26.   Edgar H. Hemminghaus, *Mark Twain in Germany* (New York: Columbia University Press, 1939), 142.

27.   *Mark Twain's Hannibal, Huck & Tom*, ed. Walter Blair (Berkeley and London: Univ. of California Press, 1969), pp. 243–324.

28.   *Mark Twain Letters*, ed. Albert Bigelow Paine (New York: Harper & Bros., 1917), II, 476–79. Significantly enough, this letter has also been published in "The Art of Saying No: Mark Twain Refuses Permission to Dramatize 'Tom Sawyer,' " *Reader's Digest* 38 (March 1941), 56.

29.   "The Original Tom Sawyer/Mark Twain's Hero That Got Into Trouble and Out Again With Huckleberry Finn Now Living in the Mission," San Francisco *Examiner*, 9 October 1892, 15:4–5.

30.   Lute Pease, "The Famous Story-Teller Discusses Characters/Says That No Author Creates, but Merely Copies," *Portland Oregonian*, 11 August 1895; rpt. in *Critical Essays on Mark Twain, 1867–1910*, ed. Louis J. Budd (Boston: G. K. Hall & Co., 1982), 108.

31.   *The Adventures of Tom Sawyer* (Berkeley, Los Angeles, London: University of California Press, 1982), xvii.

32. Robert Tracy, "Myth and Reality in *The Adventures of Tom Sawyer*," *Southern Review* 4 (Spring 1968): 530; hereafter cited as Tracy.

33. William Lyon Phelps, "Mark Twain," *North American Review*, 5 July 1907, 546.

34. Percy Boynton, "Introduction" to *The Adventures of Tom Sawyer* (New York and London: Harper & Bros., 1920), xi.

35. Bertha Evans Ward, "Introduction" to *The Adventures of Tom Sawyer* (Boston: Ginn and Co., 1931), xi.

36. Emily Fanning Barry and Herbert B. Bruner, "Introduction" to *The Adventures of Tom Sawyer* (New York and London: Harper & Bros., 1932), xi.

37. T. S. Eliot, "Introduction" to *Adventures of Huckleberry Finn* (London: Cresset, 1950), viii.

38. "The Screen," *New York Times*, 18 February 1938, 23:1.

39. Allison R. Ensor, " 'Norman Rockwell Sentimentality': The Rockwell Illustrations for *Tom Sawyer* and *Huckleberry Finn*," in *The Mythologizing of Mark Twain*, ed. Sara deSaussure Davis and Philip D. Beidler (University: University of Alabama Press, 1984), 35, 27–28; hereafter cited as Ensor.

40. Tom Tenney, *Mark Twain: A Reference Guide* (Boston: G. K. Hall, 1977), 173.

41. Frank Luther Mott, *Golden Multitudes: The Story of Best Sellers in the United States* (New York: Macmillan, 1947), 156–57. In a 1989 survey, *Tom Sawyer* was named the second favorite children's book (behind *Huck Finn*) of U.S. governors—another hint of its iconographic importance in American public life. See *Satire or Evasion? Black Perspectives on Huckleberry Finn*, ed. James S. Leonard, Thomas A. Tenney, and Thadious M. Davis (Durham: Duke University Press, 1992).

42. "An American Summer," *Variety*, 23 May 1990, 34.

43. Ron Powers, *White Town Drowsing* (Boston: Atlantic Monthly Press, 1986), 86, 87, 109, 110.

44. Walter Blair, *Native American Humor* (New York: American Book Co., 1937), 147–156, 517; and "On the Structure of *Tom Sawyer*," *Modern Philology*: 37 (August 1939), 75–88.

45. Bernard De Voto, *Mark Twain at Work* (Cambridge: Harvard University Press, 1942), 3–44.

46. DeLancey Ferguson, *Mark Twain: Man and Legend* (Indianapolis: Bobbs-Merrill, 1943), 175, 176. See also Alexander Cowie, *The Rise of the American Novel* (New York: American Book Co., 1948), 609.

47. Gladys Bellamy, *Mark Twain as a Literary Artist* (Norman: University of Oklahoma Press, 1950), 332.

48. Roger Asselineau, *The Literary Reputation of Mark Twain from 1910 to 1950* (Paris: Didier, 1954), 58.

49. George P. Elliott, "Vacation Into Boyhood," afterword to *The Adventures of Tom Sawyer* (New York: New American Library, 1959), 221.

50. Hamlin L. Hill, "The Composition and Structure of *The Adventures of Tom Sawyer*," *American Literature* 32 (January 1961): 391, 392.

51. Louis D. Rubin, Jr., "Tom Sawyer and the Use of Novels," *American Quarterly* 9 (Summer 1957): 209–16.

52. Leslie Fiedler, *Love and Death in the American Novel* (New York: Dell, 1966), 276.

53. Albert E. Stone, Jr., *The Innocent Eye: Childhood in Mark Twain's Imagination* (New Haven: Yale University Press, 1961), 64.

54. Henry Nash Smith, *Mark Twain: The Development of a Writer* (Cambridge: Harvard University Press, 1962), 88, 92, 89, 90.

55. James M. Cox, *Mark Twain: The Fate of Humor* (Princeton: Princeton University Press, 1966), 136, 137, 146.

56. Harry A. Jaffa, *The Conditions of Freedom: Essays in Political Philosophy* (Baltimore: Johns Hopkins University Press, 1975), 191–224.

57. L. Moffitt Cecil, "Tom Sawyer: Missouri Robin Hood," *Western American Literature* 4 (Summer 1969): 131; hereafter cited as Cecil.

58. Judith Fetterley, "The Sanctioned Rebel," *Studies in the Novel* 3 (Fall 1971): 297, 301, 302.

59. Helen L. Harris, "Mark Twain's Response to the Native American," *American Literature* 46 (January 1975): 499.

60. Robert Regan, *Unpromising Heroes: Mark Twain and His Characters* (Berkeley and Los Angeles: University of California Press, 1966), 116.

61. Leo Marx, *The Machine in the Garden* (London, Oxford, New York: Oxford University Press, 1964), 319.

62. John R. Byers, Jr., "The Framework of *The Adventures of Tom Sawyer*," *Studies in American Fiction* 8 (Spring 1980): 86–87.

63. Louis J. Budd, "Mark Twain," in *American Literary Scholarship 1980*, ed. J. Albert Robbins (Durham: Duke University Press, 1982), 97; *American Literary Scholarship 1984*, ed. J. Albert Robbins (Durham: Duke University Press, 1986), 106.

64. Bernard De Voto, *Mark Twain's America* (Cambridge: Houghton, 1932), 304, 306.

65. Tom H. Towers, " 'I Never Thought We Might Want to Come Back': Strategies of Transcendence in *Tom Sawyer*," *Modern Fiction Studies* 21 (Winter 1975–76): 510, 511, 512, 514, 519–520.

66. Cynthia Griffin Wolff, "*The Adventures of Tom Sawyer*: A Nightmare Vision of American Boyhood," *Massachusetts Review* 21 (Winter 1980): 641, 647–48, 651, 652.

67. John Seelye, "What's in a Name: Sounding the Depths of *Tom Sawyer*," *Sewanee Review* 90 (Summer 1982); 408–29.

68. Forrest Robinson, "Social Play and Bad Faith in *The Adventures of Tom Sawyer*," *Nineteenth Century Fiction* 39 (June 1984): 7, 9, 11, 12, 24.

69. *The Adventures of Tom Sawyer: A Facsimile of the Author's Holograph Manuscript*, ed. with an introduction by Paul Baender (Frederick, Md.: University Publications of America, 1982).

70. Edgar J. Burde, "Slavery and the Boys: *Tom Sawyer* and the Germ of *Huck Finn*," *American Literary Realism* 24 (Fall 1991); 86–91.

71. Thomas A. Maik, "The Village in *Tom Sawyer*: Myth and Reality," *Arizona Quarterly* 42 (Summer 1986): 160, 164.

72. Elizabeth G. Peck, "Tom Sawyer: Character in Search of an Audience," *ATQ*, n.s. 2 (September 1988): 224, 233.

73. Fred G. See, "Tom Sawyer and Children's Literature," *Essays in Literature* 12 (Fall 1985): 254, 258, 261, 264, 266, 268, 269. See also Wayne Fields, "When the Fences Are Down: Language and Order in *The Adventures of Tom Sawyer* and *Huckleberry Finn*," *Journal of American Studies* 24 (December 1990): 369–86.

74. Sanford Pinsker, "*The Adventures of Tom Sawyer*, Play Theory, and the Critic's Job of Work," *Midwest Quarterly* 29 (Spring 1988): 360. See also Michael Oriard, "From *Tom Sawyer* to *Huckleberry Finn*: Toward Godly Play," *Studies in American Fiction* 8 (Autumn 1980): 183–87.

CONTEMPORARY REVIEWS

◆

[Review of *The Adventures of Tom Sawyer*]

W. D. Howells

Mr. Aldrich has studied the life of A Bad Boy as the pleasant reprobate led it in a quiet old New England town twenty-five or thirty years ago, where in spite of the natural outlawry of boyhood he was more or less part of a settled order of things, and was hemmed in, to some measure, by the traditions of an established civilization. Mr. Clemens, on the contrary, has taken the boy of the Southwest for the hero of his new book, and has presented him with a fidelity to circumstance which loses no charm by being realistic in the highest degree, and which gives incomparably the best picture of life in that region as yet known to fiction. The town where Tom Sawyer was born and brought up is some such idle, shabby little Mississippi River town as Mr. Clemens has so well described in his piloting reminiscences, but Tom belongs to the better sort of people in it, and has been bred to fear God and dread the Sunday-school according to the strictest rite of the faiths that have characterized all the respectability of the West. His subjection in these respects does not so deeply affect his inherent tendencies but that he makes himself a beloved burden to the poor, tender-hearted old aunt who brings him up with his orphan brother and sister, and struggles vainly with his manifold sins, actual and imaginary. The limitations of his transgressions are nicely and artistically traced. He is mischievous, but not vicious; he is ready for almost any depredation that involves the danger and honor of adventure, but profanity he knows may provoke a thunderbolt upon the heart of the blasphemer, and he almost never swears; he resorts to any stratagem to keep out of school, but he is not a downright liar, except upon terms of after shame and remorse that make his falsehood bitter to him. He is cruel, as all children are, but chiefly because he is ignorant; he is not mean, but there are very definite bounds to his generosity; and his courage is the Indian sort, full of prudence and mindful of retreat as one of the conditions of prolonged hostilities. In a word, he is a boy, and merely and exactly an ordinary boy on the moral side. What makes him delightful to the reader is that on the imaginative side he is very much more, and though every boy has wild and fantastic dreams, this boy cannot rest till he has somehow realized them. Till he has actually run off with two other boys in the character

Reprinted from the *Atlantic Monthly* 37 (May 1876): 621–22.

of buccaneer, and lived for a week on an island in the Mississippi, he has lived in vain; and this passage is but the prelude to more thrilling adventures, in which he finds hidden treasures, traces the bandits to their cave, and is himself lost in its recesses. The local material and the incidents with which his career is worked up are excellent, and throughout there is scrupulous regard for the boy's point of view in reference to his surroundings and himself, which shows how rapidly Mr. Clemens has grown as an artist. We do not remember anything in which this propriety is violated, and its preservation adds immensely to the grown-up reader's satisfaction in the amusing and exciting story. There is a boy's love-affair, but it is never treated otherwise than as a boy's love-affair. When the half-breed has murdered the young doctor, Tom and his friend, Huckleberry Finn, are really, in their boyish terror and superstition, going to let the poor old town-drunkard be hanged for the crime, till the terror of that becomes unendurable. The story is a wonderful study of the boy-mind, which inhabits a world quite distinct from that in which he is bodily present with his elders, and in this lies its great charm and its universality, for boy-nature, however human-nature varies, is the same everywhere.

The tale is very dramatically wrought, and the subordinate characters are treated with the same graphic force that sets Tom alive before us. The worthless vagabond, Huck Finn, is entirely delightful throughout, and in his promised reform his identity is respected: he will lead a decent life in order that he may one day be thought worthy to become a member of that gang of robbers which Tom is to organize. Tom's aunt is excellent, with her kind heart's sorrow and secret pride in Tom; and so is his sister Mary, one of those good girls who are born to usefulness and charity and forbearance and unvarying rectitude. Many village people and local notables are introduced in well-conceived character; the whole little town lives in the reader's sense, with its religiousness, its lawlessness, its droll social distinctions, its civilization qualified by its slave-holding, and its traditions of the wilder West which has passed away. The picture will be instructive to those who have fancied the whole Southwest a sort of vast Pike County, and have not conceived of a sober and serious and orderly contrast to the sort of life that has come to represent the Southwest in literature. Mr. William M. Baker gives a notion of this in his stories, and Mr. Clemens has again enforced the fact here, in a book full of entertaining character, and of the greatest artistic sincerity.

Tom Brown and Tom Bailey are, among boys in books, alone deserving to be named with Tom Sawyer.

[Review of *The Adventures of Tom Sawyer*]

Anonymous

Mark Twain's appearance as a writer of a book for boys is justified by the result. His book, *The Adventures of Tom Sawyer*, though it has throughout a strong American flavour, will delight all the lads who may get hold of it. We have made the experiment upon a youngster, and found that the reading of the book brought on constant peals of laughter. That is perhaps the best testimony that can be produced as to its amusing character. There is nothing in it of an unwholesome kind, so that parents need have no fear of trusting it into the hands of their boys. It is a book in which full knowledge of the habits of thought of lads is shown; and a full appreciation of the mischief which constitutes to a large extent their chief amusement.

Reprinted from the Edinburgh *Scotsman*, 9 June 1876, 2.

Mark Twain's New Book

Moncure D. Conway

This newest work of Mark Twain increases the difficulty of assigning that author a literary *habitat*. "American humourist" has for some time been recognized as too vague a label to attach to a writer whose 'Jumping Frog' and other early sketches have been reduced to mere fragments and ventures by such productions as 'The Innocents Abroad' and 'The New Pilgrim's Progress,' in which, while the humour is still fresh, there is present an equal art in graphic description of natural scenery, and a fine sense of what is genuinely impressive in the grandeurs of the past. Those who have travelled with Mark Twain with some curiosity to observe the effect of the ancient world interpreted by a very shrewd eye, fresh from the newest outcome of civilisation, may have expected to find antiquity turned into a solemn joke, but they can hardly have failed to discover a fine discrimination present at each step in the path of the "new pilgrim"; while he sheds tears of a kind hardly relished by the superstitious or sentimental over the supposed grave of his deceased parent Adam, he can "listen deep" when any true theme from the buried world reaches his ear. Without being pathetic he is sympathetic, and there is also an innate refinement in his genius felt in every subject it selects and in his treatment of it. 'Tom Sawyer' carries us to an altogether novel region, and along with these characteristics displays a somewhat puzzling variety of abilities. There is something almost stately in the simplicity with which he invites us to turn our attention to the affairs of some boys and girls growing up on the far frontiers of American civilisation. With the Eastern Question upon us, and crowned heads arrayed on the political stage, it may be with some surprise that we find our interest demanded in sundry Western questions that are solving themselves through a *dramatis personæ* of humble folk whose complications occur in a St. Petersburg situated on the Missouri [*sic*] river. Our manager, we feel quite sure, would not for a moment allow us to consider that any other St. Petersburg is of equal importance to that for which he claims our attention. What is the deposition, death, or enthronement of a Sultan compared with the tragical death of "Injun Joe," the murderer, accidentally buried and entombed in the cavern where his stolen treasures are hid? There he was found.[1]

Reprinted from the London *Examiner*, 17 June 1876, 687–88.

＊　　　＊　　　＊

In such writing as this we seem to be reading some classic fable, such as the Persian Sâdi might point with his moral, "Set not your heart on things that are transitory; the Tigris will run through Bagdat after the race of Caliphs is extinct." Nor is this feeling of the dignity of his subject absent when the author is describing the most amusing incidents. Indeed, a great deal of Mark Twain's humour consists in the serious—or even at times severe—style in which he narrates his stories and portrays his scenes, as one who feels that the universal laws are playing though the very slightest of them. The following is a scene in which the principal actors are a dog, a boy, and a beetle, the place being the chapel:—[2]

＊　　　＊　　　＊

The scene we have selected is not so laughable, perhaps, as some others in the volume, but it indicates very well the kind of art in which Mark Twain is pre-eminent in our time. Every movement of boy, beetle, and poodle, is described not merely with precision, but with a subtle sense of meaning in every movement. Everything is alive, and every face physiognomical. From a novel so replete with good things, and one so full of significance, as it brings before us what we can feel is the real spirit of home life in the far West, there is no possibility of obtaining extracts which will convey to the reader any idea of the purport of the book. The scenes and characters cannot be really seen apart from their grouping and environment. The book will no doubt be a great favourite with boys, for whom it must in good part have been intended; but next to boys we should say that is might be most prized by philosophers and poets. The interior life, the everyday experiences, of a small village on the confines of civilisation and in the direction of its advance, may appear, antecedently, to supply but thin material for a romance; but still it is at just that same little pioneer point that humanity is growing with the greatest freedom, and unfolding some of its unprescribed tendencies. We can, indeed, hardly imagine a more felicitous task for a man of genius to have accomplished than to have seized the salient, picturesque, droll, and at the same time most significant features of human life, as he has himself lived it and witnessed it, in a region where it is continually modified in relation to new circumstances. The chief fault of the story is its brevity, and it will, we doubt not, be widely and thoroughly enjoyed by young and old for its fun and its philosophy.

Notes

    1.   Omitted is an excerpt from chapter 33, 239.9–240.21. All citations in the notes are to *The Adventures of Tom Sawyer* (Berkeley, Los Angeles, London: University of California Press, 1982).

    2.   Omitted is an excerpt from chapter 5, 40.33–43.22.

[Review of *The Adventures of Tom Sawyer*]

Richard F. Littledale

In the sketches by which Mr. Clemens, who is pleased to call himself Mark Twain, first became known to the English public, there is one of a bad little boy who didn't come to grief, which is obviously capable of being indefinitely developed. Some such idea seems to have prompted the composition of *Tom Sawyer*, who is own brother, or at least cousin-german, to the bad Jim of the *Sketches*. He goes through a variety of adventures, for whose authenticity Mark Twain pledges himself, although they did not all happen to the same person, and the book, which is a very amusing one in parts, has a certain value as showing what kind of animal the American schoolboy is, and what odd fancies and superstitions he indulges and practises, or at least did some thirty or forty years ago. Traditions of the sort have such vitality, and are so readily handed down by one generation of schoolboys to another, that there is little reason to believe them extinct now; and those who are curious in such studies will note that some at least are survivals of old English usages, themselves the *detritus* of a vanished Paganism; while the common-school discipline as depicted in *Tom Sawyer* will recall to a few at least Mr. George Macdonald's vigorous sketches of the Scottish parish-school in *Alec Forbes of Howglen*. In each case, the whole is differentiated by the conditions of American life; but the parentage cannot be mistaken, and no one could take *Tom Sawyer* for either French Canadian or Pennsylvania Dutch in descent and instincts. The book is designed primarily for boys, but older people also will find it worth looking through.

Reprinted from the *Academy*, 24 June 1876, 605.

London Letter

MONCURE D. CONWAY

London, June 10, 1876.—Next week all England will be enjoying a new story by Mark Twain, with a piquant sauce supplied by the novelty of reading it before the Centennial land. Carlyle told me that the first bound book of his he ever saw came to him by mail from New England, and presently Mark Twain may say that the last bound book of his was sent him from Old England. By what means it happens that we are to have "The Adventures of Tom Sawyer" before you I cannot tell; all I know is that, through the kindness of Messrs. Chatto & Windus, who are its publishers, by special arrangement with the author, I have before me early sheets of this story, and have good reason to believe that some notes concerning it will be "news" to the author's countrymen.

It is, as I think, the most notable work which Mark Twain has yet written, and will signally add to his reputation for variety of powers. His *dramatis personæ* are mainly some boys and girls residing in the magnificently small village of St. Petersburg, somewhere on the Missouri [*sic*], the Czar of which village is Tom Sawyer, who settled his western questions more satisfactorily, I suspect, than the chief of the larger St. Petersburg is likely to settle in his Eastern one. Under pretext of this boy-and-girl's romance, Mark Twain has written a book which will not only charm elder readers— especially if they have that age which, as the Book of Wisdom says, "consisteth not in length of years, but in having made the most of them"—but will be of value to philosophers. I shouldn't wonder if Mr. Edward Tylor, in his next book on human evolution—and we are looking for one—should find reason to refer to the survivals of ancient Oriental and Greek myths and beliefs in the elaborate folklore of Tom Sawyer and his comrades. Heine, in his "Exiled Gods," has traced a classic legend of some magnificent deity— Apollo, I believe—until he finds it interesting as an anecdote [about] an old miller in a German parish; and I think it would not be difficult to trace some of the attributes of Siva and Odin, and perhaps the Eleusynian rites, in the notions of these children about their village witch, and the power of a dead cat thrown in a graveyard with precise rules, to remove warts, and sundry other superstitions. No doubt most of us remember such things in our early

Reprinted from the *Cincinnati Commercial*, 26 June 1876, 5:1–3.

life—especially if we were born in remote southern or western villages, where the Semitic had not, as in New England, trampled out the Indo-Germanic varieties of superstition; but it was a "happy thought" in Mark Twain to recover them and twine them in with his story. It is a valuable bit of social embryology, for instance, when we find that those barefoot western boys, who know nothing of Catholicism, have somehow got the belief that the devil can't get at them if a cross is near by; and it reminds us of the fact that in the country districts of Europe the most determined Lutheran, if he thinks himself bewitched, will repair to the Catholic priest for the exorcism, and never to his Protestant pastor.

However, this is but a small part, however valuable to certain minds, of the interest of this work. Incidental, also—but very striking—are the indications in it of how, amid all the spars and fragments of a past that has gone to pieces and been washed up on the beach of a new moral continent, new tendencies are seen forming, and new themes, which are still harmonious with what is eternal in human nature. Children report the past and fore-shadow the future. Here in England the boy repeats the history of his ancestors,—aye, and the girl, too. The boy is a savage, and then a Viking and a pirate in his tastes, a nomad in his love adventure, and passing through the age of the huntsman, affects agriculture and mechanic art for a time, becomes a knight errant, and so advances to be an Englishman. These embryological stages of development are very marked at some points. Thus there is a phase in the life of English children of both sexes—and a phase which lasts inconveniently long—when they madly desire to run about in the garden naked. It requires the utmost vigilance to prevent them from doing this in the little gardens of London. Many a boy and girl here will feel an agony of envy when they contemplate the scene of Mark Twain's three boys painted with mud to look like Indians racing up and down the beach to their heart's content. Many other scenes and notions, too, will correspond to the familiar feelings of the healthy British boy and girl. But now and then they will pause with some wonder, and it will be at some point where the village of Missouri has unfolded some unprescribed tendency in human nature or, perhaps, recovering one that was lost. It will introduce a novel ethical problem in the young circles of England when they read about Tom Sawyer's lie. Tom has been deeply offended by a little girl whom he had adored. She was soon after in great trouble, having torn a valuable book belonging to the teacher while surreptitiously examining it at his desk. The teacher is going down from boy to boy and girl to girl, switch in hand, asking each if he or she had done the dreadful deed. The guilty, terrified girl is reached at last, and the fearful question is being asked: "Becky Thatcher, did you—." Just here a boy's voice sounded through the breathless school. "I done it." It was Tom; he took his unmerciful flogging. The girl's father, when he heard of this long after, declared "it was a noble, a generous, a magnanimous lie—a lie that was worthy to hold up its head and march down through history breast to breast with George Washington's lauded truth about the hatchet." Besides this perilous accident, there is an interest of an equally doubtful kind surrounding a unique and vigorously drawn character called Huckleberry Finn, the juvenile Pariah of the village, son of the town drunkard thus described:[1]

*　　*　　*

Huckleberry comes into fortune at last, or what respectable people think fortune, and is taken into a respectable home by kind people, who try to educate and civilize him, but he finds it irksome, cannot bear it, disappears, and is found afterward sleeping in such quarters as tradition assigns to Diogenes, and begging Tom to take the wealth that has befallen him and allow him to continue in his old felicity of vagabondage.

There is in this work more that is dramatic than in any of Mark Twain's previous works, and some scenes that are impressive, and even weird. There is a thrilling murder-scene, a graphic trial-scene, and a solemn retribution-scene,—the murderer, a half-breed called "Injun Joe," being barred up in a cavern where he was accustomed to hide the money got by robbery. He is entombed there accidentally, it having been thought necessary to close up the cave after Tom and Becky had been lost in it, and nearly perished. When "Injun Joe" is finally tracked to it, the villagers rush to the spot, and, opening the cave, find him there dead.[2]

*　　*　　*

The humor of the book breaks out everywhere in little touches, and is, of course, the chief characteristics of many of the chapters. The showing-off day at a boarding-school, when the young misses parade in their ribbons, is portrayed with exquisite drollery; and the poetical compositions recited on the occasion are given with a realistic exactness which cannot be surpassed. The author assures us that these compositions are genuine, and so I think I must quote some of the specimens:[3]

*　　*　　*

There are some respects in which Mark Twain excels any living humorist—if we can still so describe a writer who has shown such various powers (which is doubtful)—and one in his innate refinement and self-restraint. With perfect freedom in his style he is never coarse, and spontaneous as his fun is it never overpasses the temperance of all true art. And another unique feature of his is the stately and dignified way in which he deals with the seemingly small subject which has excited his sympathy. Landseer gave grandeur to a donkey, and Mark Twain paints a scene between a dog and a pinch-bug with such true perception of universal laws, that it is quite worthy to occur, as it does, in church, and to extinguish the parson's sermon, which is not half so important. That Mark is a philosopher is amply proved by the following incident:

Tom Sawyer, having offended his guardian, Aunt Polly, is by that sternly-affectionate dame punished, by being set to whitewash the fence in front of the garden. The world seemed a hollow mockery to Tom, who had planned fun for that day, and who knew that he would be the laughing stock of all the boys as they came past and saw him, set to work like a 'nigger.' But a great inspiration burst upon him, and he went tranquilly to work. What that inspiration was will appear from what follows. One of the boys, Ben. Rogers, comes by and pauses, eating a particularly fine apple. Tom does not see him. Ben. stared a moment, and then said:[4]

*　　　*　　　*

In a brief preface the author tells us that most of the adventures recorded in his book really occurred with himself or his schoolmates; that Huck Finn is drawn from life, and others are composite characters; and the odd superstitions touched upon are such as prevailed among children and slaves in the west thirty years ago. "Although," he says, "my book is intended mainly for the entertainment of boys and girls, I hope it will not be shunned by men and women on that account, for a part of my plan has been to try pleasantly to remind adults of what they once were themselves, and of how they felt and talked and what queer enterprises them sometimes engaged in." I feel quite sure that the book will be a favorite in England, among grown-up folk, and also among the boys and girls if the fifty thousand governesses, enumerated in the new census, who guard the Hesperides of youth, permit anything so fresh, and natural, and free from cant and pietism, to find its way into their little heads and hearts. But however this may be, Mark Twain has written a book which will cause all sensible people to love and honor him, and at the same time will inspire a doubt whether it will be really true that, as he states in an article in Temple Bar, he has found perfect happiness in Connecticut by the simple plan of killing his conscience. Meanwhile, to Americans abroad, it will be a proud centennial fact that if we have our Belknaps and Babcocks, we also have our Twain of a different stamp, and if Missouri is for the time represented in the White House by a Grant, Tom Sawyers, though at present in the rough, are growing up in the background, and may come to the front. Nay, as these things happened thirty years ago, Tom must be somewhere about, and I recommend the political conventions, in choosing our next president, to look out for him. No doubt information may be obtained in the neighborhood of Hartford. "There's millions in it."[5]

Notes

1. Omitted is an excerpt from chapter 6, 47.15–48.21.
2. Omitted is an excerpt from chapter 33, 239.9–240.21.
3. Omitted is an excerpt from chapter 21, 157.21–159.16.
4. Omitted is an excerpt from chapter 2, 13.19–16.17.
5. This phrase is Colonel Sellers' refrain in the theatrical adaptation of *The Gilded Age* (1873), a novel Mark Twain wrote in collaboration with Charles Dudley Warner.

[Review of *The Adventures of Tom Sawyer*]

Anonymous

"Mark Twain" has dropped the humorous exaggerations of his "Jumping Frog" and "Innocents Abroad" in his fresh and racy story of *Tom Sawyer* (Chatto and Windus). "Although," writes this popular American humorist in his preface, "my book is intended mainly for the entertainment of boys and girls, I hope it will not be shunned by men and women on that account; for part of my plan has been to try to write pleasantly, to remind adults of what they once were themselves, and of how they felt and thought and talked, and what queer enterprises they sometimes engaged in." So very human is "Tom Sawyer" in its faithful delineation of boy-life that it cannot fail to realize the hope of "Mark Twain," and amuse everyone who in the words of the song, "would" he "were a boy again." All the love of mischief, hopes and fears, joys and sorrows, foolhardy pranks and acts of bravery that make Tom Sawyer stand out as a veritable portrait from the life are set down by Mr. Clemens with unfailing fidelity to nature; and that element of adventure so dear to boys is supplied in a manner to satisfy the appetite for the strangest sensational fare. It is the faithful portrayal of boy-life, however—not the midnight murder in a churchyard of which Tom Sawyer and Huck Finn are eye-witnesses, nor the piratical venture of Tom and his mates, nor even the wanderings of Tom and his sweetheart whilst lost in the cave— that makes "Mark Twain's" last volume so welcome, and that will, doubtless, win for him even a wider circle of readers that he has at present.

Reprinted from the *Illustrated London News*, 24 June 1876, 611.

[Review of *The Adventures of Tom Sawyer*]

Anonymous

The name of Mark Twain is known throughout the length and breadth of England. Wherever there is a railway-station with a bookstall his jokes are household words. Those whose usual range in literature does not extend beyond the sporting newspapers, the *Racing Calendar*, and the 'Diseases of Dogs,' have allowed him a place with Artemus Ward alongside of the handful of books which forms their library. For ourselves, we cannot dissociate him from the railway-station, and his jokes always rise in our mind with a background of Brown & Polson's Corn Flour and Taylor's system of removing furniture. We have read 'The Adventures of Tom Sawyer' with different surroundings, and still have been made to laugh; and that ought to be taken as high praise. Indeed, the earlier part of the book is, to our thinking, the most amusing thing Mark Twain has written. The humour is not always uproarious, but it is always genuine and sometimes almost pathetic, and it is only now and then that the heartiness of a laugh is spoilt by one of those pieces of self-consciousness which are such common blots on Mark Twain's other books. 'The Adventures of Tom Sawyer' is an attempt in a new direction. It is consecutive, and much longer than the former books, and as it is not put forward as a mere collection of "Screamers," we laugh more easily, and find some relief in being able to relax the conventional grin expected from the reader of the little volumes of railway humour. The present book is not, and does not pretend to be a novel, in the ordinary sense of the word; it is not even a story, for that presupposes a climax and a finish; nor is it a mere boys' book of adventures. In the Preface the author says, "Although my book is intended mainly for the entertainment of boys and girls, I hope it will not be shunned by men and women on that account, for part of my plan has been to try pleasantly to remind adults of what they once were themselves, and of how they felt and thought and talked, and what queer enterprises they sometimes engaged in." Questions of intention are always difficult to decide. The book will amuse grown-up people in the way that humorous books written for children have amused before, but (perhaps fortunately) it does not seem to us calculated to carry

Reprinted from *Athenaeum*, 24 June 1876, 851.

out the intention here expressed. With regard to the style, of course there are plenty of slang words and racy expressions, which are quite in place in the conversations, but it is just a question whether it would not have been as well if the remainder of the book had not been written more uniformly in English.

[Notice of *The Adventures of Tom Sawyer*]

Anonymous

This is a capital boys's book, and will be the more amusing to English boys from the fact that the language, the doings, and all but the human nature differ so widely from those with which they are familiar. The language is certainly extraordinary. It is that strange tongue which has grown up on the other side of the Atlantic which, although founded upon English, is yet not English, whose grammar, whose idioms, and whose slang differ wholly from our own. The human nature is boys' human nature all the world over. Tom Sawyer is a true boy, up to all sorts of adventure, however risky; more precocious than a boy of the same age would be in England, as is natural in a country where boys of eighteen consider that the "old man" is behind the age and doesn't know much, but likeable boys for all that: frank, fearless, mischievous, and as full of tricks as monkeys. Boys will certainly like the book for its being so unlike anything they have ever read before.

Reprinted from the London *Standard*, 7 July 1876, 3.

[Notice of *The Adventures of Tom Sawyer*]

Anonymous

Mark Twain's *Adventures of Tom Sawyer* is a book for boys, and relates the experiences of certain bold and restless youths who, finding every-day life very monotonous, went in for living like outlaws in the woods, exploring for hidden treasures, and other romantic adventures. The story is marked by the extravagant and too often vulgar humour of the writer.

Reprinted from *Saturday Review*, 8 July 1876, 59.

[Review of *The Adventures of Tom Sawyer*]

Anonymous

This tale of boy-life on the other side of the Atlantic will amuse many readers, old as well as young. There is a certain freshness and novelty about it, a practically romantic character, so to speak, which will make it very attractive. Desert islands and the like are all very well to read about, but boys know that they are not likely to come in their way; but an island in the Mississippi where they can really play Robinson Crusoe, catch fish to eat, and in a way, actually live like real runaways, looks true. Altogether, Tom Sawyer's lot was cast in a region not so tamed down by conventionalities, as is that in which English boys are doomed to live. Hence he had rare opportunities, and saw rare sights, actual tragedies, which our tamer life is content to read about in books. Of course, what Mark Twain writes is sure to be amusing. There are passages in this volume which no gravity could resist. Notably there is that in which is detailed Tom's experience with the "pain-killer," which his too-careful aunt administered to him in the hope of benefiting his health. For a while, Tom was content to hand it over to a crack in the floor. But one day the cat came along and begged for a share, and the temptation was irresistible. The animal, of course, performed the most amazing antics before the old lady's eyes. Tom, asked for an explanation, demurely answers " 'Deed, I don't know, Aunt Polly: cats always act so when they're having a good time." Pressed with the truth, and asked why he had treated "that poor dumb beast so," he continues, "I done it out of pity for him,—because he hadn't any aunt." *Tom Sawyer* is certainly a book to be read.

Reprinted from *Spectator*, 15 July 1876, 901.

[Notice of *The Adventures of Tom Sawyer*]

Anonymous

A bright, most readable, and informing book, which we can most cordially recommend to the ever growing class who are on the outlook for such books.

Excerpted from the *Newcastle Weekly Chronicle* in *Athenaeum*, 22 July 1876, 128.

[Review of *The Adventures of Tom Sawyer*]

Anonymous

Mark Twain belongs to a somewhat different school of writers from Miss Yonge, and "Tom Sawyer" is a characteristic production of his genius. We recognize the germ of it in the stories of the good and bad little boys, which went some way towards making their author's popularity. "Tom Sawyer," as we are told in the Preface, is intended primarily for the amusement of children, but it is hoped that "it will not be shunned by men and women on that account, for part of my plan has been to try pleasantly to remind adults of what they once were themselves." How far Master Sawyer's eccentric experiences may come home in that way to American citizens we cannot pretend to say. To our English notions, Tom appears to have been a portentous phenomenon, and his eventful career exhibits an unprecedented precocity. His conceptions were as romantic as their execution was audacious. Holding all sedentary occupations in aversion, his cast of thought was as original as his quaint felicity of picturesque expression. We are very sure there are no such boys in this country, and even in the States it may be supposed that the breed has been dying out, for fully more than a generation has gone by since Tom was the glory and plague of his native village on the Mississippi. His remarkable talent for mischief would have made him an intolerable thorn in the flesh of the aunt who acted as a mother to him had it not been that his pranks and misconduct endeared him to that much-enduring woman. "Cuteness" is scarcely the word for Tom's ingrained artfulness. Take, by way of example, one of his earliest achievements. He is caught by his aunt in some flagrant delict, and condemned to whitewash the fence that runs in front of her cottage. Tom had planned to make one of a swimming party, and, what is more, he knows that he will be jeered by his playmates, and contempt is intolerable to his soaring spirit. So, when he sees Ben Rogers, whose satire he stands most in dread of, come puffing along the road, personating a high-pressure steamer, Tom buckles himself to his task with a will. He is so absorbed, in fact, in artistic enthusiasm that Ben's ribald mockery falls on unheeding ears, and Tom has actually to be twitched by the jacket before he turns to recognize his friend. Ere long Ben, who was bound for the river, is begging and praying to be permitted to have a turn

Reprinted from the London *Times*, 28 August 1876, 4:4–5.

with the brush. Tom is slow to be persuaded; had it been the back fence it might have been different, but his aunt is awful particular about this front one—

"Ben, I'd like to, honest injun; but Aunt Polly—well, Jim wanted to do it, but she wouldn't let him. Sid wanted to do it, but she wouldn't let Sid. Now, don't you see how I'm fixed? If you was to tackle this fence and anything was to happen to it." The result is that Tom, as an immense favour, trades the privilege of a few minutes' painting for an apple. Each of the other boys, as he comes up in Ben's wake, makes a similar deal on his own account. Tom amasses a wealth of miscellaneous treasure, which he subsequently barters for a sufficiency of tickets of merit at the Sunday school to entitle him to walk off with the honours for which meritorious children have been toiling; while his aunt, to her intense surprise, finds her fence covered with several coatings of whitewash, and goes into raptures over Tom's capacity for work on the rare occasions when he chooses to apply himself. But, though anything but a bookish boy, Tom had paid considerable attention to literature of an eccentric kind, and, indeed, his knowledge of men and things was very much taken from his favourite authors. He runs away with a couple of comrades to follow the calling of pirates on an island of the Mississippi, the grand inducement being "that you don't have to get up mornings, and you don't have to go to school and wash and all that blame foolishness." After some days, when the trio are bored and half-starved and rather frightened, Tom plans a melo-dramatic return, and the missing ones emerge from the disused gallery of the church and present themselves to the congregation of weeping mourners, just as the clergyman's moving eloquence is dwelling on the virtues of the dear departed. Afterwards, Tom, who "all along has been wanting to be a robber," but has never been able to find the indispensable cave, stumbles on the very thing to suit him. So he carries off a devoted follower who has been hardened for an outlaw's life by the habit of living on scraps and sleeping in empty hogsheads—Republican freedom from class prejudices seems to have been a marked feature among the boys of the Transatlantic St. Petersburg. He teaches Huck his duties as they are flying from the society of their kind out of the accumulated stores of his own erudition. "Who'll we rob?" asks Huck. "Oh, 'most anybody—waylay people; that's mostly the way." "And kill them?" "No, not always. Hide them in the cave till they can raise a ransom. You make them raise all they can off o' their friends, and after you've kept them a year, if it ain't raised, then you kill them. That's the general way. Only you don't kill the women; you shut up the women, but you don't kill them. They're always beautiful and rich and awfully scared. You take their watches and things, but you always take off your hat and talk polite. There ain't everybody as polite as robbers; you'll see that in any book. Well, the women get to loving you; and after they've been in the cave a week or two weeks they stop crying, and after that you couldn't get them to leave. If you drove them out they'd turn right round and come back. It's so in all the books." In the course of their researches in the cavern they come on what Tom pronounces "an awful snug place for orgies." "What's orgies?" inquires Huck. "I dunno," says Tom very frankly; "but robbers always have orgies and of course we've got to have them too."

We fear these elegant extracts give but a faint idea of the drollery in which the book abounds; for the fact is that the best part of the fun lies in the ludicrous individuality of Tom himself, with whom we have been gradually growing familiar. But we should say that a perusal of "Tom Sawyer" is as fair a test as one could suggest of anybody's appreciation of the humorous. The drollery is often grotesque and extravagant, and there is at least as much in the queer Americanizing of the language as in the ideas it expresses. Practical people who pride themselves on strong common sense will have no patience with such vulgar trifling. But those who are alive to the pleasure of relaxing from serious thought and grave occupation will catch themselves smiling over every page and exploding outright over some of the choicer passages.

[Review of *The Adventures of Tom Sawyer*]

ANONYMOUS

Tom Sawyer is a bit of a scamp, a kind of juvenile Gil Blas, an *enfant terrible*, a schoolboy full of practical jokes and solemn impositions, who wins a Sunday-school Bible by buying tickets, and proves his assiduous study by the astounding answer to the question, 'Who were the first two apostles?' 'David and Goliath.' He absconds from school, and with a village ne'er-do-well sets up for a pirate on an island in the river, then steals home at night to listen to his old aunt weeping over him as drowned, and is furtively present on Sunday to hear his funeral sermon preached. In one of his escapades he is witness of a midnight murder—gets lost in a cave on the Mississippi, finds the murderer and his treasure, and ends his schoolboy days by being a hero. The book is full of roaring fun, interspersed with touches of true pathos. It will have the effect of making boys think that an unscrupulous scapegrace is sure to turn out a noble man; it might therefore have given more emphasis to truth and straightforwardness. But it is irresistible; fully up to the mark of the 'Innocents Abroad.'

Reprinted from the *British Quarterly Review* 63 (October 1876): 264.

[Review of *The Adventures of Tom Sawyer*]

ANONYMOUS

Mark Twain's new novel is intended rather for boys and girls than the subscribers to Mudie's. Mark Twain's wit too often depends on mere mannerism. He relies too often upon spelling for his point. Whether English boys and girls will appreciate the humour of "Tom Sawyer" as much as their American cousins, appears to us very doubtful. We want to be born in the States to appreciate the allusions. Aristophanes himself is often dull from our ignorance of Attic slang. In an English edition of Mark Twain's works we would venture to suggest that a glossary would be useful.

Reprinted from the *Westminster Review*, 2 October 1876, 573.

[Review of *The Adventures of Tom Sawyer*]

Anonymous

Tom Sawyer, it is almost needless to remark, is an American, and his adventures are such as could only happen in a country where nature and novelists conduct their operations on a portentous scale. Mr. Twain is as daring as his hero. He heaps incident upon incident and impossibility upon impossibility with an assurance which is irresistible. We almost believe in Tom Sawyer while reading about him, and are ready to agree with some of his companions, who affirmed that "he would be President yet if he escaped hanging." Tom goes to Sunday school, but gains small moral advantage from this duty, for he is naughty enough to buy up the tickets of good boys and to receive the prize he did not merit. He displays his knowledge of Scripture by saying that the two first disciples were David and Goliath, and his piety in church by catching flies. Then he shams illness in order to stay from school, but peccadilloes like these can be committed by ordinary youths, and Tom's ambition soon leads him to more exciting adventures. First, however, he makes love to a girl who goes to the same school, and the story of the courtship is told in Mr. Twain's best style. Unfortunately, just as the course of schoolboy love promises to run quite smoothly, Tom lets out that he has been "engaged" before, and of course the new love, Becky Thatcher by name, is mortally offended, and will not accept his peace offering, a brass knob from the top of an andiron, whereupon Tom thinks there is no more hope for him in this world and wishes he could die temporarily. He finds some comfort, however, in the resolution to turn outlaw, and after the horrible experience of witnessing a midnight murder in a churchyard Tom, being a second time repulsed by his young lady, goes with two còmrades to an uninhabited island, where they determine to be pirates, but pirates of a novel description, for they say their prayers like good boys, and resolve not to steal. How they return to civilization in time to hear their virtues wept over at a funeral sermon is very humorously related. The mourners broke into sobs, the preacher cried in the pulpit, "when the three dead boys came marching up the aisle." After this date Tom's adventures multiply, and the boy apparently gets little rest either by day or night. We cannot venture to follow his erratic footsteps. Suffice it to say that, having told a lie to shield

Reprinted from the *Pall Mall Gazette*, 28 October 1876, 11.

Becky from a whipping, (do they whip school-girls in the States?) Tom, after saving a widow's life and having sundry marvellous encounters with Injun Joe, the murderer, to whose bloody deed he had been a witness, loses himself with his lady-love in a cave, and is in intimate danger of death by starvation. All turns out well at last, after the manner of story-books, to every one but Injun Joe, who dies the death which Tom and Becky have escaped. This is the bare outline of a tale full to overflowing of exciting and impossible scenes. The book is deficient occasionally in good taste, and there are allusions in it which grate unpleasantly on the ear; but the first requisite of a story-book is accomplished, for the interest is sustained throughout.

Mark Twain's New Book

Anonymous

The American Publishing company of this city have just issued Mark Twain's book, "Tom Sawyer." It is a beautiful book, both outside and in, as one might naturally expect to find it on seeing the imprint of this publishing house upon it—a house that has established a well-earned reputation in the book publishing lines. The illustrations in the book are of a merit beyond praise. They are of the eloquent kind that speak for themselves, as well as for the print they illustrate. Those who imagine this to be a tame story for little boys will discover their mistake on reading it. It is safe to predict that no one will read the first page without reading all the rest. There is a power of attraction about it that doesn't "let up," but grows stronger to the end. Though claiming to be a book for boys and girls it will not be monopolized by them. There's rich entertainment in it for young and old. The author says most of the adventures recorded in it really occurred, and that one or two of them were his own. Perhaps his well-known modesty forbids his claiming any larger proportion. The story dates back some forty years ago, in one of the southwestern slave states. The hero, Tom Sawyer, is a unique individual, to state it mildly. The author says he belongs to the composite order of architecture. Perhaps that is as good a description of him as can be given in brief. He isn't one of the orthodox boys who loves their Sunday schools, and love to read about the good little boys who die early and go to heaven. He evidently preferred the other place where they don't have any Sunday schools, and the boys don't have to keep quiet every seventh day in the week. He doesn't believe in early deaths, nor early piety. Tom is a reckless, daredevil fellow, ready to hazard life for an adventure any time; but under the rollicking air of the book there appears an occasional bit of philosophy in the peculiarly dry, sarcastic vein of the author, as this, for instance:[1]

*   *   *

Here's a hit at ministers:[2]

*   *   *

Reprinted from the *Hartford Daily Times*, 20 December 1876, 1:1.

The following, especially the account of the fly's toilet is particularly good:[3]

*　　*　　*

During the sermon that followed—a sermon that thinned the elect down to a company so small as to be "hardly worth the saving"—Tom had further interesting adventures which helped to give variety and keep awake "other people uninterested in the sermon" as well as himself.

The account, some chapters further along, of the village school graduating exercises, and the prize poems and compositions of the young ladies, is racy and rich, but not in the least exaggerated. Its beauty consists in its truth to life. The slim, melancholy girl, with a cast of countenance "that comes of pills and indigestion," who reads a poem as indigestible as her ordinary diet, is to be found in any average school of the present day, as can likewise be found her bilious companion who reads a composition which "wound up with a sermon so destructive of all hope to non-Presbyterians that it took the first prize."

Perhaps the most pointed paragraph in the book is the following in relation to a petition for pardon for a murderer:[4]

*　　*　　*

If there is any defect in the book it is in the love scenes, where a boy of Tom Sawyer's size wanders off to be an outlaw. This part is a little overdrawn. But the whole story is so exquisitely told that the book will be widely sought. It is a capital gift for the holidays.

Notes

1. Omitted is an excerpt from chapter 2, 16.3–16.13.
2. Omitted is an excerpt from chapter 5, 39.14–40.11.
3. Omitted is an excerpt from chapter 5, 40.13–40.31.
4. Omitted is an excerpt from chapter 33, 240.36–241.7.

[Notice of *The Adventures of Tom Sawyer*]

Anonymous

We have already alluded to Mark Twain's new book, "The Adventures of Tom Sawyer." The work has just been published, and is a most capital subject for a holiday gift. Like all of its author's works, it overflows with rare and quaint humor; and, in addition to its attractive subject-matter, it has the advantage of being bound very handsomely, printed on heavy tinted paper, and beautified with 150 illustrations, and is to be obtained at a far lower price than Twain's other works. It contains about 300 pages. The lady agent for this city may be found at 88 Court Street, where any subscriber omitted by her may obtain the book.

Reprinted from the New Haven *Morning Journal and Courier*, 21 December 1876, 1:8.

[Review of *The Adventures of Tom Sawyer*]

[CHARLES DUDLEY WARNER?]

Mark Twain's *Adventures of Tom Sawyer* was published in England last June, and immediately many of the most easily detached and quotable portions of it found their way into the American press, and a wide circulation. The COURANT printed at the time two or three extracts from the book—Tom's adventure with the beetle in church, a most delightful study as well as a piece of profound philosophy, and the whitewashing of the fence, a bit of genuine fun with an artistic finish that would give the author a deserved reputation if he had never written anything else. The volume has just been brought out here in a very handsome style, copiously illustrated with drawings by Mr. J. W. Williams, who has happily entered into the spirit of the book, and produced excellent and on the whole the best set of character sketches we have ever seen from his pencil. The engravings do not all do justice to the original drawings, but they are more than fair, and as the text is beautifully printed on broad pages, the whole effect is very pleasing, and the volume is attractive at the first glance.

Tom Sawyer is in some respects an advance on anything that Mr. Clemens has before done—an advance we mean as a piece of literary work, careful in finish, and thought out more maturely. It has not the large, original force of that uncontrolable, spontaneous humor that in "The Innocents Abroad" carried an irrepressible burst of merriment round the globe, from San Francisco to India by way of Europe, but it has passages as exquisitely humorous as any in that book, and as a general thing it is more finely wrought. The passages we have spoken of above amply sustain this assertion; you can read them again and again with new delight, and indeed, we find it difficult not to read them every time we take up the book. They could not have been written without the spark of genius. We find in this book, too, the author's style, not more virile and sparklingly clear than formerly, but more carefully finished; and the author has toned down a little those excursions into the impossible, which are intensely amusing, but do not commend themselves to the judgment on a second reading. And in doing this he has lost nothing of his extraordinarily forceful use of the English language. There is no one

Reprinted from the *Hartford Daily Courant*, 27 December 1876, 1:8. Also printed in the *Boston Globe*, 29 December 1876, 4:5–6.

writing today who has a finer intuitive sense of the right word in the right place.

The book is all about boys, and it is said to be written for boys. It is a masterly reproduction of boy's life and feeling, but, at the same time, it is written above boys: that is, the best part of it—the wit, the humor, the genius of it will fly miles above every boy's head in the country. The boys can appreciate the adventure in it as a mere narrative, but not that which makes the adventure valuable to older readers, who recall their own boyhood in it. The boy has not the least sense of humor; there is nothing funny to him in having his pocket in measure of useless trash; the tricks he plays upon his comrades are not amusing to him; he is a non-humorous, dead, in earnest creature, and it is this characteristic that makes him amusing to us (to himself in retrospect); but his serious life does not take in what we call humor. It is for this reason that we say that Tom Sawyer will be enjoyed most by mature readers, who will have a great delight in seeing how faithfully boy life is recalled.

Boy nature is the same everywhere, and the characteristics here given are of universal acceptance; but local coloring (as it is now called) is different, and the boys of this book are of Missouri and not of New England in a good many of their ways; and so they ought to be, being studies from life. We should not counsel New England boys to expect or to imitate some of the adventures in this book, but they doubtless are true enough to the society they sketch. The Missouri boy who has mighty stirrings in his soul and feels deeply the desperate injustice of his tender home, may want to go away and be a noble river pirate, just as the New England boy is sometimes moved to run away to sea. But neither of them we fancy ever finds or makes a pot of money by any sudden streak of luck.

We do not believe that Tom Sawyer or his comrades ha[ve] the least idea how bright a boy he is, or what exceedingly funny things he says; he is as bright as Mark Twain himself. And probably no boy will appreciate the deep fun and satire of the following passage. In a midnight adventure of Tom and his companion, Huckleberry, the boys think they are lost and fall into a panic. Huckleberry whispers:—[1]

*　　*　　*

The Sunday-school chapter, in which Tom's financial abilities come out strong, and he trades himself into the possession of the first prize, and in which he exhibits his Biblical knowledge, is saturated with the keenest humor; but a boy will hardly comprehend the fine observation and deep satirical humor of the scene. It is prize day and company is present. On the platform is the great Judge Thatcher, the county judge, and it is an important hour for Mr. Walters, the superintendent, and for the whole school. It was an impressive silence when Jeff Thatcher, the brother of the judge, observed by "ranks of staring eyes," went forward to be familiar with the great man and be envied by the school:—[2]

*   *   *

Tom is a genuine boy and his Aunt Polly is a genuine woman; both are capitally drawn; and the author has given to both some noble traits and elements of pathos which make them remain our friends long after the laughter they excite has ceased. The book is full of quotable things, scenes as amusing as anything Mr. Clemens has written, with now and then a stroke of good humored satire that is as well deserved as it is artistically administered—take the school examination and exhibition as a specimen; the remarks on the "compositions" of the young ladies might well be framed and hung up in every school room. But it is unnecessary to quote from a book which everybody will read.

Notes

1. Omitted is an excerpt from chapter 10, 81.32–82.5.
2. Omitted is an excerpt from chapter 4, 33.24–34.5.

[Review of *The Adventures of Tom Sawyer*]

Anonymous

Mark Twain's "Adventures of Tom Sawyer" having first appeared in Canadian print, and thus been made familiar to admirers of "Mark," has at last been published by an American firm, "The American Publishing Company, of Hartford," namely, and it is made more attractive than the foreign edition by numerous illustrations and excellent print and paper. If "Mark" had not proved himself unpatriotic enough to sell his wares first to a "Kanuck" we should possibly have dwelt longer upon this book. As it is, we can but commend it as exceedingly funny, and apologize to our readers (not to "Mark"—not at all to "Mark") for the brief mention which we make of it, on the ground that everybody will have Mr. Clemens's "brain-work" whether it is issued here or across the border, and that, consequently, everybody has already read of the astute "Tom" and his fence-whitewashing experience as well as of numberless other episodes in that precocious and peculiar youth's career. We hope that in future Mr. Clemens will be more patriotic and mingle his efforts to secure an international copyright with his sense of duty to the country which gave him birth.

Reprinted from the New York *World*, 1 January 1877, 2:5.

Mark Twain's Lively Juvenile

ANONYMOUS

One of the best books ever written by the genial Mark Twain is this fascinating history of the comical Tom Sawyer. Of the little barefooted hero and his humorous associates Mr. Clemens says in this preface: "Most of the adventures recorded in this book really occurred. One or two were experiences of my own, the rest those of boys who were schoolmates of mine. Huck Finn is drawn from life; Tom Sawyer also, but not from an individual. He is a combination of the characteristics of three boys whom I knew, and therefore belongs to the composite order of architecture." The story is told in an episodical way and with an individual completeness of chapters that permits of felicitous quotation. As a consequence the different sketches have been torn from their places in the symmetrical whole, and in still symmetrical and most laughable form have been scattered about the world in a lavish and indiscriminate style, often without the slightest credit to either author or publisher. The scene of the story is laid in Missouri, and at some point on or near the Mississippi river. Tom's mother is dead, and he and his brother "Sid" live with an old but very affectionate aunt. The boy is full of life and activity, averse to the path of knowledge, and with a limited inclination to that of rectitude. His escapes, subterfuges, dodges, tricks, and escapades of all kinds, afford abundant opportunity for amusing description and for the exercise of that quaint fancy which characterizes all of the writer's efforts. The volume is intended mainly for the entertainment of boys and girls, but the hope is expressed in the preface that it will not be shunned by men and women on that account, as it may serve to remind grown people of how they once felt and talked, and in what absurd childish adventures they were once engaged. We select one of those episodes as a fair sample of the contents of the volume:[1]

*   *   *

The illustrations are handsome, and fit the text in their graphic and fanciful character. Other mechanical features are equally admirable.

Notes

1. Omitted is an excerpt from chapter 6, 44.1–47.13.

Reprinted from the San Francisco *Sunday Chronicle*, 7 January 1877, 6:5–6.

[Review of *The Adventures of Tom Sawyer*]

Anonymous

Shades of the venerable Mr. Day, of the instructive Mrs. Barbauld, of the persuasive Miss Edgeworth! Had you the power of sitting to-day beside the reviewer's desk, and were called upon to pass judgment on the books written and printed for the boys and girls of today, would you not have groaned and moaned over their perusal! If such superlatively good children as Harry and Lucy could have existed, or even such nondescript prigs as Sandford and Marton had abnormal being, this other question presents itself to our mind: "How would these precious children have enjoyed Mark Twain's Tom Sawyer!" In all books written for the amusement of children there are two distinct phases of appreciation. What the parent thinks of the book is one thing; what the child thinks of it another. It is fortunate when both parent and child agree in their conclusions. Such double appreciation may, in most instances, simply be one in regard to the fitness of the book on the part of the parent. A course of reading entirely devoted to juvenile works must be to an adult a tax on time and patience. It is only once in many years that such a charming book as *Little Alice in Wonderland* is produced, which old and young could read with thorough enjoyment. If, thirty years ago, *Tom Sawyer* had been placed in a careful father's hands to read, the probabilities would have been that he would have hesitated before giving the book to his boy—not that Mr. Clemens' book is exceptional in character, or differs in the least, save in its cleverness, from a host of similar books on like topics which are universally read by children to-day. It is the judgment of the book-givers which has undoubtedly undergone a change, while youthful minds, being free from warp, twist, or dogma, have remained ever the same. Returning then to these purely intellectual monstrosities, mostly the pen-and-ink offspring of authors and authoresses who never had any real flesh and blood creations of their own, there can be no doubt that had Sandford or Merton ever for a single moment dipped inside of *Tom Sawyer's* pages, astronomy and physics, with all the musty old farrago of Greek and Latin history, would have been thrown to the dogs. Despite tasseled caps, starched collars, and all the proprieties, these children would have laughed uproariously over *Tom Sawyer's* "cat and the pain-killer," and certain new ideas

Reprinted from the *New York Times*, 13 January 1877, 3:2–3.

might have had birth in their brains. Perhaps, had these children actually lived in our times, Sandford might have been a Western steam-boat captain, or Merton a filibuster. *Tom Sawyer* is likely to inculcate the idea that there are certain lofty aspirations which Plutarch never ascribed to his more prosaic heroes. Books for children in former bygone periods were mostly constructed in one monotonous key. A child was supposed to be a vessel which was to be constantly filled up. Facts and morals had to be taken like bitter draughts or acrid pills. In order that they should be absorbed like medicines it was perhaps a kindly thinker who disguised these facts and morals. The real education swallowed in those doses by the children we are inclined to think was in small proportion to the quantity administered. Was it not good old Peter Parley who in this country first broke loose from conventional trammels, and made American children truly happy? We have certainly gone far beyond Mr. Goodrich's manner. There has come an amount of ugly realism into children's story-books, the advantages of which we are very much in doubt about. We draw our pictures, utterly indifferent as to the subjects. Now, it is perfectly true that many boys do not adopt drawing-room manners. Perhaps it is better that little paragons—pocket Crichtons—are so rare. Still, courage, frankness, truthfulness, and self-reliance are to be inculcated in our lads. Since association is everything, it is not desirable that in real life we should familiarize our children with those of their age who are lawless or dare-devils. Granting that the natural is the true, and the true is the best, and that we may describe things as they are for adult readers, it is proper that we should discriminate a great deal more as to the choice of subjects in books intended for children. To-day a majority of the heroes in such books have longings to be pirates, want to run away with vessels, and millions of our American boys read and delight in such stories. In olden times the *Pirate's Own Book* with its death's-head and crossbones on the back had no concealment about it. It is true, edition after edition was sold. There it was. You saw it palpably. There was no disguise about it. If a father or mother objected to their child's reading the *Pirate's Own Book*, a pair of tongs and a convenient fireplace ended the whole matter. To-day the trouble is this: That there is a decidedly sanguinary tendency in juvenile books. No matter how innocent, quiet, or tame may be the title of a child's book, there is no guarantee that the volume your curly-headed little boy may be devouring may not contain a series of adventures recalling Capt. Kidd's horrors. In the short preface of *Tom Sawyer*, Mr. Clemens writes, "Although my book is intended mainly for the entertainment of boys and girls, I hope it will not be shunned by men and women on that account." We have before expressed the idea that a truly clever child's book is one in which both the man and the boy can find pleasure. No child's book can be perfectly acceptable otherwise. Is *Tom Sawyer* amusing? It is incomparably so. It is the story of a Western boy, born and bred on the banks of one of the big rivers, and there is exactly that wild village life which has schooled many a man to self-reliance and energy. Mr. Clemens has a remarkable memory for those peculiarities of American boy-talk which the grown man may have forgotten, but which return to him not unpleasantly when once the proper key is sounded. There is one scene of a quarrel, with a dialogue between Tom and a city boy which is perfect of its kind. Certain chapters in Tom's life, where his love for the school-girls is told, make us believe that for an urchin who had just lost his milk-teeth the affections out West have an awakening even earlier than in Oriental climes. In fact, Tom is a preternaturally precocious urchin. One admirable character in the book, and touched with the hand of a master, is that of Huckleberry Finn. There is a reality about this boy which is striking. An honest old aunt, who adores her scapegrace nephew, is a homely picture worked with exceeding grace. Mr. Clemens must have had just such a lovable old aunt. An ugly murder in the book, over-minutely described and too fully illustrated, which Tom and Huck see, of course, in a graveyard, leads somehow or other, to the discovery of a cave, in which treasures are concealed, and to which Tom and Huck fall heirs. There is no cant about Mr. Clemens. A description of a Sunday-school in *Tom Sawyer* is true to the letter. Matters are not told as they are fancied to be, but as they actually are. Mr. Walters is the Superintendent of the village Sunday-school, and this is Mr. Clemens' idea about him and his actions:[1]

*   *   *

Have any readers ever seen a Sunday-school "show off"? If they have, it was done exactly as Mr. Clemens tells it:[2]

*   *   *

Tom, like all boys, gets good and bad by fits and starts, and becomes a member of the order of the Cadets of Temperance, "being attracted by the showy character of their regalia." Tom swears to abstain from smoking, chewing, and profanity, in order to wear the uniform of the Cadets of Temperance on the occasion of the expected death of a rural Judge, when the regalia is to be sported at his funeral. But as the Judge don't die soon enough, Tom, disgusted with waiting, throws off his regalia and relapses again.[3]

*   *   *

If Mr. Clemens has been wanting in continuity in his longer sketches, and that sustained inventive power necessary in dovetailing incidents, *Tom*, as a story, though slightly disjointed, has this defect less apparent. As a humorist, Mr. Clemens has a great deal of fun in him, of the true American kind, which crops out all over the book. Mr. Clemens has an audience both here and in England, and doubtless his friends across the water will re-echo the hearty laughs which the reading of *Tom Sawyer* will cause on this side of the world. We are rather inclined to treat books intended for boys and girls, written by men of accredited talent and reputation, in a serious manner. Early impressions are the lasting ones. It is exactly such a clever book as *Tom Sawyer* which is sure to leave its stamp on younger minds. We like, then, the true boyish fun of Tom and Huck, and have a foible for the mischief these children engage in. We have not the least objection that rough boys be the heroes of a story-book. Restless spirits of energy only require judicious training in order to bring them into proper use. "If your son wants to be a pirate," says Mr. Emerson somewhere, "send him to sea. The boy may make a good sailor, a mate, maybe a Captain." Without advocating the utter suppression of that wild disposition which is natural in many a fine lad, we think our American boys require no extra promptings. Both East and West our little people are getting to be men and women before their time. In the books to be placed, then, into children's hands for purposes of recreation, we have a preference for those of a milder type than *Tom Sawyer*. Excitements derived from reading should be administered with a certain degree of circumspection. A sprinkling of salt in mental food is both natural and wholesome; any cravings for the contents of the castoras, the cayenne and the mustard, by children, should not be gratified. With less, then, of Injun Joe and "revenge," and "sitting women's ears," and the shadow of the gallows, which throws an unnecessarily sinister tinge over the story, (if the book really is intended for boys and girls,) we should have liked *Tom Sawyer* better.

Notes

1. Omitted is an excerpt from chapter 4, 31.14–32.15.
2. Omitted is an excerpt from chapter 4, 33.27–34.5.
3. Omitted is an excerpt from chapter 22, 161.29–162.7.

[Review of *The Adventures of Tom Sawyer*]

Anonymous

Tom Sawyer was a boy, not one of the sort that you read about in good books, but a little devil, never malicious and always at some trick, and in the course of years he engaged in a multitude, all of which are here recorded in Twain's style. He had special aversions for church, Sunday school, pious people, devout conversation and the company of his sedate but good old aunt. In spite of his efforts to escape from such inflictions he had to suffer them once in a while, but in his efforts to get some diversion on such occasions he more than once made lively sensations. Too lazy to get his Sunday school lessons, he managed by sharp trading to buy up a lot of the tickets given to the best pupils, and when a distinguished visitor came the children were requested to step forward with their tickets so that the one who had the most should receive the prize. To the astonishment of all Tom Sawyer was the hero, and, after a great time had been made over him, the visitor thought Tom should have a chance to show his learning, so he asked him who were the first two of the twelve Apostles to follow Jesus, it being presumed that the prize boy knew such things perfectly, for the lesson of the term had been in the study of the four Gospels. Tom felt the necessity of giving some answer, and his was "David and Goliath," to the surprise of the visitor, the consternation of the head teacher and the amusement of the school. When Tom went to church he took a large snapping bug (which has a grip like a crab) with him, and it got hold of a church-going dog, which rushed around the building and howled in a manner highly unbecoming to the place. When he was sick his aunt gave him pain-killer, and when she went out he gave a dose to the cat, which squawled, rushed around like mad, upsetting everything, and then jumped through the window, breaking a pane of glass in the way. Aunt Polly hearing the disturbance and finding the cause, scolded Tom for being so cruel to the cat, but Tom said she had compelled him to take pain-killer when he protested, and he had not given it to pussy till she came and begged for a taste when she saw him pour it into a spoon. He went to school, and got into trouble on account of a little girl—both about ten years old. Having read about the romantic life of pirates, Tom and two companions of the same age stole a little raft, on which

Reprinted from the San Francisco *Daily Alta California*, 15 January 1877, 2:3.

they floated a few miles on the Mississippi to a small uninhabited island, where they remained three days, while their relatives mourned their supposed death by drowning, and when they were discovered and brought back [*sic*] there was great rejoicing, and Tom was looked at by other little boys as a wonderful hero, and he put on awful airs on account of the sensation he made. What we have told here is merely part of the outline of the story; the chief merit is in the filling in, which is full of humorous and acute delineation of the follies, superstitions and peculiarities of boys, girls and older people.

[Review of *The Adventures of Tom Sawyer*]

Anonymous

Whatever Mark Twain writes is pretty sure of an eager popular recognition. And it is due to him to say that he finds his readers and admirers among all classes, here and in England. His humor has that eclectic quality that makes itself appreciated alike by the tutored and untutored, by the refined and coarse natured; for it appeals to the instinctive love of the ludicrous and the exaggerated, which dwells in all human souls. His last book, *The Adventures of Tom Sawyer*, is not unworthy his well-earned fame. Nowhere else do his peculiar gifts appear more conspicuous, does his lawless fancy have more free play, is his drollery more unctuously genuine. The book we suspect to have some of the characteristics of an autobiography. *Tom Sawyer* is too vividly realistic to be entirely a creation of fancy. If the author had not told us that it was drawn in part at least from life we would have been irresistibly forced to the conclusion that the master-touches were evolved from his "inner consciousness." He must have *felt* in his deepest experience what he so vividly and with such intense truthfulness describes. "Tom Sawyer" is the story of a harum scarum reckless boy, not bad, but full to the brim of childish perverseness. The old Adam possesses him from the very cradle, making him the plague of the household, the terror of goody-goody folks, the persecutor of those colorless little seraphs known as "good boys." He will lie, he will cheat at play, he will steal in a small way, he will impose upon the credulity of guileless Sunday-school superintendents by palming other boys' "reward of merit" tickets as his own; he will desecrate the Lord's Day by taking a snapping bug to church with him and fixing it to a pious dog's tail. He is taken sick, and his aunt gives him a painkiller to alleviate his bodily torments, but instead of taking it himself as a good boy should, he administers it to the cat, to the great bodily agony of that persecuted quadruped. And so he goes from bad to worse, capping the climax of his wicked ways by turning amateur pirate—floating off on a raft with two boon companions, taking possession of a desolate island in the Mississippi river, where they remain three days, to the great anguish of their friends, who gave them up for drowned. Discovered and brought back [*sic*], Tom

Reprinted from the San Francisco *Evening Bulletin*, 20 January 1877, 1:3.

assumes the air of a hero, and is looked upon with awe and envy by his less adventurous play-fellows. For his later exploits, we refer the reader to the narrative, which will be found almost as absorbing in its interest as *Robinson Crusoe*.

[Review of *The Adventures of Tom Sawyer*]

ANONYMOUS

In the first half of "The Adventures of Tom Sawyer" there are some of Mark Twain's best and most characteristic touches. In the last half the exaggeration is marked and the piece loses much of its charm, becoming a commonplace story, grotesquely told, instead of the singularly faithful picture of life in a little town on the banks of the Mississippi River which it sets out to be. The book is meant for children's reading chiefly—unless this pretension is one of its author's broad jests, as it may be. Certainly it will be in the last degree unsafe to put the book into the hands of imitative youth, and as certainly every grown reader will enjoy it heartily.

The tale is simply a record of the doings of Tom Sawyer and his companions, chief among whom is Huckleberry Finn, the outcast of the village; and their doings afford a setting for as graphic and realistic a picture of the life of the western river towns a generation ago as has been produced anywhere. With apparent unconsciousness, which may be only apparent, and seemingly with no more earnest purpose than to amuse himself and his readers, Mr. Clemens has given us, in the earlier chapters of this book, a bit of very genuine art, which is fairly entitled to rank with Mr. Aldrich's "Story of a Bad Boy." Like Mr. Aldrich's story, it is intensely funny; but it is like that work also in other and better ways.

Reprinted from the New York *Evening Post*, 1 February 1877, 1:1.

[Review of *The Adventures of Tom Sawyer*]

ANONYMOUS

Our city of Hartford can boast the greatest humorist in current literature. Mr. Clemens owes nothing to erratic spelling like "Artemas Ward," or to exciting political themes like some other witty writers. He is altogether original and unique. "The Innocents Abroad," is an ex[h]austless feast vastly entertaining and full of information as a book of travels. The same charm of genius in an unusual direction fills the fascinating pages of "Tom Sawyer." The boy hero and the other children are so lifelike that the reader hardly needs the author's assurance that real boys and genuine parts are in the book. One gets very fond of Tom notwithstanding his grave faults, some of which you almost wish had been omitted. But he is a brave, manly boy after all, and the finest scene in the whole story to one reader at least, is where he receives a whipping to shield a little, terrified girl. The childish attachment between these two and the manly protection Tom accords to little Becky both at school and amid the horrors of being lost in the cave, are very finely described. To one who had only seen the other side of Tom's character these noble traits would have seemed impossible. The "pain-killer" adventure is funny beyond expression as is much of Tom's career. The last few chapters are extremely sensational and strike one as too remarkable to be natural adventures for little boys. One cannot help regretting that so fine a fellow as Tom lies and smokes, but the intention was not to describe a model boy. Yet these traits solely detract from the hero. Those who regard Mark Twain as only "a funny man," greatly underestimate his power. Wit is the spice of his books not the substance. In this story are some most exquisitely beautiful descriptions. That of early morning in one place particularly, is delicious in its perfect picture of nature and its beautiful poetry.

Reprinted from the *Christian Secretary*, 17 May 1877, 2.

CRITICAL ESSAYS

◆

[Review of *The Adventures of Tom Sawyer*]

Anonymous

Our city of Hartford can boast the greatest humorist in current literature. Mr. Clemens owes nothing to erratic spelling like "Artemas Ward," or to exciting political themes like some other witty writers. He is altogether original and unique. "The Innocents Abroad," is an ex[h]austless feast vastly entertaining and full of information as a book of travels. The same charm of genius in an unusual direction fills the fascinating pages of "Tom Sawyer." The boy hero and the other children are so lifelike that the reader hardly needs the author's assurance that real boys and genuine parts are in the book. One gets very fond of Tom notwithstanding his grave faults, some of which you almost wish had been omitted. But he is a brave, manly boy after all, and the finest scene in the whole story to one reader at least, is where he receives a whipping to shield a little, terrified girl. The childish attachment between these two and the manly protection Tom accords to little Becky both at school and amid the horrors of being lost in the cave, are very finely described. To one who had only seen the other side of Tom's character these noble traits would have seemed impossible. The "pain-killer" adventure is funny beyond expression as is much of Tom's career. The last few chapters are extremely sensational and strike one as too remarkable to be natural adventures for little boys. One cannot help regretting that so fine a fellow as Tom lies and smokes, but the intention was not to describe a model boy. Yet these traits solely detract from the hero. Those who regard Mark Twain as only "a funny man," greatly underestimate his power. Wit is the spice of his books not the substance. In this story are some most exquisitely beautiful descriptions. That of early morning in one place particularly, is delicious in its perfect picture of nature and its beautiful poetry.

Reprinted from the *Christian Secretary*, 17 May 1877, 2.

The Composition and Structure of
The Adventures of Tom Sawyer

Hamlin L. Hill

The structure of *The Adventures of Tom Sawyer* has for some time marked a point of divergence among Twain scholars. Walter Blair's study "On the Structure of *Tom Sawyer*" suggested that the book was organized as the story of a boy's maturation, presented to the reader through four lines of action—the Tom and Becky story, the Muff Potter story, the Jackson's Island adventure, and the Injun Joe story—each of which begins with an immature act and ends with a relatively mature act by Tom.[1] Blair's interpretation has been accepted by Dixon Wecter, who agreed that "Tom and Huck grow visibly as we follow them,"[2] by Gladys Bellamy,[3] and E. H. Long.[4] But it has been ignored by DeLancey Ferguson, who claimed that "*Tom Sawyer*, in short, grew as grows the grass; it was not art at all, but it was life."[5] It was disclaimed by Alexander Cowie, who stated that *Tom Sawyer* "lives in small units which when added up (not arranged) equal the sum of boyhood experience."[6] And most recently, Roger Asselineau dismissed Blair's hypothesis as a mere tour de force when he suggested, "This attempt at introducing logic and order into a book which had been rather desultorily composed was interesting, but not fully convincing. Such *a posteriori* conclusions, however tempting, smacked of artificiality and could only contain a measure of truth."[7]

These, then, are the two poles: that *Tom Sawyer* has a narrative plan and exhibits what was for Twain a high degree of literary craftsmanship; or that it is a ragbag of memories, thrown together at random with little or no thought to order or structure. My suggestion is that the original manuscript, now in the Riggs Memorial Library of Georgetown University, Washington, D.C.,[8] holds the solution to the problem of the book's structure and that a more intention intensive examination of it than De Voto made in *Mark Twain at Work*[9] provides the secret of Mark Twain's methods of composition of *Tom Sawyer*.

Reprinted from *American Literature* 32 (January 1961): 379–92. Copyright 1961, Duke University Press. Reprinted by permission of the publisher.

I

Twain's own statements about the book's composition support the "ragbag" theory. He began work on *Tom Sawyer* itself, as distinguished from its several precursors, [10] probably in the summer of 1874. By September 4, he "had worked myself out, pumped myself dry,"[11] so he put the manuscript aside until the spring or summer of 1875, and on July 5, 1875, announced its completion.[12] Years later, he described the crisis which presumably came in September, 1874:

> At page 400 of my manuscript the story made a sudden and determined halt and refused to proceed another step. Day after day it still refused. I was disappointed, distressed and immeasurably astonished, for I knew quite well that the tale was not finished and I could not understand why I was not able to go on with it. The reason was very simple—my tank had run dry; it was empty; the stock of materials in it was exhausted; the story could not go on without materials; it could not be wrought out of nothing.[13]

And Brander Matthews, reporting a discussion with Twain, confirmed this haphazard method of composition:

> He began the composition of "Tom Sawyer" with certain of his boyish recollections in mind, writing on and on until he had utilized them all, whereupon he put his manuscript aside and ceased to think about it, except in so far as he might recall from time to time, and more or less unconsciously, other recollections of those early days. Sooner or later he would return to his work and make use of memories he had recaptured in the interval.[14]

The manuscript provides many examples of this plot development through recollection and association.

While writing or reading over the early parts of *Tom Sawyer*, Twain apparently remembered ideas and incidents from his earlier writings or his own boyhood which he felt might be of use to him later. Accordingly, he wrote notes and suggestions in the margins of his manuscript, mentioning material which would either be utilized later in the book or be discarded.[15] A few of these notations are so cryptic that I have been unable to identify them: "The dead cigar man" on manuscript page 210, "The old whistler" on page 85, and "Silver moons" on page 322. But in most cases his intention is perfectly clear.

Among the marginal reminders which Twain discarded was the name of a steamboat, the *City of Hartford*, which he wrote on manuscript page 89, opposite the Sunday school superintendent's speech (Chapter IV). Evidently his first thought was to utilize an anecdote from his May, 1870, "Memoranda" column for this speech. The episode went thus:

> "Just about the close of that long, hard winter," said the Sunday-school superintendent, "as I was wending toward my duties one brilliant Sabbath morning, I glanced down toward the levee, and there lay the City of Hartford!—no mistake about it, there she was, puffing and panting, after her long pilgrimage through the ice. . . . I should have to instruct empty benches, sure; the youngsters would all be off welcoming the first steamboat of the season. You can imagine how surprised I was when I opened the door and saw half the benches full! My gratitude was free, large, and sincere. I resolved that they should not find me unappreciative. I said: 'Boys, what renewed assurance it gives me of your affection. I confess that I said to myself, as I came along and saw that the City of Hartford was in—'
>
> " 'No! *But is she, though!*'
>
> "And as quick as any flash of lightning I stood in the presence of empty benches! I had brought them the news myself."[16]

In the margin of a page for Chapter VIII (MS p. 210), he wrote "Rolling the rock," a reference to the Holliday's Hill episode which he had utilized in *The Innocents Abroad* (Chapter LVIII) and which he rejected for *Tom Sawyer*. And three pages later Twain noted, "candy-pull," apparently toying with the idea of having "Jim Wolfe and the Cats" make an appearance in the book.[17] He also suggested to himself on page 464, "Becky had the measles," and "Joe drowned." One suggestion which was not eliminated entirely but was greatly altered in the book appeared on manuscript page 161: "burnt up the old sot." The story recalled the time that Clemens gave a tramp some matches which "the old sot" used to burn up the jail and himself, and Twain referred to it in *Life on the Mississippi* and the *Autobiography*[18] as well as *Tom Sawyer*. The character corresponding to the tramp was Muff Potter, and Tom did smuggle "small comforts" to Muff in jail and was bothered with nightmares, just as young Sam Clemens was in 1853. But since burning Muff Potter would have made it necessary to omit the trial chapter, Twain used only those portions of the story which we find in the book.

Some of the marginal notations bore fruit immediately. On page 15 Twain wrote "coppers" and on page 19 mentioned that the "new boy" whom Tom was challenging "took two broad coppers out of his pocket and held them out with derision" (Chapter I). On page 409 he wrote "storm" and on page 432 began describing the storm on Jackson's Island (Chapter XVI).

Several of the notes were not incorporated into the manuscript until much later. In the margin of a page of Chapter VIII (MS p. 209), he wrote, "Cadets of Temp.," a suggestion for including material which would appear in Chapter XXII of the book. On the next page, 210, he wrote, "Learning to smoke" and "Burying pet bird or cat." The first note was amplified in

Chapter XVI, where Huck instructs Tom and Joe Harper in the art of smoking; and the other received brief mention in Chapter XXII: "He drifted listlessly down the street & found Jim Hollis acting as Judge in a juvenile court that was trying a cat for murder, in the presence of her victim, a bird" (MS p. B-12).

In another hand, probably Mrs. Clemens's, there was a note on page 160 (Chapter VI) which read, "Take of[f] his wig with a cat." Twain himself reiterated the suggestion on page 573 (Chapter XXIII, but written before the graduation ceremony chapter), noting "(Dropping cat)."[19] Finally, in Chapter XXI, the humorist incorporated the incident of lowering a cat from the ceiling to remove the schoolmaster's wig.

Incidentally, the graduation chapter, although it utilized these notes, was greatly assisted by a book Twain possessed: *The Pastor's Story and Other Pieces; or Prose and Poetry* by Mary Ann Harris Gay, of which seven editions were published between 1858 and 1871.[20] It was this author and this book which Twain acknowledged in his note at the end of the graduation chapter: "The pretended 'compositions' quoted in this chapter are taken without alteration from a volume entitled 'Prose and Poetry, by a Western Lady'— but they are exactly and precisely after the school-girl pattern and hence are much happier than any mere imitations could be." The elocutions in this chapter, "Is This, Then, Life?," "A Missouri Maiden's Farewell to Alabama," and "A Vision," were not, then, as Dixon Wecter suggested,[21] Twain's own satiric efforts. On the contrary, the humorist pasted actual pages torn from Mary Ann Gay's book in his manuscript. His page A-14 (547–548) is actually pages 31 and 32 of her selection, "Is This, Then, Life?" His pages A-16 (550) and A-17 (551) are her pages 118 and 119, "Farewell to Alabama," written, her footnote explained, in imitation of Mr. Tyrone Power's "Farewell to America." And finally, Twain's page A-19 (553) was her pages 189 and 190, "A Vision."

All this material supports the theory that *Tom Sawyer* was structureless. The author's own statements suggested that he wrote those memories of his childhood which came to mind, waited until he remembered some more, and then added them to his manuscript. The marginal notations show that as he wrote he thought of other incidents by association and made his notes to keep them in mind. In one instance the associative link between the material he was writing and the marginal note is apparent. On page 209 he was describing Tom Sawyer's daydream of returning to St. Petersburg as a pirate wearing a "crimson sash." A red sash was the enticement which the author could not resist as a boy when joining the Cadets Temperance, and, remembering this, he wrote the "Cadets of Temp." note in his margin. This was sheer opportunism, but it was the way he collected the material for the book—from immediate memory and from brief notes in his margins which he would later expand.[22]

II

On the other hand, some of the material in the manuscript supports the "maturation" theory. In the margin of manuscript page 276, in the hand I believe is Mrs. Clemens's, there appeared, "Tom licked for Becky." Twain repeated the suggestion on page 464: "T takes B's whipping." And in Chapter XX, he expanded the note into one of the chapters which Blair suggests are crucial,[23] delaying the use of his wife's note until fairly late in the book. Conversely, he manipulated the Cadets of Temperance episode to emphasize Tom's immaturity. He first mentioned the Cadets of Temperance in a brief paragraph of a letter for the *Alta California:*

> . . . And they started militia companies, and Sons of Temperance and Cadets of Temperance. Hannibal always had a weakness for the Temperance cause. I joined the cause myself, although they didn't allow a boy to smoke, or drink or swear, but I thought I never could be truly happy till I wore one of those stunning red scarfs and walked in procession when a distinguished citizen died. I stood it four months, but never an infernal distinguished citizen died during the whole time; and when they finally pronounced old Doctor Norton convalescent (a man I had been depending on for seven or eight weeks,) I just drew out. I drew out in disgust, and pretty much all the distinguished citizens in the camp died within the next three weeks.[24]

In *Tom Sawyer* (Chapter XXII), the material was almost as short:

> Tom joined the new order of Cadets of Temperance, being attracted by the showy character of their "regalia." He promised to abstain from smoking, chewing, and profanity as long as he remained a member. Now he found out a new thing—namely, that to promise not to do a thing is the surest way in the world to make a body want to go and do that very thing. Tom soon found himself tormented with a desire to drink and swear; the desire grew to be so intense that nothing but the hope of a chance to display himself in his red sash kept him from withdrawing from the order. Fourth of July was coming; but he soon gave that up—gave it up before he had worn his shackles over forty-eight hours—and fixed his hopes upon old Judge Frazer, justice of the peace, who was apparently on his death-bed and would have a big public funeral, since he was so high an official. During three days Tom was deeply concerned about the Judge's condition and hungry for news of it. Sometimes his hopes ran high—so high that he would venture to get out his regalia and practice before the looking-glass. But the Judge had a most discouraging way of fluctuating. At last he was pronounced upon the mend—and then convalescent. Tom was disgusted; and felt a sense of injury, too. He handed

in his resignation at once—and that night the Judge suffered a relapse and died. Tom resolved that he would never trust a man like that again.

The four months of membership were shortened to less than a week in *Tom Sawyer*, making Tom much less steadfast than young Clemens. And the overwhelming desire to drink and swear made Tom much more irresolute and immature. Both changes tended to emphasize the boy's inability to abide by his decisions at this point in the book.

But the most important support for Blair's interpretation occurs on the first page of the manuscript. Here Twain wrote a long note, never before discussed, which merits careful study:

> I, Boyhood & youth; 2 y & early manh; 3 the Battle of Life in many lands; 4 (age 37 to [40?],) return & meet grown babies & toothless old drivelers who were the grandees of his boyhood. The Adored Unknown a [illegible] faded old maid & full of rasping, puritanical vinegar piety.

This outline was written, if not before he began the book, before he reached page 169 of his manuscript. Before that page, the "new girl" was referred to as "the Adored Unknown" (Chapter III of the published book). And on that page the name "Becky Thatcher" appeared for the first time (Chapter VI). If Becky had been "christened" when Twain wrote this outline, it seems likely that he would have used her name in it. The marginal note represents, then, a very early if not the earliest plan for the plot of the new novel. The book was to be in four parts, clearly progressing from boyhood to maturity and ending with Tom's return to St. Petersburg and a puritanical Becky. The "return" idea was a recurrent one, appearing in Twain's notebooks several times.[25] Rudimentary though it is, this outline assumes enormous importance, for the only "theme" it conveys is one of the maturation of a person from boyhood to manhood. It is obviously crucial to determine exactly when this plan was discarded, because if Twain composed the book by this formula the "maturation" theory stands vindicated.

Even after the book was finished, Twain was uncertain about the wisdom of having stopped with Tom's youth. "I have finished the story and didn't take the chap beyond boyhood," he told Howells. "See if you don't really decide that I am right in closing with him as a boy."[26] But the decision to alter the original outline was not made until after September 4, 1874, and perhaps as late as the spring of 1875.

Page 403 of the manuscript, where the change is noticeable, appears toward the end of Chapter XV. Tom, Joe Harper, and Huck have run away to Jackson's Island to become pirates. Joe and Huck, homesick and ready to return to St. Petersburg, have been "withered with derision" by Tom, who has no desire to go back to civilization. The cannons on the ferry boat have failed to bring up the boys' bodies. Just as in *Huckleberry Finn*, the stage has been set, the devices prepared, for an imminent departure. After the other boys go to sleep, Tom scrawls a note to Joe Harper on a piece of sycamore bark and leaves it, together with his "schoolboy treasures of almost inestimable value." This leavetaking from Joe thus sounds much more final than would be necessary merely for Tom to deliver a note to his aunt. Tom writes another note for Aunt Polly, returns to his home in St. Petersburg, and at page 403 is standing over his sleeping aunt.

Preparations were thus made for Tom to begin his "Battle of Life in many lands," to leave both St. Petersburg and his comrades who were about to return there. But Mark Twain's manuscript shows that he pondered the wisdom of having Tom depart. Aware that a critical point in the story was at hand, he sprinkled the page with signs of his indecision. Deliberating what course to take, he wrote at the top margin, "Sid is to find and steal that scroll," and "He is to show the scroll in proof of his intent." In the left margin, he wrote two further lines and cancelled them. Across the page itself he wrote, "No, he leaves the bark there, & Sid gets it." Then he suggested, "He forgets to leave the bark." This was the point at which he had "pumped myself dry"[27] and found that "at page 400 of my manuscript the story made a sudden and determined halt and refused to proceed another step."[28]

If the note was merely to contain the message, "We ain't dead—we are only off playing pirates," the author's ruminations over what would happen to it were completely out of proportion. If Tom left Jackson's Island to deliver this message and then return, the bequest of his proudest possessions to Joe Harper was equally absurd. If, as one of the notes suggested, he was to forget to leave the scroll after swimming part of the river and sneaking under his aunt's bed, he would be completely unbelievable. But if the bark was to contain a farewell message to Aunt Polly and was to be stolen by Sid, this scene might prepare for Tom's return at age thirty-seven to St. Petersburg. Though the possible development of the plot is conjectural, it is plausible to suggest an identification scene, perhaps a court trial, in which the stolen bark would be the crucial evidence.[29] Almost literally, the piece of bark with a scrawled message separated the reader from something very similar to *Adventures of Huckleberry Finn*; the scroll of sycamore bark became the key to the further progress of *Tom Sawyer* that the resurrected raft would later be in Twain's masterpiece.[30] Used in one way, the plot would continue on the course Twain outlined on the first page of his manuscript; used in another, the direction of the novel would be altered.

Twain chose not to have Tom start his travels. The boy returns the scroll to his jacket pocket, where Aunt Polly discovers it a few chapters later. It was undoubtedly after he made his decision that he also turned back to page 401 and inserted a paragraph: "This was Wednesday night. If the OVER [then on the back of the page] bodies continued missing until Sunday, all hope would be given over, & the funeral would be preached on that morning. Tom shuddered." *Now* the stage was set for the boy's return to their own funeral.

In several places the author reminded himself marginally to insert Aunt Polly's discovery of the message: on page 409 he jotted down, "The piece of bark at Aunt Polly's," and on page 464, "Aunt P's bark." Finally, on manuscript page 512 he related her discovery of the scroll and rounded off the awkward solution of that problem. He never explained Tom's similar message to Joe or his strange bequest of his "treasures" to his friend. Whether from expediency, indifference, or, most likely, the realization that Tom Sawyer was not the boy to send off on the "Battle of Life in many lands," Twain decided not to start Tom's journeying. Evidence that he realized Tom's shortcomings for such a role is offered by his own statement to Howells that "by and by I shall take a boy of twelve and run him on through life (in the first person) but not Tom Sawyer—he would not be a good character for it."[31] The decision committed him to center the book in his protagonist's boyhood in St. Petersburg.

Even though Twain thus determined the direction of his plot on manuscript page 403, the second half of the book gave him some problems in organization. For two hundred pages, beginning at manuscript page 533 and therefore in the late spring and summer of 1875, he juggled and rearranged his chapters extensively. For the two hundred pages following page 533 the manuscript is paginated thus (brackets indicating cancelled page numbers):

			A-1	to	A-24		
			B-1	to	B-13		
		[534]	573	to	[642]	694	
	[535]	[643]	695	to	[345]	[653]	705
		[654]	706	to	[669]	721	

The two inserts, A-1 to A-24 and B-1 to B-13, related the graduation ceremonies and the Cadets of Temperance episode (Chapters XXI and XXII). The latter chapter may have been composed separately when the author wrote a note about it the previous fall; but since a marginal note referring to the graduation chapter occurred at page 573, that material must have been composed after the note (in Chapter XXIII) was written. Obviously neither insert was placed in its present position until after Twain had written beyond them to page 722 (Chapter XXX). The third section listed above contained Chapters XXIII through the first paragraph of XXIX. The fourth contained eleven pages of Chapter XXIX relating some preliminary details about the picnic. The final section related the last paragraphs of Chapter XXIX, those concerning Huck, Injun Joe, and Widow Douglas. From the pagination it appears that Twain originally intended the picnic section to follow the scene in which Tom took Becky's whipping.[32] Then Muff Potter's trial was substituted. While writing of the aftereffects of Muff's trial, Twain cancelled a passage which was to lead to the capture or death of Injun Joe. In Chapter XXIV, just before the final sentence of the published book, he wrote regarding Tom's apprehension of Injun Joe's revenge: "But Providence lifts even a boy's burden when it begins to get too heavy for him. The angel sent to attend to Tom's was an old back-country farmer named Ezra Ward, who had been a schoolmate of Aunt Polly's so many. . . ." The page (MS p. 600) ended and Twain discarded whatever other pages carried the idea further. Ezra Ward became an enigma, the only clue to his intended function in the story being the cryptic marginal note, "Brick pile." At this spot, probably, Twain replaced whatever plan he had for Injun Joe with the "buried treasure" chapters culminating in Joe's death in the cave. For he began writing the treasure chapters (XXV–XXIX) immediately after cancelling the "Ezra Ward" material. These chapters then followed the trial chapter, and the beginning of the picnic was placed in Chapter XXIX. At this point, apparently realizing the climactic possibilities of the cave chapters, Twain placed the two sections on the graduation exercises and on the Cadets of Temperance between the whipping scene and Potter's trial. This manipulation of material which was written more or less at random was accurately described by Brander Matthews:

> When at last he became convinced that he had made his profit out of every possible reminiscence, he went over what he had written with great care, adjusting the several instalments one to the other, sometimes transposing a chapter or two and sometimes writing into the earlier chapters the necessary preparation for adventures in the later chapters unforeseen when he was engaged on the beginnings of the book.[33]

Furthermore, this rearrangement of his material tends to support the theory that Twain was working with the deliberate intention of showing Tom's maturation. The school graduation depicting the high jinks at the expense of the school master and the painfully amateurish orations, and the Cadets of Temperance material revealing a youthful, irresolute Tom Sawyer were inserted in a relatively early spot in the manuscript, forcing three of the four chapters which Blair suggests are crucial into later positions.[34] The trial of Muff Potter was followed by the treasure chapters which portrayed a superstitious and fanciful pair of boys, and before this line of action was completed in Chapter XXIX by "showing Huck conquering fear to rescue the widow,"[35] the author inserted some preliminary paragraphs originating the picnic scene, paragraphs which had originally been intended for Chapter

XXI. Next came Huck's bravery (MS pp. 706–721), completing the Injun Joe line of action. Finally the picnic material developed into the adventures in the cave, which not only completed the Tom and Becky line of action but also showed Tom at his most manly. Though terms like *maturation, boyhood, youth,* and *early manhood* are ambiguous and ill-defined, nevertheless the rearranging of these climactic chapters allowed Twain to present Tom in a group of critical situations toward the end of the book where maturer judgment and courage were vital. These events required a Tom Sawyer who was nowhere apparent in the idyllic first half of the book.

III

In composing *Tom Sawyer*, then, Twain faced and solved two problems. First, when he was about half way through his manuscript, he paused at a crucial point and determined to keep his story centered in youth in St. Petersburg. An early scheme had included taking Tom on a "Battle of Life in many lands," and the moment for his departure was reached on manuscript page 403. Even though he altered the structure of the novel then, the author was nevertheless progressing through several stages of childhood mentioned in his outline, a progression which would be, as Blair observed, a "working out in fictional form . . . of a boy's maturing."[36]

Then in 1875, in the second half of the book, Twain very deliberately shifted his chapters so that climactic actions were placed after childish and immature incidents. Though the various anecdotes and episodes which he mentioned in his margins came to him chaotically and without formal significance, the humorist's selectivity and rearrangement of the material provided him with the structure he envisioned, roughly, in his early outline of the book. The marginal notations were identical with the working notes of *Huckleberry Finn*: though they were a ragbag of memories, the book which resulted was not structureless.

The manuscript of *Tom Sawyer* thus provides convincing evidence to corroborate Blair's interpretation of the book. The original outline indicated that it was begun with a definite structure in the author's mind. And the rearrangement of the later material shows that, instead of growing "as grows the grass," the book was considerably altered to conform to a bisected version of the outline when Twain determined to keep it, as he stated in the "Conclusion," "strictly a history of a *boy* . . . the story could not go much further without becoming the history of a *man*."

Notes

1. Walter Blair, "On the Structure of *Tom Sawyer*," *Modern Philology*, XXXVII, 75–88 (August, 1939).
2. "Mark Twain," *Literary History of the United States*, ed. Robert E. Spiller *et al.* (New York, 1953), p. 930.
3. *Mark Twain as a Literary Artist* (Norman, 1950), pp. 334–335.
4. *Mark Twain Handbook* (New York, 1957), pp. 316–318.
5. *Mark Twain: Man and Legend* (Indianapolis, 1943), p. 176.
6. *The Rise of the American Novel* (New York, 1948), p. 609.
7. *The Literary Reputation of Mark Twain from 1910 to 1950* (Paris, 1954), p. 58.
8. I am grateful to Mr. Joseph Jeffs of the Riggs Memorial Library for making a microfilm of the manuscript available to me. I also thank the Mark Twain Estate for granting permission to quote previously unpublished notations in the manuscript, which are copyright 1959, by the Mark Twain Company.
9. Bernard De Voto, *Mark Twain at Work* (Cambridge, Mass., 1942), pp. 3–18. Cited hereafter as MTAW.
10. See MTAW, pp. 3–9.
11. *Mark Twain's Letters*, ed. Albert B Paine (New York, 1917), p. 224.
12. *Ibid.*, p. 258.
13. *Mark Twain in Eruption*, ed. Bernard De Voto (New York, 1940), p. 197.
14. Brander Matthews, *The Tocsin of Revolt and Other Essays* (New York, 1922), p. 265.
15. De Voto (MTAW, p. 6) mentions only one of these many marginal notations, the one on the first page of the manuscript: "Put in thing from Boy-lecture." The reference was probably to a lecture Twain proposed for the 1871–1872 lecture season. In the *American Publisher*, a magazine published by the American Publishing Company, Twain's publisher, and edited by Orion Clemens, Twain's brother, Orion revealed, "We have the pleasure to announce that Mark Twain will lecture in New England during the ensuing fall, and later, in the Western States. The subject is not yet decided upon. He has *two* new lectures, one an appeal in behalf of Boy's Rights, and one entitled simply 'D.L.H.' " (*American Publisher*, I, 4, July, 1871).
16. "Memoranda," *Galaxy*, IX, 726 (May, 1870), reprinted in *Mark Twain at Your Fingertips*, ed. Caroline T. Harnsberger (New York, 1948), pp. 30–31.
17. "Jim Wolfe and the Cats" was frequently reprinted. According to Merle Johnson, *A Bibliography of Mark Twain* (New York, 1935), p. 229, it appeared in the *Californian*, the New York *Sunday Mercury*, the "Buyer's Manual of 1872," "Beecher's Readings and Recitations," and in book form in *Mark Twain's Speeches* (New York, 1910), I, pp. 262–264, and *Mark Twain's Autobiography*, ed. Albert B. Paine (New York, 1924), 1, 135–138.
18. *Life on the Mississippi*, Chapter LVI, and *Autobiography*, I, 130–131. See Dixon Wecter, *Sam Clemens of Hannibal* (Boston, 1952), pp. 253–256, for a succinct account of the actual incident.
19. This and one other note of Livy's, considered below, are the only comments I have found in the manuscript which are by his wife; neither smacks of censorship. Mr. Fred Anderson, curator of the Mark Twain Papers, has suggested that since the language of these two notes does not sound like Mrs. Clemens, she may well have written them at her husband's dictation, perhaps while they were reading the manuscript aloud together.
20. See L. H. Wright, *American Fiction, 1851–1875* (San Marino, 1957), p. 131.
21. Wecter, *Sam Clemens of Hannibal*, p. 257, speaks of saccharine poetry "which he later satirized in *Tom Sawyer*, when at school exercises a 'slim, melancholy girl' arose and recited 'A Missouri Maiden's Farewell to Alabama.' "
22. On at least one occasion, however, Twain wrote some separate notes relating to

his book. In the Aldis Collection of the Yale University Library there is a single page of notes for the graveyard scene:

> Potter & Dr.
>> objects to job
>> quarrell [*sic*]
>> fight
>> Potter knocked down with Tom's
> shovel.
>> Joe rushed in & stabs Dr.
>> Potter insensible
>> Joe will bury Dr in Tom's hole &
> will make Potter think *he* is accessory.
>> Finds treasure—goes & hides it
> —returns & finds P up.
>> No use to bury body, for Potter
> thinks *he* did it.
>> When boys leave, they carry their
> tools with them & will never tell.
>> Somewhere previously it is
> said Joe lives in the cave.

Since Injun Joe has been substituted for Pap Finn (who originally played this part in the manuscript [see MTAW, p. 17]), and since the graveyard and the treasure scenes have been combined, this was probably a note for a lecture or a dramatization.

23. "On the Structure of *Tom Sawyer*," pp. 84–87.

24. *Mark Twain's Travels with Mr. Brown*, ed. Franklin Walker and G. Ezra Dane (New York, 1940), p. 146.

25. See MTAW, p. 49, and *Mark Twain's Notebook*, ed. Albert B. Paine (New York, 1935), p. 212.

26. *Mark Twain's Letters*, pp. 258–259. See also his letter of June 21, 1875, to Howells (MTAW, p. 10, n. 2).

27. Sept. 4, 1874, *Mark Twain's Letters*, p. 224.

28. *Mark Twain in Eruption*, p. 197.

29. Court trials with surprise witnesses and sensational evidence were the ingredients of one of Mark Twain's favorite plots. They occurred in "Ah Sin," "Simon Wheeler, the Amateur Detective," and several of the trials analyzed in D. M. McKeithan, *Court Trials in Mark Twain and Other Essays* (The Hague, 1958), pp. 10–114.

30. See Walter Blair, "When Was *Huckleberry Finn* Written?" *American Literature*, XXX, 1–25 (March, 1958), and Henry Nash Smith, "Introduction," *Adventures of Huckleberry Finn* (Boston, 1958), p. ix.

31. *Mark Twain's Letters*, p. 259.

32. The first three pages of the picnic material were originally numbered "535" to "537." The next eight pages were "338" to "345." The two-hundred-page drop in pagination was apparently inadvertent. There is no indication in the manuscript that this material might have belonged at page 338; Twain was making preparations for the picnic in Chapter XVIII, MS pp. 487–490.

33. Matthews, p. 266.

34. "On the Structure of *Tom Sawyer*," p. 87: "And well in the second half of the book, in a series of chapters—xx, xxiii, xxix, xxxii—come those crucial situations in which he acts more like a grownup than like an irresponsible boy."

35. *Ibid.*, p. 85.

36. *Ibid.*, p. 84.

[Discovery of River and Town]

Henry Nash Smith

The germ of *The Adventures of Tom Sawyer* was an unfinished sketch called "Boy's Manuscript" apparently written in 1870, that is, during the first year of the writer's married life. This is a literary burlesque, possibly suggested by David Copperfield's courtship of Dora. But the comic device of reducing the principals of a story to children was familiar on the popular stage; even as far west as Carson City, Mark Twain had seen the R. G. Marsh troupe of Juvenile Comedians, whose entire repertory consisted of burlesques of this sort. The "Boy's Manuscript" translates the story of an adult courtship (possibly with some reference to Mark Twain's own) into the vocabulary provided by the Matter of Hannibal. Instead of the conventional flower given by the woman to her lover, Mark Twain's hero, Billy Rogers, receives from his beloved a piece of molasses candy. He wears it next his heart until it melts and sticks to him so that he cannot get his shirt off. Billy Rogers became Tom Sawyer as the book unfolded in the author's mind, and the original love story was modified somewhat by a narrative pattern depicting Tom's growth toward maturity. But the childish love affair remains as a central component of what conventional plot the novel has. Tom's wanderings, intended and actual, are motivated by his despair over being rejected by Becky Thatcher. After their first quarrel he contemplates suicide, then decides to run away in order to become a pirate, but meets Joe Harper and falls to playing Robin Hood instead. After a later rejection Tom actually embarks on his career as a pirate to the extent of escaping to Jackson's Island with Huck Finn and Joe Harper.

The repetition of plot material in these two sequences suggests that Mark Twain found Tom's amorous experiences deficient in variety and exciting incident. He supplements the burlesque love story with two subplots: the rivalry between Tom and his half brother Sid (which is itself a burlesque of Sunday-school stories about the Bad Boy and the Good Boy), and the melodramatic sequence of events set in motion when Tom and Huck by accident become witnesses of the midnight grave-robbing and Injun Joe's murder of young Dr. Robinson. This material might be one of Tom Sawyer's

Reprinted by permission of the publishers from *Mark Twain: The Development of a Writer* by Henry Nash Smith, Cambridge, Mass.: The Belknap Press of Harvard University Press, copyright © 1962 by the President and Fellows of Harvard College.

fantasies except that we are expected to take it seriously. It is another example of Mark Twain's susceptibility to infection from "wildcat literature."

Neither the love story nor the Injun Joe subplot provides a good framework for the Matter of Hannibal, and the rivalry of Tom and Sid serves merely to introduce such boyish crimes as Tom's swimming without permission. Nothing comes of the hint that Sid picks up about the murder of Dr. Robinson from Tom's talk in his sleep. The Matter of Hannibal gets into *The Adventures of Tom Sawyer* primarily through episodes having little connection with the plot. Yet these are the passages for which the book is remembered: the whitewashing of the fence, the Sunday school and church services, examination day at school.

The structural problems of the novel, like those of Mark Twain's earlier books, reflect the instability of his attitudes toward his material. He was not clear in his own mind whether he was writing a story for boys or a story about boys for adults. The burlesque love story presupposes a grown-up audience; it depends for its effect on the reader's perception of the comic parallels between Tom's behavior and that of an adult. Tom's fantasies about pirates and robbers and Robin Hood, again, are relatively meaningless unless the reader can enjoy the ironic contrast between the glamorous fantasy world of romance and the everyday reality of life in St. Petersburg. Both these modes of burlesque interpose a considerable psychological distance between the novelist and his characters, and make it difficult for him to do justice to whatever values may be latent in the Matter of Hannibal. Thus at the end of the whitewashing episode Mark Twain remarks patronizingly that Tom

had discovered a great law of human action, without knowing it—namely, that in order to make a man or a boy covet a thing, it is only necessary to make the thing difficult to attain. If he had been a great and wise philosopher, like the writer of this book, he would now have comprehended that Work consists of whatever a body is *obliged* to do, and that Play consists of whatever a body is not obliged to do.

The incident is reduced to an exemplum illustrating a generalization that has nothing to do with the story. Something tells the writer he is on the wrong tack and he confuses things further by mocking at himself.

His uncertain attitude is even more apparent in his efforts to lend importance to the Injun Joe subplot. When the half-breed is found dead of hunger and thirst just behind the iron door Judge Thatcher has had installed at the entrance to the cave, Mark Twain inserts a serious version of Jim Blaine's rumination about special providences, with touches reminiscent of the rhapsody on the Sphinx in *The Innocents Abroad*:

In one place near at hand, a stalagmite had been slowly growing up from the ground for ages, built by the water-drip from a stalactite overhead. The captive had broken off the stalagmite, and upon the stump had placed a stone, wherein he had scooped a shallow hollow to catch the precious drop that fell once in every three minutes with the dreary regularity of a clocktick—a dessert-spoonful once in four-and-twenty hours. That drop was falling when the Pyramids were new; when Troy fell; when the foundations of Rome were laid; when Christ was crucified; when the Conqueror created the British empire; when Columbus sailed; when the massacre at Lexington was "news." It is falling now; it will still be falling when all these things shall have sunk down the afternoon of history and the twilight of tradition and been swallowed up in the thick night of oblivion. Has everything a purpose and a mission? Did this drop fall patiently during five thousand years to be ready for this flitting human insect's need? and has it another important object to accomplish ten thousand years to come?

*　　　*　　　*

The emphasis on Injun Joe's thirst is implausible in view of numerous earlier references to water in the cave; Tom and Becky had encountered him near a spring. Furthermore, such a burst of eloquence is quite out of keeping with the tone of the book. It serves no purpose except to demonstrate that the narrator can produce the kind of associations held in esteem by the dominant culture. The diction of the novel often has a similar effect. Take for example the introduction to the whitewashing incident:

> Saturday morning was come, and all the summer world was bright and fresh, and brimming with life. There was a song in every heart; and if the heart was young the music issued at the lips. There was cheer in every face and a spring in every step. The locust trees were in bloom and the fragrance of the blossoms filled the air. Cardiff Hill, beyond the village and above it, was green with vegetation, and it lay just far enough away to seem a Delectable Land, dreamy, reposeful, and inviting.

The elegantly archaic verb form "was come"; the genteel impersonality of "the lips"; "fragrance" in place of "odor"; the literary allusion in "Delectable Land"; and the telltale reference to dreams, all mark this as polite prose. The imagery and the tone are intended to establish a mood of peace and joy as a foil to Tom's "deep melancholy" over being sentenced to whitewash the fence: "Life seemed to him hollow, and existence but a burden." But the rhetorical effect is overdone.

Another illustration of the psychological distance between the writer and his material is the description of the superintendent's address to the pupils in the Sunday school, with satirical comments like the following.

> When a Sunday-school superintendent makes his customary little speech, a hymn-book in the hand is as necessary as is the inevitable sheet of music in the hand of a singer . . . at a concert—though why, is a mystery: for neither the hymn-book nor the sheet of music is ever referred to by the sufferer.

The patronizing air is maintained:

> The latter third of the speech was marred by the resumption of fights and other recreations among certain of the bad boys, and by fidgetings and whisperings that extended far and wide, washing even to the bases of isolated and incorruptible rocks like Sid and Mary.

In themselves, the witty understatement of "recreations" and the equally witty comparison of Sid and Mary to rocks with waves breaking against them are amusing, but they represent a kind of exhibitionism on the part of the writer.

Fortunately, Mark Twain is sometimes able to get rid of his self-consciousness and render Tom's experience directly, without comment or moralizing. Such a moment comes during the church service that follows the Sunday-school scene just quoted. The minister is inviting the attention of the Almighty to a long list of persons in need of divine guidance.

> In the midst of the prayer a fly had lit on the back of the pew in front of [Tom] and tortured his spirit by calmly rubbing its hands together, embracing its head with its arms, and polishing it so vigorously that it seemed to almost part company with the body, and the slender thread of a neck was exposed to view; scraping its wings with its hind legs and smoothing them to its body as if they had been coat-tails; going through its whole toilet as tranquilly as if it knew it was perfectly safe. As indeed it was; for as sorely as Tom's hands itched to grab for it they did not dare—he believed his soul would be instantly destroyed if he did such a thing while the prayer was going on. But with the closing sentence his hand began to curve and steal forward; and the instant "Amen" was out the fly was a prisoner of war. His aunt detected the act and made him let it go.

The language used in describing the fly is easy and effective without being either high or low: it is an almost imperceptible medium of communication. The insect is not a symbol, but the minuteness with which it is described conveys with admirable force Tom's agony of boredom during the prayer. He seizes upon any distraction that offers itself as a relief from his suffering. The austere language in which the fly is depicted is quite different from Mother Utterback's richly colloquial speech. At its best this prose is devoid of vernacular color as well as of all other idiosyncrasies. But Mark Twain could not have achieved such a command of his medium if he had not learned how to free himself from the preoccupation with eloquence that permeated the American literary tradition, and the means of his emancipation had been the skeptical attitude toward ornate rhetoric developed in his repeated exposures of it to comic juxtaposition with vernacular speech.

The description of Tom's secret journey back to St. Petersburg from Jackson's Island is a comparable example of the spare, flat rendering of experience. The series of declarative statements imparts an appropriate forward motion to the prose and engenders a mood of expectancy. Mark Twain carefully refrains from telling us what Tom is about. There is no reason why the information should be withheld except that the writer wishes to fix the reader's attention by something like suspense. Perhaps the result is impressive because it simulates the inner movement of our feelings in many actual situations: we recognize a strong current impelling us in a general direction, but we do not know what the exact outcome or destination will be. It may be also that stripping away rhetorical ornament fosters vividness by suggesting that the actual situation absorbs all the writer's attention. The passage sounds like Hemingway. Whatever the means by which the effect is achieved, it is an all but complete recapture of the past:

> A few minutes later Tom was in the shoal water of the bar, wading toward the Illinois shore. Before the depth reached his middle he was halfway over; the current would permit no more wading, now, so he struck out confidently to swim the remaining hundred yards. He swam quartering upstream, but still was swept downward rather faster than he had expected. However, he reached the shore finally, and drifted along till he found a low place and drew himself out. He put his hand on his jacket pocket, found his piece of bark safe, and then struck through the woods, following the shore, with streaming garments. Shortly before ten o'clock he came out into an open place opposite the village, and saw the ferry-boat lying in the shadow of the trees and the high bank. Everything was quiet under the blinking stars. He crept down the bank, watching with all his eyes, slipped into the water, swam three or four strokes, and climbed into the skiff that did "yawl" duty at the boat's stern. He laid himself down under the thwarts and waited, panting.
>
> Presently the cracked bell tapped and a voice gave the order to "cast off." A minute or two later the skiff's head was standing high up, against the boat's swell, and the voyage was begun. Tom felt happy in his success, for he knew it was the boat's last trip for the night. At the end of a long twelve or fifteen minutes the wheels stopped, and Tom slipped overboard and swam ashore in the dusk, landing fifty yards down-stream, out of danger of possible stragglers.

The information that the current swept Tom downstream faster than he expected lends a peculiar vividness to the passage. Since this had no effect on the outcome of the trip, it does not need to be reported for the sake of logic or coherence. The narrator's remark has the artless, circumstantial air of a witness determined to tell everything he remembers without presuming to judge what is relevant and what is not. The same comment could be made about the statement that the skiff's head stood up high, and the epithet "blinking" applied to the stars: that was the way they looked, although their appearance had no bearing on Tom's mission.

Another moment of almost completely unself-conscious recovery of the past—a moment that must lie close to the emotional center of the Matter of Hannibal for Mark Twain—comes a few pages later, but still in the Jackson's Island sequence:

> After breakfast they went whooping and prancing out on the bar, and chased each other round and round, shedding clothes as they went, until they were naked, and then continued the frolic far away up the shoal water of the bar, against the stiff current, which latter tripped their legs from under them from time to time and greatly increased the fun. And now and then they stooped in a group and splashed water in each other's faces with their palms, gradually approaching each other, with averted faces to avoid the strangling sprays, and finally gripping and struggling till the best man ducked his neighbor, and then they all went under in a tangle of white legs and arms, and came up blowing, sputtering, laughing, and gasping for breath at one and the same time.
>
> When they were well exhausted, they would run out and sprawl on the dry, hot sand, and lie there and cover themselves up with it, and by and by break for the water again and go through the original performance once more. Finally it occurred to them that their naked skin represented flesh-colored "tights" very fairly; so they drew a ring in the sand and had a circus—with three clowns in it, for none would yield this proudest post to his neighbor.

The language here is again almost without color, but what coloring it has is colloquial. "Whooping" and "prancing" are applied more often to animals than to human beings, and the actions they describe are distinctly indecorous. "Round and round" belongs to colloquial rather than exalted diction, and so does "chase" in the sense of "pursue." (One would prefer, incidentally, to omit "latter" in the last clause of the sentence.) "Averted faces" is somewhat literary in place of "faces turned away," but "ducked," "sputtering," "sprawl," and "break for the water" are drawn from a basic oral vocabulary. The writer is directing more attention to his subject than to his diction; it subordinates itself to the actions described.

As in the description of the fly, the minute detail with which the scene is rendered gives it an air of meaning more than it seems to on the surface. The lavish particularity testifies to the value the author attaches to what he is describing. It would never have occurred to Mark Twain to say that natural facts are symbols of spiritual facts, but the memory of such a frolic had for him thirty years later a significance comparable to what Emerson tried to express in metaphysical terms. Although the value is perhaps too deeply buried ever to be brought to the surface and given precise statement, it is value just the same, and it is not derived from the sources or supported by the sanctions acknowledged in the traditional culture. In contrast with the revulsion against the body implicit in the notion of refinement or ideality, this scheme of values lays stress on sensory experience—of sunlight, water, bodily movement, and physical contact with other human beings—and on impulse rather than schedules as a guide to behavior.

*   *   *

The images of Tom in church or Tom whooping and prancing along the sand bar remain in the reader's mind after Mark Twain's struggles with plot and subplot and point of view are forgotten. They belong to his primary alphabet of symbols. Their importance for his subsequent career requires us to examine them with care.

Tom is a kind of embryonic Everyman. In church and school he confronts institutions that seem to him alien and at times hostile; on Jackson's Island he enjoys comradeship with his fellows and he responds to the physical environment. Natural man beleaguered by society, but able to gain happiness by escaping to the forest and the river: this is undoubtedly an important aspect of the meaning that thousands of readers have found in the novel. In situations of this sort nineteenth-century writers were likely to be led by the heritage of Romantic thought to identify themselves with the virtuous hero and to ascribe evil exclusively to society. The signs of such a tendency on the part of Mark Twain himself can be discerned in *Tom Sawyer*. But the church and the school are not truly evil, they are merely inconvenient and tedious; Tom doesn't really intend running away for good; his playing pirate is a child's fantasy, and can with perfect appropriateness have its climax in the boys' return:

> Suddenly the minister shouted at the top of his voice: "Praise God from whom all blessings flow—SING! and put your hearts in it!"
> And they did. Old Hundred swelled up with a triumphant burst, and while it shook the rafters Tom Sawyer the Pirate looked around upon the envying juveniles about him and confessed in his heart that this was the proudest moment of his life.
> As the "sold" congregation trooped out they said they would almost be willing to be made ridiculous again to hear Old Hundred sung like that once more.

Here Tom is fully integrated with the community (which is identical with the congregation in the church); the community is completely harmonious within itself; and the general exultation finds expression in the singing of a Christian hymn at the command of the minister. The official culture of St. Petersburg could hardly receive a more absolute affirmation.

It is the absence of a basic conflict between Tom and the society of the village that obliges Mark Twain to look elsewhere for the conflict he considered essential to the plot of a novel. He solves his problem by introducing evil in the form of Injun Joe, whose mixed blood labels him an outsider. Tom and Huck fear him, and Tom is sufficiently aggressive to testify against him in court, but a direct collision is out of the question and Injun Joe has to be destroyed unintentionally by Judge Thatcher when he seals up the mouth of the cave.

While acknowledging, at least tacitly, the artificiality of this subplot, Bernard De Voto emphasized its importance in contributing to *Tom Sawyer* "murder and starvation, grave-robbery and revenge, terror and panic, some of the darkest emotions of men, some of the most terrible fears of children." He believed such materials were an important aspect of the book's fidelity to human experience. It is an idyll, he pointed out, but it is enclosed in dread; and this keeps it true to the world of boyhood. The argument has weight. Yet a melodramatic villain tends to evoke a melodramatic hero, and Mark Twain does not entirely resist the temptation. He evades the naïve moral categories of the Sunday-school books by making Tom a boy who is "bad" according to their standards yet "good" according to more profound criteria. The demonstration, however, is not enough to give Tom real depth of character. The reader is evidently meant to see Tom's badness as nothing more than endearing mischief, indicative of a normal amount of imagination and energy; it is not bad at all. Mark Twain has written the Sunday-school story about the Good Little Boy Who Succeeded all over again with only a slight change in the hero's make-up and costume.

If the Matter of Hannibal is to be explored by means of a plot involving a protagonist of this sort, two basic situations are possible. We may have the naturally good hero enjoying a triumphant and harmonious relation with his society (Tom in church while the Doxology is being sung), or the naturally good hero at odds with his society (Tom suffering during the minister's prayer). The first of these alternatives could yield nothing except an endorsement of conventional values. The second alternative was more promising; it at least offered a built-in conflict and a point of view adapted to satire of existing institutions. But *Tom Sawyer* shows how dangerous the idea of the hero's natural goodness was as literary material. It constantly threatened to become merely a stereotype because of the difficulty of imagining a kind of goodness basically different from that endorsed by the accepted value system. Francis Parkman, for example, wishing to praise his French-Canadian guide across the plains, Henry Chatillon, said he had a "natural refinement."

Mark Twain would ultimately need a hero more hostile toward the dominant culture than Tom Sawyer was—Tom, the devotee of the "rules," the exponent of doing things by the book, the respectable boy who took out his impulses toward rebellion in harmless fantasies of escape. It is appropriate that *The Adventures of Tom Sawyer* ends with Tom made wealthy by the treasure he has found, acclaimed as a hero, and basking in the approval of both his sweetheart and her father. His last act is to persuade Huck to return to the Widow Douglas' and be "respectable." No doubt this wind-up of the plot was dictated by "the exigencies of romantic literature" which Mark Twain later said accounted for the death of Injun Joe in the cave. In the brief Conclusion he almost explicitly confesses that the conventions of the novel as he has adopted them in *Tom Sawyer* have proved to be poorly suited to his materials.

This perception was probably aided by the fact that even before he had finished the book he had recognized the solution for several of his technical problems. It lay in using Huck Finn as a narrative persona. The outcast Huck was far more alienated than Tom from conventional values. Telling a story in Huck's words would allow Mark Twain to exploit fully the color of vernacular speech. At the same time, the use of a narrator who was also a principal actor in the story would virtually compel the writer to maintain a consistent point of view.

In a fashion that recalls Cooper's discovery of unexpected possibilities in Leatherstocking while he was writing *The Pioneers*, Mark Twain seems to grow suddenly aware of Huck's potential importance only a few pages before the end of *Tom Sawyer*. Huck performs his first significant act in Chapter 29 by giving the alarm to Mr. Jones and his sons, who frustrate Injun Joe's plot against the Widow Douglas. The conversation between Huck and the Joneses is reported at surprising length. Mark Twain has evidently become interested both in the workings of Huck's mind and in his speech; he exhibits him in the process of inventing a cover story—an activity that would become almost compulsive in *Adventures of Huckleberry Finn*. Huck's impulse to run away when he learns that the townspeople have gathered to honor him and Tom in a great civic ceremony and his sufferings under the regimen imposed on him by the well-intentioned Widow Douglas are not merely prophetic of the sequel, they merge imperceptibly with the opening chapters that Mark Twain would begin to write as soon as he had finished *Tom Sawyer*. Indeed, Tom figures too prominently for the taste of most readers in both the opening and the closing chapters of the later novel. But the differences between the two books—aptly illustrated by the contrast between the tone of the chapters of *Huckleberry Finn* in which Tom appears and the tone of those in which he does not—greatly outweigh the similarities. *Tom Sawyer* provides relatively little opportunity to deal with the problem of values to which Mark Twain had devoted so much attention in his early work; *Huckleberry Finn* is his major effort in this direction.

[Idyl]

JAMES M. COX

Roughing It and "Old Times on the Mississippi" had carried the autobiography of Mark Twain backward in time by successive stages to the threshold of Samuel Clemens' boyhood. With *The Adventures of Tom Sawyer*, Mark Twain crossed into the enchanted territory of childhood, where he was to make his greatest discoveries as a writer. It is possible to argue that he had crossed the threshold before completing "Old Times," for *Tom Sawyer* was actually begun before the first *Atlantic* sketch was written. In a real sense, the beginning of *Tom Sawyer* may have made possible "Old Times" itself, for in terms of chronology of composition, "Old Times" comes between the beginning and end of *Tom Sawyer*. Certainly the two books illuminate each other. For although the opening passage of "Old Times" is an overture to the sketches, its tone and substance are much more characteristic of the *matter* of *Tom Sawyer*. The cub Mark Twain has more in common with the boy Tom Sawyer than he probably had with the young Sam Clemens who became a pilot in 1857. The boy and the cub are so much alike that at times their experience almost seems to merge. Indeed, the scene in "Old Times" in which a certain "Tom" steals the cub's girl by virtue of a lucky escape could easily double as an adventure of Tom Sawyer. Though Samuel Clemens was twenty-two when he became a pilot, the cub Mark Twain seems scarcely older than Tom Sawyer; he is a pre-adolescent, interested in nothing but puppy love, and his fantasies are essentially the same as Tom's.

Short though the step is from the cub pilot to the dreaming boy, it involves a passage from one world to another. For in crossing the frontier dividing apprenticeship from boyhood, Mark Twain made the great transition from tall tale to fiction. The necessity which defined Mark Twain's life had been the experience of Samuel Clemens. Although Mark Twain might enlarge and be an enlargement upon that experience, he was nonetheless held in bondage to it by the ligature of actuality. The fictive element in the reconstruction of the past was actually an aspect of the humorous personality—it was, after all, Mark Twain's *humor* to exaggerate. As long as "Mark Twain" remained in the foreground of the action, there could be no fiction,

Reprinted from James M. Cox, *Mark Twain: The Fate of Humor* Copyright © 1966 Princeton University Press. Excerpt, pp. 127–155 reprinted with permission of Princeton University Press.

but only more tall tale. To achieve true fiction, Mark Twain had to invent a character to take his place and discover a plot which would free him from history.

The Adventures of Tom Sawyer, as its title discloses, is that discovery. The road there had been long and involved. Mark Twain had first to discover, exploit, and exhaust the myth of himself—which he had done in the course of *The Innocents Abroad, Roughing It*, and "Old Times on the Mississippi"— so that he would need to develop another claim. Yet even as he proceeded with the tall tale of himself, he was laying tentative and casual claims in the territory of fiction, some of which presaged *Tom Sawyer*. There is, for example, "The Story of the Bad Little Boy Who Did Not Come to Grief," a burlesque of the sentimental moral fables about good and bad little boys, which appeared in 1866. As burlesque, it depends much more upon inverting the parent form than inventing a new plot. Yet even in the idea of The Bad Boy, Mark Twain is pointing toward the figure of Tom Sawyer. Then there is the fragmentary "A Boy's Manuscript," probably written in 1870, which is actually a kind of scenario of *Tom Sawyer*. Written in dramatic form, this fragment contains the rudimentary character and situations of the novel. Yet the very facts that it is a fragment and is in the form of a drama suggest not how close Mark Twain was to the form of the novel, but how far he had to go to reach it.

The book which both defined that distance and helped span it was *The Gilded Age*, Mark Twain's first extended effort in fiction. Significantly enough, the book is a collaboration, in which Mark Twain contributed the character and Charles Dudley Warner furnished the plot. Much later, Mark Twain said that Colonel Sellers, the one memorable character in *The Gilded Age*, was his only real property in the book. Though he is not to be freed completely from the responsibility of the flimsy plot detailing the fortunes of Philip Sterling, there is no question that Sellers is Mark Twain's property and the plot is Warner's. The point is not whether Mark Twain is better than Warner, but that Mark Twain's invention lay primarily in character, not in plot—that, in fact, he needed someone else to provide the plot.

The whole process should not be surprising, for his invention of "Mark Twain" had been to impose a character upon a form. Thus, in *The Innocents Abroad*, he gave the world not so much a new travel book as a new traveler— a new perspective, a new point of view. In *The Gilded Age*, he left the narrative design to Warner and contented himself with inventing a character who would, and did, steal the show. Yet for all Sellers' grandiose imagination, for all his instant appeal, he cannot accomplish the "fiction" of the book; he exists as a creature unto himself rather than a character involved in the action. What the two writers fully share is the satiric-burlesque perspective. Yet here again, the point is that they share it. Each was only half a satirist by himself, but together they were able to write the satiric novel of their age which gave the age its name.

In the character of Tom Sawyer, however, Mark Twain fully entered the realm of fiction. The preface to the novel makes clear the different order of conception between fiction and the tall tale:

> Most of the adventures recorded in this book really occurred; one or two were experiences of my own, the rest those of boys who were schoolmates of mine. Huck Finn is drawn from life; Tom Sawyer also, but not from an individual— he is a combination of the characteristics of three boys whom I knew, and therefore belongs to the composite order of architecture.
>
> The odd superstitions touched upon were all prevalent among children and slaves in the West at the period of this story—that is to say, thirty or forty years ago.
>
> Although my book is intended mainly for the entertainment of boys and girls, I hope it will not be shunned by men and women on that account, for part of my plan has been to try to pleasantly remind adults of what they once were themselves, and of how they felt and thought and talked, and what queer enterprises they sometimes engaged in.[1]

To be sure, Tom Sawyer is said to be based on real people, but he is a composite character freed from the "experience" in which he had his origins. He is not bound by the laws of biography but by the laws of fiction, which is to say plot and character. It does not finally matter whether "most of the adventures recorded . . . really occurred," and by insisting they did, Mark Twain was doing no more than echoing a convention familiar to the novelist from the earliest emergence of the novel form.

The entire preface discloses how much Mark Twain relied upon the conventions of narrative structure and fictive reality. What Mark Twain discovered was the character of Tom himself—a boy in action. That is why Tom's presence has remained in the national memory while the organization of the narrative has been forgotten. For the reality of the adventures lies not so much in their order as in their relation to Tom. They are *his* adventures, and remain in the reader's memory as extensions of his character. Having come to accept Tom's freedom from the context in which he appeared, readers forget that it was the book itself which set him free.

There are four essential elements which make up the world of Tom Sawyer. First there is, of course, the figure of Tom himself, standing at the center of the stage. Second, there is the stage, the summer world of St. Petersburg. Third, there is the audience—the society of St. Petersburg, composed of adults as well as children, all of whom function at one time or another as Tom's audience inside the action. Finally, there is the narrator, who acts as an indulgent audience himself. Though he exercises as much power over his characters as Thackeray does in *Vanity Fair*, the narrator creates the illusion of being a spectator who draws the curtain at his performance rather than a puppet master pulling the strings. Although the perspective upon the characters is equally remote in both novels, Thackeray exercises control in terms of plot and history, Mark Twain in terms of age and time. Thackeray's genius, following mock-heroic strategies, reduces adult rituals and momentous events to the status of acts upon a dwarfed stage. Tom Sawyer and his gang, on the other hand, are children at play—their world is a play world in which adult rituals of love, death, war, and justice are reenacted in essentially harmless patterns. To be sure there is violence in the play world of Tom Sawyer, and Bernard De Voto was in a certain way right to observe that the idyl of Hannibal is surrounded by dread. Yet the boy's world is charmed; it is safe simply because the narrator's perspective enchants whatever terror and violence exist inside the world. Like the "once upon a time" of the fairy tale, this perspective reduces the size of the action by keeping it at a distance from the reader.

The distance is maintained in two ways—through the perspective of burlesque and the perspective—of indulgence. Franklin Rogers, in his study of Mark Twain's burlesque patterns, observes that the seminal "Boy's Manuscript" was in all probability a burlesque aimed at *David Copperfield*. He goes on to show how the first part of *Tom Sawyer* burlesques the good-boy cliché by showing how a bad boy prospers.[2] The soundness of Rogers' observations is evident throughout *Tom Sawyer*, from the blustering fight in the first chapter to the discovery of the treasure in the last. The relationship between Tom and Becky burlesques romantic conventions; the conversions of Tom and Huck, after the graveyard murder, parody religious conversions; lamentations of the village over Tom's apparent death mock funeral rituals and conventional language of grief. In brief, the entire action of the boys' world burlesques adult rituals.

And yet *Tom Sawyer* is neither burlesque nor primarily satiric novel. The reason is that the narrator's impulse toward burlesque and satire is largely assimilated in his indulgent posture. The burlesque personality of Mark Twain has undergone a genuine transformation. No longer the traveler or autobiographer, he is the observer of an action which, though intimate, is so remote in time that he patronizes the behavior of the actors at almost every point. The second chapter begins:

> Saturday morning was come, and all the summer world was bright and fresh, and brimming with life. There was a song in every heart; and if the heart was young the music issued at the lips. There was cheer in every face and a spring in every step. The locust trees were in bloom and the fragrance of the blossoms filled the air. Cardiff Hill, beyond the village and above it, was green with vegetation, and it lay just far enough away to seem a Delectable Land, dreamy, reposeful, and inviting.[3]

Thus the scene is set, the idyl defined. In this scene the whitewashing episode takes place. The opening sentence of Chapter IV, "The sun rose upon a tranquil world, and beamed down upon the peaceful village like a benediction,"[4] provides an unobtrusive but nevertheless clearly evident "screen" for the Sunday school recitations. In Chapter XIV, Tom awakens on Jackson's Island:

> It was the cool gray dawn, and there was a delicious sense of repose and peace in the deep pervading calm and silence of the woods. Not a leaf stirred; not a sound obtruded upon great Nature's meditation. Beaded dewdrops stood upon the leaves and grasses. A white layer of ashes covered the fire, and a thin blue breath of smoke rose straight into the air. Joe and Huck still slept.
>
> Now, far away in the woods a bird called; another answered; presently the hammering of a woodpecker was heard. Gradually the cool dim gray of the morning whitened, and as gradually sounds multiplied and life manifested itself. The marvel of Nature shaking off sleep and going to work unfolded itself to the musing boy.[5]

Each of these passages at once qualifies and generalizes the scene—qualifies it by screening out the impact of unpleasurable impulses; generalizes it by stabilizing and stylizing action into the form of tableau. Though there is murder in the world, its impact does not reach the reader but is used up in the explosion it has upon the boys who move at a great distance from the reader. And though there is "realism" in the book, if one means by realism an antitype of romance, there is neither uniqueness of character nor particularity of incident. Instead of individuals, the book generates types. Thus there is not even a minute description of Tom Sawyer; it is impossible to tell what he looks like—how tall, how heavy, how handsome or ugly he is. He emerges as the figure, the *character*, of the Boy. Yet he is not allegorical, simply because he is a *character* and not a personification.[6]

The indulgent and burlesque perspectives do not exist in isolation; they are combined to form the particular humor of the invisible narrator. A fairly typical example of this humor occurs at the beginning of Chapter VIII, in which Tom, stung by Becky's angry rejection at discovering his earlier affection for Amy Lawrence, rushes away to solitude:

> Tom dodged hither and thither through lanes until he was well out of the track of returning scholars, and then fell into a moody jog. He crossed a small "branch" two or three times, because of a prevailing juvenile superstition that to cross water baffled pursuit. Half an hour later he was disappearing behind the Douglas mansion on the summit of Cardiff Hill, and the schoolhouse was hardly distinguishable away off in the valley behind him. He entered a dense wood, picked his pathless way to the center of it, and sat down on a mossy spot under a spreading oak. There was not even a zephyr stirring; the dead noonday heat had even stilled the songs of the birds; nature lay in a trance that was broken by no sound but the occasional far-off hammering of a woodpecker, and this seemed to render the pervading silence and sense of loneliness the more profound. The boy's soul was steeped in melancholy; his

feelings were in happy accord with his surroundings. He sat long with his elbows on his knees and his chin in his hands, meditating. It seemed to him that life was but a trouble, at best, and he more than half envied Jimmy Hodges, so lately released; it must be very peaceful, he thought, to lie and slumber and dream forever and ever, with the wind whispering through the trees and caressing the grass and the flowers over the grave, and nothing to bother and grieve about, ever any more. If he only had a clean Sunday-school record he could be willing to go, and be done with it all. Now as to this girl. What had he done? Nothing. He had meant the best in the world, and been treated like a dog—like a very dog. She would be sorry some day—maybe when it was too late. Ah, if he could only die *temporarily*!

But the elastic heart of youth cannot be compressed into one constrained shape long at a time. Tom presently began to drift insensibly back into the concerns of this life again.[7]

The indulgent and burlesque impulses are inextricably joined throughout the passage to create an essential condescension to the scene, making the narrator a tolerant adult observer fondling yet patronizing the world he evokes. Tom's retreat to the woodland, the solitude of the scene, and his brooding meditations are impersonations of conventionalized romantic melancholy; the whole scene and action lead up to Tom's boyish death wish. The entire passage is utterly characteristic of the narrator's attitude toward his subject. The humor of the burlesque personality of *The Innocents Abroad* was characterized by irreverence; that of the autobiographer was the tall tale, the lie. The humor of the narrator of *Tom Sawyer* is a gently indulgent irony, a tender yet urbanely superior attitude toward the subject of his affection, which defines his focus upon the boy he creates.

This perspective is not some mere device for seeing Tom; it contributes immeasurably to the illusion Tom sustains—the illusion of Tom as performer. The fact that the society of St. Petersburg, both old and young, is involved in watching Tom's play from the inside world of the novel while the narrator is engaged in watching it indulgently from the outside goes far toward creating Tom's role of chief actor in a drama which the juvenile reader can believe and the adult reader can indulge with a mixture of nostalgia and gentle irony. The narrator, an almost invisible agent with whom the adult reader unwittingly identifies, provides the perspective through which Mark Twain meant to reach an adult audience.[8] What Mark Twain did was to treat his fiction as a performance rather than a story. If, in the preface, he alluded to the adult audience he was creating, he defined the nature of his characters in the conclusion. "Most of the characters that perform in this book still live," he said, "and are prosperous and happy." He continued, "Some day it may seem worth while to take up the story of the younger ones again and see what sort of men and women they turned out to be; therefore it will be wisest not to reveal any part of their lives at present."[9] Here in the midst of the conventional Victorian epilogue is the disclosure that Mark

Twain visualizes his characters in performance rather than in action, on stage rather than in the world.

Though the sense of a double audience contributes greatly to the illusion of a performance, there is still the performer—the actor and his "act." Tom Sawyer fully collaborates with the audience watching him; he puts on a show throughout the novel, one of the chief aspects of his character being his desire to be stage center. He is a performer in almost everything he does, whether he is showing off for Becky, parading with Joe and Huck into the arena of his own funeral, becoming the central figure in the trial of Muff Potter, or proudly producing the bags of gold before the startled eyes of St. Petersburgers. In a word, he is the show-off, and though he is not simply that, he cannot resist the temptation to perform to an audience. Thirty years after the writing of *Tom Sawyer*, Mark Twain observed that Theodore Roosevelt was a political incarnation of Tom Sawyer. "Just like Tom Sawyer," he remarked of Roosevelt's eagerness to keep the public eye; "always showing off."[10] This sense of showmanship defines Tom's desire to be a hero, for it is the spectacle of heroism as much as its achievement which fascinates Tom. The narrator gives us the image: "Tom was a glittering hero once more,"[11] he observes after Tom's performance at the trial, and the adjective tells the story. Tom simply has to shine if he can, and he utilizes every resource at his command to do so. In this respect he is a forerunner of Hank Morgan, whose chief character trait is his inveterate love of the effect. Morgan, like Tom, can never resist the temptation to be the central attraction, and both characters rely on electrifying their audiences. They nourish the tactics of the grand entrance, the great surprise, the splendid disclosure.

But Tom is a boy. His age, his size, and the security of his world—accentuated by the adult perspective upon it—place severe limits on the range of effects he can achieve. There are two areas of heroic achievement open to him in this enchanted world. The one is to be a hero on the St. Petersburg stage—in Becky's eyes, the school's, the church's, the court's, or the town's. The other is to be victorious in the world of make-believe, in the world of play. Tom's genius lies in his ability to realize the possibilities of make-believe in the life of the village, combining both possibilities of achievement into a single act. Thus he succeeds in playing out his fantasies for the entertainment and salvation of the town.

The best example is the mock funeral, the motive or seed of which appears in the long passage in which Tom wants to die temporarily. At this early moment of the book, it is no more than a desire, an almost ineffectual and childish death wish which the narrator can patronize. But in the course of the narrative not only does Tom's wish become a reality—if that were all, the book would be no more than a juvenile success story—but the entire village is made to play the dupe in the performance. And not simply made to play the dupe but made to like the role.

The boy's resurrection, occurring precisely at the center of the book, is the central episode. By central, I mean characteristic or characterizing, for it dramatizes the full union between narration and action. First, the narrator sets the scene. In contrast to the joyous plans of the fugitives on Jackson's Island, he describes the village grief:

> But there was no hilarity in the little town that same tranquil Saturday afternoon. The Harpers, and Aunt Polly's family, were being put into mourning, with great grief and many tears. An unusual quiet possessed the village, although it was ordinarily quiet enough, in all conscience. The villagers conducted their concerns with an absent air, and talked little; but they sighed often. The Saturday holiday seemed a burden to the children. They had no heart in their sports, and gradually gave them up. [12]

The two adjectives in the initial sentence define the narrator's visual and auditory perspective on the action. He discloses to the reader a scene so remote in distance that the village is a *little* town hung in a tranquil air. This distance is not something physical or definite in time and space—the narrator never says that the action happened so many miles away or so many years ago—but an objectification of a mental state. Thus the action and scene which the narrator unfolds in his first paragraph do not have the status of actuality; they are themselves an image, an idyl, which reflects in turn the narrator's role of complacent and superior observer.

His superiority is not simply one of size and actuality; it is superiority of knowledge which he shares with the reader. For the villagers do not know what the narrator and his readers are only too aware of—that Tom is not dead. Thus their grief, though real to them, is ultimately unreal because it has a false object and the narrator is free to ridicule it at will. He accomplishes his burlesque by exposing the clichés of conventional grief. The entire episode is handled remarkably, for the target of the burlesque—the threadbare clichés of conventional grief—is perfectly paralleled by the nature of the villagers' grief, which like their platitudes, is *sincere*, but nevertheless essentially unreal.

Tom's resurrection before the stunned townspeople who have ceremoniously gathered to lament his death is the surprise performance which he has prepared for the purpose of electrifying his audience. For Tom it is the act by which he gains the center of the stage; he has carefully made the resurrection his drama in which Huck and Joe will be supporting actors. Tom, completely unaware of the burlesque, remains imprisoned in his ego. While the choir bursts into song, "Tom Sawyer the Pirate looked around upon the envying juveniles about him and confessed in his heart that this was the proudest moment of his life." [13]

In the world of *Pudd'nhead Wilson*, such a practical joke would have provided the source of unrelenting hostility and hatred, but here in the idyl, where burlesque commingles with indulgence, the townspeople are tolerant of Tom's boyish pranks and forgive him, as does his Aunt Polly, for making them ridiculous. They expect him to be bad and, like Aunt Polly, they love him for it—not because Mark Twain's world is "realistic" but because they are his audience and collaborate with Tom in creating the illusion that the world is ultimately given over to play. Thus what was to have been a funeral is transmogrified by Tom into an entertainment, enhancing rather than undermining the burlesque element. For Tom's joke, his play funeral, provides the ultimate definition of what the "sincere" funeral was to have been for the town in the first place—an entertainment! A tearful, lugubrious, and hackneyed production in which each of the participants was fully working up his part—but an entertainment nonetheless.

Tom's resurrection offers in fairly clear outline the essential realization of his character. He is of course the bad boy, but not simply the bad boy, though he breaks rules and plays practical jokes. Thomas Bailey Aldrich's Tom Bailey in *The Story of a Bad Boy* broke rules, and Peck's Bad Boy existed by means of an endless succession of practical jokes on his Pa. Neither is it Tom's subtler psychology nor his more realistic character which set him apart. Nor is it his celebrated independence and pluck, nor his essentially good heart. Tom is really no freer than Sid and clearly has no better heart. Though the indulgent Mark Twain felt a deep invitation to sentimentalize Tom in this way and thus affirm that he was for all his badness really a good good boy, the burlesque perspective afforded protection against such sentimentality. As it had been for Mark Twain in the beginning and as it was throughout his career, burlesque functioned as a reality principle—a reliable anchor in a storm of dreams.

Tom's play *defines the world as play*, and his reality lies in his commitment to play, not in the involuntary tendencies which are often attributed to him. Actually Tom is in revolt against nothing. To be sure, he feels the pinch of school and the discipline of Aunt Polly, but he has no sustained desire to escape and no program of rebellion. What he does have is a perennial dream of himself as the hero and a commitment to the dream which makes it come true not once, but as many times as he can reorganize the village around his dream. The truth the dream invariably comes to is *play*—a play which converts all serious projects in the town to pleasure and at the same time subverts all the adult rituals by revealing that actually they are nothing but dull play to begin with.

Thus in the famous whitewashing episode, the ritual of the chore is converted into pleasure by Tom's stratagem. And not simply converted, but shrewdly exploited by Tom. To be sure, the episode discloses that Tom is an embryo businessman and that he has a bright future in the society of commerce and advertising, but such a criticism of Tom's character ignores the essential criticism the episode itself makes of the original chore. The chore was, after all, a kind of dull-witted stratagem for getting work done at low pay in the name of duty. Tom discovers—and surely it is a discovery worth making—that the task can be done four times as thick and as well in the name of pleasure. Though Tom shows off his handiwork, he does no more than Aunt Polly meant to do with him and the fence.

The adults throughout the book are engaged in showing off as much as are the children. If Tom apes the authorities of romance, Mr. Walters, the Sunday school superintendent, has his own authorities which he likewise strives to emulate:

> This superintendent was a slim creature of thirty-five, with a sandy goatee and short sandy hair; he wore a stiff standing-collar whose upper edge almost reached his ears and whose sharp points curved forward abreast the corners of his mouth—a fence that compelled a straight lookout ahead, and a turning of the whole body when a side view was required; his chin was propped on a spreading cravat which was as broad and as long as a bank-note, and had fringed ends; his boot-toes were turned sharply up, in the fashion of the day, like sleigh-runners—an effect patiently and laboriously produced by the young men by sitting with their toes pressed against a wall for hours together. Mr. Walters was very earnest of mien, and very sincere and honest at heart; and he held sacred things and places in such reverence, and so separated them from worldly matters, that unconsciously to himself his Sunday-school voice had acquired a peculiar intonation which was wholly absent on week-days.[14]

Mr. Walters, like Tom, puts on style. Indeed, the whole village, adults as well as children, puts on style of various sorts on various occasions—all for the purpose of showing off. On the opening page of the book, Aunt Polly has to look for Tom over the top of her spectacles because "they were her state pair, the pride of her heart, and were built for 'style,' not service—she could have seen through a pair of stove-lids just as well." The style of *Tom Sawyer* is the vision which at once looks over and exposes the old dead styles which are impersonated and gently burlesqued as the boy stages his action.

If Tom must stage his shows, he is doing no more than the adults who are busily engaged in staging their own performances, casting the children as characters. At the end of the Sunday school episode, for example, as the Thatchers make their impressive entrance, Tom occupies himself by showing off for Becky and the rest of the society shows off for the impressive Judge Thatcher.

> Mr. Walters fell to "showing off," with all sorts of official bustlings and activities, giving orders, delivering judgments, discharging directions here, there, everywhere that he could find a target. The librarian "showed off"— running hither and thither with his arms full of books and making a deal of the splutter and fuss that insect authority delights in. The young lady teachers "showed off"—bending sweetly over pupils that were lately being boxed, lifting pretty warning fingers at bad little boys and patting good ones lovingly.

> The young gentlemen teachers "showed off" with small scoldings and other little displays of authority and fine attention to discipline. . . . The little girls "showed off" in various ways and the little boys "showed off" with such diligence that the air was thick with paper wads and the murmur of scufflings. And above it all the great man sat and beamed a majestic judicial smile upon all the house, and warmed himself in the sun of his own grandeur—for he was "showing off," too.[15]

The satiric direction of this passage points to the activity which unites the entire community, from the revered Judge down to the youngest child. The entire Sunday school is a show in which everyone is showing off. No sooner are the Thatchers seated than Mr. Walters proceeds to the next act of his performance—the delivery of the Bible prize to the student who had earned the most tickets for memorizing Bible verses. This little act gives him a chance—the language of the book unfailingly discloses the terms of the action—to "exhibit a prodigy." Tom, however, steals the scene. Having traded spoils taken at the whitewashing exploit for tickets awarded to Bible quoters, he emerges with the largest number of tickets, to the amazement and envy of the little showmen he has outmaneuvered. His performance elevates him to the height of Judge Thatcher. "It was the most stunning surprise of the decade, and so profound was the sensation that it lifted the new hero up to the judicial one's altitude, and the school had two marvels to gaze upon in place of one."[16]

The Sunday school is merely one of the shows in St. Petersburg. The sermon which follows is another. While the minister drearily enacts his performance, Tom, again cast into the background, becomes interested only upon hearing the minister say that at the millennium when the lion and lamb should lie down together a little child should lead the world's hosts. This is the minister's verbal effort to produce a great scene. "But the pathos, the lesson, the moral of the great spectacle were lost upon the boy; he only thought of the conspicuousness of the principal character before the onlooking nations; his face lit with the thought, and he said to himself that he wished he could be that child, if it was a tame lion."[17] Unable to effect such a miracle, Tom does the next best thing, which is to set up a competing act. Releasing a pinch bug, he succeeds in diverting attention from the minister and—when a dog chances to sit upon the beetle—breaking up the minister's performance completely.

Like church, school is also a dull show over which the schoolmaster Mr. Dobbins presides. Almost the only way Tom is able to gain attention from the audience, and particularly Becky Thatcher, is to secure a thrashing at the hands of the teacher. Interestingly enough, the two times Tom receives whippings at school are results of his having sought out the punishment in order to show off. First, when Becky enters school, he blatantly announces to Mr. Dobbins his tardiness is a result of talking to Huckleberry Finn, and is thus flogged before his lady love. Much later, he sacrificially offers himself to Mr. Dobbins' wrath to keep Becky from receiving the whipping due her for tearing Mr. Dobbins' anatomy book. When Tom is not consciously engaged in securing attention, he unconsciously secures it by entertaining himself to the point of forgetting Mr. Dobbins and the schoolroom until the entire audience fixes its attention on his self-absorption. At one moment he is so engaged in teaching Becky to draw that he does not realize Mr. Dobbins is at hand observing the instruction; at another, he and Joe Harper are so deeply engrossed in entertaining themselves with a tick as to be unaware of becoming the center of attention:

> A tremendous whack came down on Tom's shoulders, and its duplicate on Joe's; and for the space of two minutes the dust continued to fly from the two jackets and the whole school to enjoy it. The boys had been too absorbed to notice the hush that had stolen upon the school awhile before when the master came tiptoeing down the room and stood over them. He had contemplated a good part of the performance before he contributed his bit of variety to it.[18]

The language here discloses the essential psychology of the schoolroom. The whipping does not hurt Tom; it does not humiliate him. The other children do not shiver under Mr. Dobbins' tyranny, nor do they suffer for Tom. Though such responses would be possible and even necessary in the world of *David Copperfield*, they do not exist in the world of St. Petersburg. Instead of carrying in the roots of his memory the scars of Mr. Dobbins' blows, Tom never reflects upon the flogging he has received. And Mr. Dobbins' fall comes not in the form of a series of disasters or crimes which bring him low enough to ask mercy from the boys he has tormented; rather, it comes in the form of a trick played upon him during the commencement exercises, when he is at the height of his annual effort to show off. After the long series of dreary exercises which make up the tedious performance, the monotony is broken when the boys lower a cat from the garret to lift the master's wig, exposing a bald pate elegantly gilded by the sign painter's boy.

This episode, with all its slapstick elements, is directly appropriate to the form of the book. For once again the boys have defined to the community the essential boredom of the adult theatricals. The source of that boredom, as the narrator's burlesque perspective discloses, is the utter lack of spontaneity in the exercises. Like little machines, the children go through the motions of performing without in any way expressing themselves. Their gestures and their expressions are as manufactured as the occasion itself; and their selections are characterized by a dead language. The appearance of the cat in this program is the surprise which redeems the deadly performance, converting it into genuine entertainment for the adults who have gathered to suffer through it.

What every episode of *Tom Sawyer* enacts is the conversion of all "serious" community activity—all duty, pain, grief, and work—into pleasure and play. Tom Sawyer himself is the agent of this conversion. His imaginative force, his *reality*, lies precisely in his capacity to make his dreams and fantasies come "true" in the form of "acts" which entertain the villagers. Nowhere is David Riesman's fine observation, that glamor in an actor measures the apathy in the audience, better borne out than in the world of *Tom Sawyer*.[19] For Tom's glittering power, his heroism, invariably defines at the same time it feeds upon the boredom of the villagers.

In discovering Tom, Mark Twain had actually gained a new perspective on himself as entertainer, for he had managed to objectify in a new character the possibilities of the pleasure principle. The method of objectification was the burlesque-indulgent perspective upon the world of boyhood. Such a perspective enabled Mark Twain to see, in a way no writer had seen before him, an entire area of action where entertainment dissolved into play. In seeing it he recognized possibilities of both entertainment and play which he himself could have but dimly imagined prior to the emergence of Tom Sawyer.

For the real audacity of *Tom Sawyer* is its commitment to the pleasure principle. Though the book participates in parody, burlesque, and satire, it clearly cannot be characterized by any of these terms. It is, after all, a tale— an *adventure*—and its commitment is not to exposing sham, as in the case of satire; nor is it to mocking a prior art form as in the case of parody and burlesque. Instead, the positive force—the force to which the world of St. Petersburg succumbs—is play itself.

Play is the reality principle in the book. What makes Tom Sawyer seem more real than the adults who submit to his power is his capacity to take his pleasure openly in the form of make-believe while they take theirs covertly under the guise of seriousness. Tom's virtue lies not in his good heart, his independence, or his pluck—none of which he really has—but in his truth to the pleasure principle which is the ultimate reality of the enchanted idyl. The very enchantment results from the indulgent perspective the author assumes toward the action. The narrator's indulgence is none other than the pleasure he takes in disclosing the play world.

The coupling of the outer pleasure with the inner world of play causes Tom's make-believe to seem true, whereas the adult "reality" and "duty" appear false and pretentious. This conversion, not so much process as point of view, is at once the humor and truth of the book. By inventing Tom Sawyer, Mark Twain had actually succeeded in dramatizing in a fictional narrative the possibilities of entertainment. He had projected through Tom Sawyer's imagination a world of boyhood in which play was the central reality, the defining value. The money Tom discovers in the cave in the final episode is a reward not for his courage or heroism—the indulgent perspective discloses his cowardice and essential self-love—but for his capacity to have dreamed it into reality with his make-believe imagination. And Tom quite characteristically appears before the townspeople to show off his treasure in one last exhibitionistic fling before the final curtain. The world of boyhood as it emerges in the pages of *Tom Sawyer* is a world where play, make-believe, and adventure are the living realities defining the false pieties and platitudes which constitute the dull pleasure of the adult world.

Mark Twain's invention of Tom Sawyer and his invention of the novel are thus one and the same thing. The reality principle of this first independent fiction is, as we have seen, play. The approach to fiction through the boy-character of a master player is an index to Mark Twain's inability to "believe" in conventional fiction. The exaggerated contempt in which he held fiction was his characteristic "humor" embodying his true perception. Mark Twain had no real use for conventional fiction because his entire genius—the "Mark Twain" in Samuel Clemens—had his being in the tall tale, a form which presented the truth as a lie, whereas the fiction he condemned presented the lie as the truth. That is why Mark Twain could say to Howells that he would not take Tom Sawyer into manhood because he "would just be like all the other one horse men in literature." Though he had promised in his conclusion to trace his figures into adult life, he never did; he could only call the changeless Tom Sawyer back on stage for more—and poorer—"acts."

In moving to the form of fiction, Mark Twain subverted the conventions of the form, not only by means of the burlesque and indulgent perspectives, but also through the character of Tom himself, whose "adventure" or plot is projected in terms of play and make-believe. The enchantment, the idyl, and the boy—the chief components of the book—create fiction as play instead of as truth. The book is no testimonial to the child's unfettered imagination transcending the materialism of the adult world. Instead, it creates existence under the name of pleasure, and portrays all human actions, no matter how "serious," as forms of play. Thus the imagination is shorn of the religious, romantic, and transcendental meanings with which Coleridge invested it; in Mark Twain's world of boyhood, the imagination represents the capacity for mimicry, impersonation, make-believe, and play. That is why the boy of Mark Twain's idyl is so different from the child of Wordsworth's vision. The child of the romantic poet has a direct relationship to God and Nature. Mark Twain's boy has a direct relationship to pleasure. The romantic child *is*, has being; Mark Twain's boy plays, has pleasure.

Notes

1. *Writings*, XII, vii.
2. Rogers, *Burlesque Patterns*, pp. 102–104.
3. *Writings*, XII, 12.
4. *Ibid.*, p. 29.
5. *Ibid.*, p. 121.
6. Mark Twain's characterization of Tom Sawyer is similar in method to Chaucer's

in the *Canterbury Tales*. Two assumptions lie at the base of such characterization: (1) that people are not unique but ultimately similar in motive and behavior; (2) that social and psychological reality are wedded rather than divorced. Thus neither Chaucer nor Mark Twain develops characters with singular personalities; rather, they emphasize the traits, motives, and behavior which are easily recognizable by being individually manifest yet socially held in common. Thus, also, they have the capacity to typify characters (as knight, miller, friar, or boy) without in any way seeming to threaten their individuality. Indeed, both Chaucer and Mark Twain achieve the effect of reinforcing individuality by emphasizing typifying aspects of character.

7.   *Writings*, XII, 73.

8.   After initially recommending that Mark Twain take Tom Sawyer on into manhood, Howells, upon seeing the manuscript, wrote: "It will be an immense success. But I think you ought to treat it explicitly as a boy's story. Grown-ups will enjoy it just as much if you do; and if you should put it forth as a study of a boy character from the grown-up point of view, you'd give the wrong key to it" (*Mark Twain–Howells Letters*, I, 110–11). In seeing it as a boy's story, Howells was evidently advising Mark Twain to avoid the narrow *Atlantic* audience in favor of the mass audience, advice Mark Twain was eager enough to have.

9.   *Writings*, XII, 292.

10.   *Mark Twain in Eruption*, ed. Bernard De Voto (New York, 1940), p. 49.

11.   *Writings*, XII, 198.

12.   *Ibid.*, p. 149.

13.   *Ibid.*, p. 153.

14.   *Ibid.*, pp. 35–36.

15.   *Ibid.*, p. 38.

16.   *Ibid.*, p. 39.

17.   *Ibid.*, p. 47.

18.   *Ibid.*, p. 67.

19.   David Riesman, *The Lonely Crowd* (New Haven, 1950), p. 313.

Myth and Reality in *The Adventures of Tom Sawyer*

ROBERT TRACY

With prophetic malice, Mark Twain began *Adventures of Huckleberry Finn* by threatening any critic who should find motive, moral, or plot in his narrative. But he began *The Adventures of Tom Sawyer* rather more gently, with some helpful information about the characters and story, and with a statement wrung from him by Howells, that the book "is intended mainly for the entertainment of boys and girls." The statement has frightened off critics far more effectively than the *No Trespassing* sign posted in front of *Huckleberry Finn*. Few critics have bothered to discuss *Tom Sawyer* other than as a prelude to *Huckleberry Finn*, Mark Twain's unsuccessful dress rehearsal of the subject matter and method which he was to use in the later book. As a character, Tom interests them only because of his adventures in the sequel or because he shares some traits with his creator.

In terms of absolute literary merit this neglect is justified, to be sure, but in the very failure of *The Adventures of Tom Sawyer* as a work of art there are important clues to Mark Twain's methods and preoccupations, and to some of the attitudes of his contemporaries. Tom, he tells us, is "drawn from life . . . but not from an individual . . . and therefore belongs to the composite order of architecture"—the highly eclectic style so popular among nineteenth century American builders, found at its startling best in the "English violet" house in Hartford, where the book was completed in a wing built to resemble the pilothouse of a Mississippi steamboat. Twain's comment about the origin of his character is, in fact, probably an unintentional description of his method in *Tom Sawyer* and most of his other novels—a composite method which tries to combine reality and romantic melodrama, just as the architects of the day added fantastic spires and turrets and wooden lace to the basic structure of an ordinary house. There is a similarity of method in nineteenth-century American literature and architecture, because writers and architects alike tried to make a democratic and uniform landscape more interesting by adding a dimension of history or romance to a land that seemed destitute of both qualities. Melville compares the forecastle of the *Pequod* to a cathedral crypt, Poe invokes vaults and gloomy castles, Tom Sawyer turns

Reprinted from *Southern Review* 4 (Spring 1968): 530–41. By permission of the author and the publisher.

a Sunday school picnic into an Arab caravan and doughnuts into heaps of jewels, F. E. Church created a "provincialized Persian" villa on the Hudson, the "architectural composer" Alexander Jackson Davis built Gothic cottages, and Leopold Eidlitz turned an ordinary design into the fantastically domed and minareted "Iranistan," P. T. Barnum's home in Bridgeport, Connecticut.

Mark Twain's method is precisely that of the composite architect. *The Adventures of Tom Sawyer* is basically realistic, "mostly a true book, with some stretchers," as Huck describes it. Tom lives in the sentimental but carefully rendered atmosphere of St. Petersburg. But he also has extraordinary adventures with robbers and murderers who disrupt his placid routine of school and childish games. Two worlds, one of reality and one of melodramatic romance, are continually interpenetrating in the book. The substance of the book is this interpenetration. To control this novel of diametrically disparate elements and to relate these elements to one another, Twain employs a third element which can share in both the real world and the romantic world— archetypal myth, which can unify the two kinds of experience with which the book deals and at the same time can give them an added significance. The presence of myth brings into the work a dimension of human experience which mere realism or mere melodrama cannot supply; the realistic and the melodramatic events of the book are given importance and resonance in terms both of universal human myths and of the particular national myths which disturb the American consciousness.

Mark Twain is not alone among American writers in thus combining realism, romantic and bookish melodrama, and archetypal myth. Cooper's Indians have a degree of reality, but at the same time they derive from the literary traditions of the Noble Savage and the outlaws of Walter Scott, and from the traditional body of demonic lore. Irving combines accurate sketches of Hudson River village life with obvious and often explicit elements from literature and from Germanic mythology. *Moby-Dick* is at once a realistic depiction of life aboard a whaler, a storehouse of literary allusions, and an archetypal quest. Hawthorne combines a picture of life among American artists in Rome with echoes of Gothic novels and elements of classical myth in *The Marble Faun*; James revises the combination in *Daisy Miller*, merging his realistic Americans abroad with such romantically literary scenes as the Castle of Chillon and the Coliseum, and with the Proserpina myth in a properly classical setting.

This attempt at a coalescence of realistic observation, literary echoes, and myth is clearly a common method among American writers of the last century, and it is not surprising that Mark Twain should use it. It is almost a commonplace to recognize the simultaneous presence of all three elements in *Huckleberry Finn*, but a reminder of how they operate in the better known novel is a useful preamble to an examination of *Tom Sawyer*. We can apply to both books the song sung by the townspeople in "The Man That Corrupted Hadleyburg": "the Symbols are here, you bet!"

Huckleberry Finn is a realistic portrait of life along the banks of the antebellum Mississippi and a commentary on the moral problem of slavery. These elements are combined with a reworking of traditional picaresque material, and the whole is given resonance by the continual presence of mythic themes. An obvious example is the archetypal theme of resurrection, which begins with Huck's careful staging of his own murder, and his birth or resurrection out of a hole (Pap has already risen from the dead on one occasion, and resembles a corpse). Huck rises into freedom, and the episode is bookishly parodied in Jim's "escape" from the Phelps farm, this time with Tom Sawyer at hand to "throw in the fancy touches." The first of these is a spontaneous act by Huck, the natural man, and he comments ruefully on how much more literary Tom Sawyer would have made it. The parody escape is contrived by the overbookish and overromantic brain of Tom, already corrupted by literature and by social conformity. Mark Twain also introduces into *Huckleberry Finn* such recognizably mythic themes as the lost prince (doubled by the presence of the Duke *and* the Dauphin), and the buried treasure guarded by its dead owner for the rightful heirs. Even the "Royal Nonesuch," with its overtones of a ritualized sexual indecency, contributes to the book's mythic dimension and helps it to touch depths below that of the conscious story. Mark Twain has successfully fused mythic, literary, and realistic elements, and if one theme is the confrontation of the romantic mind and the moral mind, another is the coalescence of romance, reality, and myth.

In its balanced use of these elements *Huckleberry Finn* (written 1876–84, published 1885) represents a transition between the more realistic *The Adventures of Tom Sawyer* (published 1876) and such determinedly symbolic works as *Puddn'head Wilson* (published 1894), "The Man That Corrupted Hadleyburg" (1898), and "The Mysterious Stranger" (1916). Only in *Huckleberry Finn* does Mark Twain have complete control over the three elements which he has employed, and over the relationship between them. The presence of this control causes the book to stand out sharply from the novels which immediately preceded and succeeded it, *The Prince and the Pauper* (1882) and *A Connecticut Yankee in King Arthur's Court* (1889), where one element or the other is overstated and the work is flawed.

In *The Adventures of Tom Sawyer*, Mark Twain's earliest novel, we find the same striving for a balancing of the three elements of reality, bookish romance, and myth. The presence of reality and romance in the book is obvious enough. We have the subtle insight into the mind of boyhood and the careful evocation of the little Southern town, while Tom's literary imagination, nourished on tales of chivalry and adventure, provides a romantic counterpoint to the story's incidents. Mark Twain's sentimental idealization of childhood introduces another romantic element. But what of myth? In what sense does this book, so much shallower and barer than *Huckleberry Finn*, contain the motifs which indicate the presence of myth? What is the mythic element, and how is it evoked? What universally archetypal figures and motifs appear, and what specifically American preoccupations does the book reflect?

First of all, there is the overt element of folklore in the carefully presented superstitions current among the children and slaves of St. Petersburg. These are mere fragments of an older and infinitely more complex set of European and African beliefs in sympathetic magic, witchcraft, and the like. They are introduced primarily as local color, secondarily as a means of giving the story atmosphere and a sense of past experience and tradition—a usable past, in James's sense. They have more important functions, however, for they also add a certain darkness to the story, a shading which prepares us for the uncovered corpse in the moonlight, the murder of Dr. Robinson, and the sight of Injun Joe in the depths of the great cavern. Twain also uses them to add a supernatural dimension to the child's sense of being at the mercy of inexplicable adults and their mysterious laws, and to provide a kind of ironic undertone, a supplement to the central myths of the book.

These central myths are the resurrection of the dead, the golden age, and the capture of the demon's hoard. The operation of this ironic relationship between these major themes and the minor key of folklore used to provide local color can be seen in the graveyard episode, where Tom and Huck fear devils only to find themselves present while a corpse is exhumed and Dr. Robinson is murdered by Injun Joe. The episode follows an hourglass pattern: a dead man is brought to the world of the living, a living man is sent down to death, while the unconscious Muff Potter is halfway between the two states. This neat pattern emphasizes the motif of resurrection, to be utilized more elaborately later in the Island episode and in the Cave episode. It is introduced through the boy-slave folklore of the little town. The corpse of a dead cat, so Tom and Huck believe, can cure warts. Their superstition is an ironic childish parody of Dr. Robinson's belief that the corpse of a recently dead man will help him to cure. In his search for this cure, Dr. Robinson is killed by Injun Joe and Muff Potter comes close to death; Tom's search for a cure for warts has led him into the same danger of death at the hands of Injun Joe. The boys have waited for devils to come for the dead Hoss Williams's soul, and they plan to hurl their cat corpse after the devils; instead grave robbers come to take the dead man's corpse, and the boys witness a murder.

It is round the savage figure of Injun Joe that the mythic elements of the book most obviously cluster, and, not surprisingly, he appears when the superstition about dead cats has led the boys to expect the appearance of a demon. Child folklore is thus used to introduce into the novel a figure who will satisfactorily play the role of an archetypal demon. At the same time,

Joe is a figure out of specifically American myth. He is half Indian and so a token of the enigmatic savagery and wildness that lurks at the center of the American experience. He is related to Cooper's Indians and to savages like Tashtego and Queequeg, but unlike them he is all savagery and malevolence. Dispossessed, he does not function as guide, friend, and companion to the white man, as do the savages of Cooper and Melville, or Faulkner's Sam Fathers. He is an enemy. A half-breed, he has retained only the savagery of the Noble Savage, and has none of the nobility. His resentment against white civilization for its mistreatment of him is explicit in his murder of the Doctor, and in his cynical foisting off of the deed on drunken old Muff Potter.

As a savage, Injun Joe is related to the universally mythic elements in the book. As an Indian he is an American mythic figure, related to the book's theme of retreating to the wilderness which is expressed in the Jackson's Island episodes. The Island-Forest represents the American dream of untamed and uncivilized wilderness, the "territory" of Huck Finn's final words, even while Tom is busily insisting that it is also Sherwood Forest, the place of bookishly idyllic and romantic happenings. Idyllic, the island is a sharp contrast to the grim and dangerous and sordid life of St. Petersburg, while that life, which is civilization, represents a double threat—a threat to freedom and happiness, and a threat to life itself. Civilization masks savagery as well as restraint, as it does more obviously in the river towns of *Huckleberry Finn*. Only in the wilderness is there safety from the comic threat of school and the serious threat of death. The pirate life of the island, an attempt to live a bookish romance, masks the fact that the boys are living a very American myth of freedom. They also play at being Indians while on the island; ironically, the real Indian-outlaw is hiding in the sleepy little village itself.

But Injun Joe is not only a figure out of American myth. The characters of *Tom Sawyer* live and move in a world that is simultaneously the Missouri of the 1840s and the landscape of universal myth: the River, the Wilderness, the Island, the Cave. Deep in the cave, at the heart of its mystery, the figure of Injun Joe appears again, guarding a treasure like all the legendary dark malevolent figures who lurk in the earth—trolls, gnomes, kobolds, Fafnir, Grendel, all, like Joe, treasure guardians who are also representatives or survivors of a once dominant race. The American myth of the savage and the European myth of the dark underground dweller have coalesced.

Injun Joe's treasure-guarding functions are obvious. His demonic nature is also quite explicit throughout the book, and contributes largely to the graveyard scene. "When it's midnight a devil will come, or maybe two or three, but you can't see 'em, you can only hear something like the wind, or maybe hear 'em talk." Thus Huck explains the conditions necessary to cure warts, and his speech, delivered in the language of myth, is an accurate prophecy of what really does happen. It is also a clue to the book's method, which depends in large part on a kind of thematic resonance or echo: a myth, a superstition, or an incident from romance is evoked, and this is followed by a sudden startling realization of that myth or romance. The boys pretend to be pirates and find themselves tracked by a murderer. They speculate about treasure according to Tom's half-baked romantic ideas, and behold, a treasure appears. The haunted house *is* haunted, by dangerous criminals. They dream of a "Delectable Land" of freedom, and with the Jackson's Island episode they really do sojourn in that land. Tom imagines situations in which he will die for Becky, and then finds himself in a situation in which he must truly act heroically to save her life. The robbers' cave is available for the boys' games only after a real robber has died trying to escape from it. Reality is continually interpenetrated by the mythic and the romantic worlds. Tom himself, ironically, remains unaware of this interpretation. Like American writers of the day who dreamed only of Europe, or like the Southerners who redefined their lives in the clichés of Sir Walter Scott, Tom goes through a drama of the Old Southwest with his eyes firmly fixed on the drama in his books, hardly recognizing his own drama. At the end of *Huckleberry Finn* we find him still making the same mistake, ignoring the saga of Huck and Jim on the raft and restaging Jim's heroic escape in effete literary terms.

The unexpected appearance of the grave robbers to satisfy Huck's folk-medicine need for devils is perhaps the most typical use of this method of thematic resonance. When Injun Joe first appears he is described by Huck as "that murderin' half-breed" (Chapter IX) and "That Injun devil" (X) and the word *devil* is applied to him on almost every one of his subsequent appearances. From his arrival in the graveyard Joe carries with him the aura that surrounds the devil in legend, and we are not at all surprised to find him showing blue lights in the haunted house (the traditional demon-haunted ruin), or dwelling in the depths of the earth beneath a cross.

There is perhaps more than a hint of Caliban in the continual association of Injun Joe with the earth, with graves and burial. We see him first at Hoss Williams's opened grave, later digging the treasure from beneath the hearthstone of the haunted house or hiding deep in the earth in McDougal's Cave. Prospero addresses Caliban as "Thou earth," and Caliban upbraids his master in words that the corrupted Indian might have used to reproach the white world: "You taught me language, and my profit on't/Is, I know how to curse." There are other curious and probably accidental resemblances to *The Tempest* in *Tom Sawyer*. Both works preserve a dream of the innocent new world, the Delectable Land, and it is worth recalling that the new world was a part of Shakespeare's inspiration in that play, for Prospero's island owes something to the newly discovered Bermudas and Caliban is in part a response to the news of the Indians. Both works portray a golden age; both present an island which is a haven out of the world of men and affairs; both present civilization as a place of danger. Prospero's Island and Jackson's Island are both miniature golden ages. One moves Gonzalo to a meditation on the legendary golden age, the other is used by Mark Twain to invoke a double golden age, boyhood before it has been swallowed by adult conventionality and the wilderness before it has been spoiled by civilization. Other elements which recall *The Tempest* are the false deaths of the boys, the real violence which threatens them in their innocence, and the obsession with death by water which is so marked in both works.

Jackson's Island performs a further mythic function in providing a still center to the story, a place that is outside the stream of time, like Rip Van Winkle's hollow or Poe's Maelstrom. It is no-man's-land, belonging neither to the town nor to the forest nor to the river, and Tom and his friends return from the island after they have been considered dead, just as Rip Van Winkle returns from the green knoll in the Catskills, or the Seven Sleepers of Ephesus return from their cave. Like Rip and the Sleepers, Tom, Huck, and Joe Harper have been out of life in a dream. Their return is a return not from the world of the dead but from the world of those who are dead to life. They return to the world of the living across the symbolic river which keeps the two worlds separated, just as Avalon or the islands visited by Oisin in his wanderings are separated from the ordinary world by water, and they become marvels to the village for doing so.

River, Wilderness, Island, Cave. The first three of these traditional mythic landscapes are chiefly present in the Jackson's Island episodes (the name of the island may suggest frontier democracy, just as the village's name, St. Petersburg, suggested despotism and slavery to nineteenth-century Americans). In all three landscapes the idyllic tone persists, and it is reinforced by the return from paradise to ordinary life, from the happy other world to the life of the village.

In many traditional legends the Cave has a similar role. In it the hero often finds that long sleep which is not death; it is often a place of a temporary dropping out of life. Mark Twain chooses to use it rather differently, however. In *The Adventures of Tom Sawyer* the Cave suggests that visit to the underworld which is part of the adventures of Dante, Aeneas, Odysseus, and other epic heroes, an underworld ruled over by a devil. The word *labyrinth* is often used, and the Cave's echoes turn cries for help into meaningless peals of laughter, just as Forster's Marabar Caves turn all sounds to a meaningless "boum . . . oum." The Cave is dark and meaningless and unexplored. It is a place of horror and death. But, although a place of symbolic death and burial, the Cave resembles the catacombs in *The Marble Faun* in that it is also a symbol of birth or rebirth. A new Tom emerges from the Cave after his care for Becky makes him a true hero. Like Aladdin (after whom one of the chambers in McDougal's Cave is named) and Ali Baba, he emerges rich, leaving the evil criminal trapped inside.

For the Cave is also the dwelling-place—"No. 2, under the cross"— of Injun Joe. It is there that he dies, and with his death there is a glimpse of a complex series of references. The demon's death frees the treasure, and it can be taken up into the outside world of everyday and "put . . . out at six per cent" interest. We learn that the treasure which the Indian has guarded will be used to send Tom to West Point and then to law school, where he will learn to extend civilization by the arts of war and peace. Huck's share will be used to civilize him, to enchain him in conformity. Tom assists this chaining process, for he refuses to allow Huck to join his projected robber gang unless he conforms. Indulgence in the romantic pretense of robber-hood is only for the respectable. Free Huck would make a mockery of it.

The treasure, then, found and guarded by the doubly mythical Indian-devil, a coalescence of American myth and universal myth, becomes a servant of conformity and progress, an enforcer of civilization's mores, and the relevance of all this to the ambiguous American myth about the conquest of the wilderness is not hard to see. Like Faulkner's Bear, the Indian and his treasure have kept the wildness alive and have helped the atmosphere of a quest to continue. But the Indian dies and the treasure disappears into a bank—a neat and accurate symbol for the fate of the trans-Mississippi frontier. Civilization's progress exorcises the devils, exterminates the Indians, and banks the proceeds.

To the identification of Injun Joe with the archetypal devil Twain has thus added some elements which relate him to the American myth of the Indian, and he hints at the mixture of guilt and fear which the American feels in the presence of this dispossessed owner of the land. Injun Joe's hatred of whites is savage, but motivated. He hates Dr. Robinson because "Five years ago you drove me away from your father's kitchen one night, when I come to ask for something to eat, and you said I warn't there for any good; and when I swore I'd get even with you if it took a hundred years, your father had me jailed for a vagrant. Did you think I'd forget? The Injun blood ain't in me for nothing." As for the Widow Douglas, Joe plans to "slit her nostrils . . . notch her ears like a sow" because her late husband "was rough on me—many times he was rough on me—and mainly he was the justice of the peace that jugged me for a vagrant. And that ain't all. It ain't a millionth part of it! He had me *horsewhipped*!—horsewhipped in front of the jail, like a nigger!—with all the town looking on! HORSEWHIPPED!—do you understand?"

Mark Twain thus expresses the American's ambivalent attitude towards the Indian, presenting him as devil and victim at the same time, an evil figure to be sure, and a threat, but a figure whose evil has been provoked by white injustice and mistreatment. This ambiguous attitude is given its fullest expression at Injun Joe's death, and Tom's response to the fact:

When the cave door was unlocked, a sorrowful sight presented itself in the dim twilight of the place. Injun Joe lay stretched upon the ground, dead, with his face close to the crack of the door, as if his longing eyes had been fixed, to the latest moment, upon the light and the cheer of the free world outside. Tom was touched, for he knew by his own experience how this wretch had suffered. His pity was moved, but nevertheless he felt an abounding sense of relief and security, now, which revealed to him in a degree which he had not fully appreciated before how vast a weight of dread had been lying upon him since the day he lifted his voice against this bloody-minded outcast.

The whole of the American attitude towards the wilderness and the Indian is summed up in this passage—the fear of the wild and the unknown, the mixture of relief and regret at the passing of that wildness. Civilization, represented by the Doctor and the late Judge Douglas, has motivated Joe's crime by treating him as an outcast. His death is caused by another manifestation of American civilization, an artifact imposed upon the wilderness, that "big door sheathed with boiler iron . . . triple-locked" with which Judge Thatcher has closed the entrance to the cave. A machine-made barrier closes the path to the underworld, to mystery, and that barrier imprisons the Indian and so kills him.

In *The Adventures of Tom Sawyer* Mark Twain attempts a subtle interplay of reality, bookish romance, and myth in order to express an ambiguous attitude to both American civilization and the savage American wilderness. He exploits a universal human fear, the fear of demons, and simultaneously evokes the American myth of the Indian who is civilization's threat, victim, and rival attraction. The problem is ultimately a moral one, and for Mark Twain, as for Tom Sawyer, it is insoluble. Tom endorses freedom and conformity in almost the same breath. His creator submerges the book's moral problem and heightens the melodrama in order to conceal this evasion. It is perhaps this evasion that causes us to rate the book below many of Twain's other books, but it is important to remember that in *Tom Sawyer* he has set himself a moral problem more complex than the problem of slavery which is at the center of *Huckleberry Finn*. His problem is that of defining an attitude towards American civilization and progress, a problem he returns to, again unsuccessfully, in *A Connecticut Yankee in King Arthur's Court* (1889). A mixture of freedom and restraint characterizes boyhood life in St. Petersburg, and the boys' discovery of the treasure is a triumph and a captivity. The archetypal figure of the Indian summarizes this ambiguity, for the book views him as a devil and a threat, an object of fear. "There may be a devilish Indian behind every tree," Hawthorne's Goodman Brown speculates as he travels through the forest, "What if the devil himself should be at my very elbow!" Mark Twain invokes the same set of fears, but simultaneously he looks at the Indian as a figure out of romance, a victim whose destroyers feel a slight twinge of pity and a slight stirring of conscience, a mythic figure evoking fear and then discomfort. The Cave—that "blackness ten times black" that Melville recognized in Hawthorne—swallows and becomes a prison for the Indian, in Whitman's phrase a "dusky demon and brother," whose brotherhood is denied and whose demonhood is exaggerated. And to justify and deepen this local myth and this specifically American attitude, Mark Twain invokes continually the archetypes of universal myth.

Tom Sawyer: Missouri Robin Hood

L. MOFFITT CECIL

The tick-running episode in Chapter VII of *The Adventures of Tom Sawyer* is a mock reduction of the major contending forces in Mark Twain's novel. The Monday on which the episode occurred represented merely a typical schoolday in Tom's experience. His pretending to be sick that morning did not fool Aunt Polly, who promptly pulled his loose tooth and sent him off to school. The chance meeting with outcast Huck Finn, from whom he secured the tick, caused Tom to be tardy and resulted in his first licking of the day. Having to "sit with the girls" gave him an opportunity to make up to pretty Becky Thatcher, but all too soon he was in disgrace again, back in his own desk beside Joe Harper. Then came the tick-running. Mark Twain describes the momentary upsurge of joy the tick must have experienced upon being released from the box: "The creature probably glowed with gratitude that amounted to prayer, too, at this moment, but it was premature: for when he started thankfully to travel off, Tom turned him aside with a pin and made him take a new direction."[1] Thwarting the tick soon developed into a fierce and fascinating game the boys played. Tom drew a line, the equator, down the center of Joe's slate; so long as one of the two players could keep the scurrying tick within his half of the planisphere, he alone could bedevil the creature. For a time the tick, rebuffed at every turn, inhabited a grim world indeed. Only the intervention of the schoolmaster, Mr. Dobbins, minion of a higher order, put an end to the contest. For distracting the class on this occasion, Tom was awarded his second licking of the morning.

In the first six chapters of the novel Mark Twain has shaped events in such a way that readers cannot miss the point of the tick-running. Imaginative, energetic, venturesome Tom is shown to be in constant conflict with the village authority represented by the home, the church, the school. Each of these three institutions in turn is seen trying to curb Tom's natural exuberance and make him conform to the village notion of a good boy. On Friday, after stealing the jam, Tom manages to evade Aunt Polly's threatening switch; but on Saturday morning, to expiate an accumulation of transgressions, he submits to the letter of her judgment in the whitewashing of

From Cecil, L. Moffitt. "Tom Sawyer: Missouri Robin Hood." *Western American Literature*, 4 (Summer 1969), 125–31.

the fence. On Sunday, forced to attend both Sabbath school and church, he is shown comically disrupting the pious solemnities of the day. His eventful morning at school on Monday has already been detailed. The meaning of the tick-running is unmistakable. The lowly tick, defined by Webster as "any of certain degraded parasitic dipterous insects," becomes beleaguered Tom. And the cruel obstructing pins, in the hands of frustrated schoolboys, represent those forces in the village, social, moral, and legal, which insist upon conformity and operate to deter the free and natural development of personality.

The identification of Tom with the lowly tick in Chapter VII makes all the more remarkable the heroic proportions he assumes in Chapter VIII. Frustrated, humbled, he does not return to the schoolhouse for the afternoon session but flees instead to nearby Cardiff Hill, "just far enough away to seem a Delectable Land, dreamy, reposeful, and inviting" (p. 11). He goes straight to his hidden treasures and performs certain superstitious rites which help to revive his depressed spirit. When he hears the approaching sound of Joe's toy trumpet, he joyfully takes up his own bow and arrow, wooden sword, and tin trumpet and stands suddenly revealed as Robin Hood. Thus freed in spirit, he enacts with Joe Harper the ritual life and death of one of his heroes, a champion of all oppressed peoples. Considerably later, in Chapter XXVI, he initiates Huck Finn into the cult of Robin Hood:

". . . Do you know Robin Hood, Huck?"

"No. Who's Robin Hood?"

"Why, he was one of the greatest men that was ever in England—and the best. He was a robber."

"Cracky, I wish I was. Who did he rob?"

"Only sheriffs and bishops and rich people and kings, and such like. But he never bothered the poor. He loved 'em. He always divided up with 'em perfectly square."

"Well, he must 'a' been a brick."

"I bet you he was, Huck. Oh, he was the noblest man that ever was. They ain't any such men now, I can tell you. . . ." (p. 196)

Thus early in the book two conflicting views of Tom Sawyer, Missouri hobbledehoy, emerge. A tick or a Robin Hood—which is it to be? Already in this first of his novels (his "first solo-flight in fiction")[2] Mark Twain's tendency to see man as puny, hopeless, and ridiculously inept is indicated. But by 1876 life had not yet dealt its ample quota of stunning rebuffs and bereavements to Samuel Clemens, successful author, or to his enterprising generation, the Gilded Age. *Tom Sawyer* is an affirmative book, an optimistic one. It signs the potentialities of the human spirit, rising above the limitations of time, place, and ignorance, to create through human desire and ingenuity a better world in which truth and justice prevail. Mark Twain said of the book: "*Tom Sawyer* is simply a hymn put into prose to give it a worldly air."[3] His description is accurate as well as poetic. It helps to explain why the novel, which had sold more than two million copies by 1904, "is still the most popular of Twain's books."[4]

To grasp fully the romantic optimism of the book, one should follow the lead Twain has offered and examine the kinship that exists between Tom Sawyer and Robin Hood. Obviously Tom possesses an intimate knowledge of his hero's exploits. It would seem that Twain, when he was writing Chapter VIII, may have had a version of the Robin Hood legend near at hand, for he made the boys talk "by the book" in their playacting. When they perform "Robin Hood and Guy of Guisborne," Joe forgets his lines and Tom has to supply them for him. Later in the midst of their sword fight, when Joe refuses to fall wounded as he should, Tom quotes the text to him: " 'Then with one backhanded stroke he slew poor Guy of Guisborne' " (p. 74). A comparison of this line, as Tom recites it, with an authentic version of the ballad shows how accurate Tom's knowledge is. Joseph Ritson gives the passage as follows: "And strait he came with an awkwarde stroke/ And he sir Guy hath slayne."[5] In a footnote Ritson reports that Bishop Thomas Percy, in his *Reliques*, emended the manuscript word *awkwarde to backward*. Ritson retains the original manuscript form, defining *awkwarde stroke* to mean "an unusual or out of the way stroke, . . . a sort of left or backhand stroke."[6] Tom's precise knowledge of this detail in the life of his hero testifies to the sincerity of his devotion.

Tom's hero worship goes far beyond mere idle adulation, mere play-acting. Subconsciously at least he identifies with Robin Hood: he recognizes a correlation between the world of St. Petersburg and Robin's England, and he takes the initiative, as Robin had done centuries before, to oppose or circumvent the well-meaning, though too often self-defeating, village tyrannies. There can be little doubt that Mark Twain intended his readers to be aware of this larger parallel. As author, he fashioned a narrative made up of a sequence of events which bring young Tom Sawyer to triumph and to that special kind of fame reserved for rebels who prove finally to have been right.

Tom is in fact an outlaw, though not in quite the same sense as was his hero, Robin Hood, who lived in open and declared defiance of the oppressive authorities of his day. Robin's principal antagonists, the ballads tell us, were the Abbot of Saint Mary's in York and the Sheriff of Nottinghamshire, representatives of the church and state in the community. He knew that if he remained docilely within their jurisdiction, if he lived by the laws they had established for their own protection, he would be powerless against them; so he retreated to the forest in Sherwood and enacted there his own laws. Tom, too, finds his efforts to improve his lot hampered by the reigning authorities in St. Petersburg—the home, the church, the school. He knows that if he yields unresistingly to their well-intentioned regimen he cannot serve his private dream of a better world in which joy and justice abound. Instead of openly defying the community as Robin had done, he merely disregards those precepts and regulations which, if he honored them, would defeat his good intentions. He lies to Aunt Polly, plays hooky from school, slips out of his room at night, runs away to Jackson's Island, and "borrows" things which he has a special need for. To the village authorities he is an obstreperous boy, but in his own mind he is an outlaw, a distant disciple of the illustrious Robin Hood.

Tom is the leader of a band. Robin Hood had gathered about himself a company of like-minded companions who acknowledged him as their leader. Most famous among them, the ballads reveal, were Little John, Friar Tuck, Will Scarlet, George a Green, and Much, the miller's son—men whose exploits rivaled and sometimes even surpassed those of Robin himself. In the same way Tom's gang, proportionately small, is made up of the disgruntled and the dispossessed. But Joe Harper and Huck Finn prove to be worthy rebels in their own right. With Tom they run away to Jackson's Island, their Sherwood forest, where they live as pirates and outlaws, ritually strengthening themselves for the deeds they must perform. Eventually Huck plays a major role in the thwarting of Injun Joe.

Though at times Tom finds it expedient to operate contrary to the village authority, he is a well-meaning youngster, motivated, as was his hero before him, by a love of life and a desire to help those in distress. Joseph Ritson, in his introductory chapter, "The Life of Robin Hood," defends the English outlaw. He admits that Robin was a thief but adds, ". . . He took away the goods of rich men only; never killing any person, unless he was attacked or resisted . . . he would not suffer a woman to be maltreated; nor ever took anything from the poor, but charitably fed them with the wealth he drew from the abbots."[7] Of Robin's personal character, Ritson says, ". . . it is sufficiently evident that he was active, brave, prudent, patient; possessed of uncommon bodily strength, and considerable military skill; just, generous, benevolent, faithful, and beloved or revered by his followers or adherents for his excellent and admirable qualities."[8] Many of these same attributes can justly be ascribed to Tom, allowing for the fact, of course, that Tom is a mere stripling. His compassion is demonstrated by the results of his successful machinations. If it had not been for him, the disreputable Muff Potter probably would have been executed for a crime he did not commit, and the Widow Douglas have suffered the vengeance of Injun Joe.

It must be acknowledged that the success of Tom's endeavors, the good that returns to the community and to him because of his escapades, comes as a direct result of his refusal to accede to the village rule. Had he not slipped out of his window and visited the graveyard at midnight, he could not have witnessed the murder of Dr. Robinson and thereby prevented a miscarriage of justice. Had he not ventured deep into the cave, far beyond the area considered safe for excursionists, he could not have discovered Injun Joe's hiding place and gained the treasure. At the end of the story Tom is the rebel justified. His fame and fortune are rewards for his having defied the "law" and triumphed over it.

I have said that *Tom Sawyer* is an optimistic book. I should add that it is also a subversive one. It supposes that continuing revolution is a necessity; that the establishment, whether national or local, tyrannical or benign, will become increasingly oppressive as it becomes entrenched and secure. Existing authority must constantly be challenged, prodded to broaden its concepts of freedom and justice. An alerted citizen or band of citizens who would redirect the course of an established society might at times have to disregard or defy the laws and modes of conduct approved by that society. These assumptions, I say, make *Tom Sawyer* a subversive book. It is optimistic because it affirms that a courageous, imaginative individual can stand successfully against the establishment and thereby further the cause of individual and collective freedom. Robin Hood did so in medieval England; and Tom Sawyer, in St. Petersburg, Missouri. Tom's triumph was an especially happy one, for his revolution was bloodless.

One revolutionary element in the book should be of special interest to today's reader. Long ago Mark Twain recognized the generation gap. His distrust of the establishment extended to include most adults. He saw that what the world calls "experience" tends to make people bitter or bigoted or afraid. On the other hand, he admired the vitality and honesty of the young. Uncontaminated by the world, they are quick to recognize hypocrisy and bold to dream, to dare, and do. Mark Twain saw that there is a constant state of undeclared war in progress between adults and the young: adults strive to curb the enthusiasm, or what they call the "ignorance," of youth and hand down traditional prejudices and taboos; on their part the young struggle to make real a dream of an ideal world—a dream which their elders shared a long while ago but which now they distrust and fear. In *Tom Sawyer*, a story about this struggle, Mark Twain resolves the issue in favor of the young: he makes Tom and Huck the guardians of freedom and justice in St. Petersburg. It is his way of suggesting that the adult generations may well be in default and that the hope of humanity resides in youth. As innocent and mirth-provoking as the book may first appear, *Tom Sawyer* could well serve as a primer for those young activists and hippies who are protesting (sometimes too strenuously, it is true) against outmoded forms and attitudes today.

While he lived, Samuel Clemens never lost his concern for individual freedom; he never ceased to decry injustices, but eventually he lost his conviction that man can control his destiny and make his dreams come true. Much has been written in the effort to account for Twain's final cynicism, but whatever the causes, his view of man as tick, metaphorically hinted in *Tom Sawyer*, gradually gained the ascendency over his faith in man as Robin Hood. His loss of hope can be charted throughout his novels which followed

Tom Sawyer. *The Adventures of Huckleberry Finn*, another great affirmation, shows Huck and Tom helping goodness to triumph over ignorance and vice. In *A Connecticut Yankee* Hank Morgan, a confident, clever, democratic American of the nineteenth century, strives to bring freedom and justice to a benighted land, but his efforts result in a holocaust. For a moment Twain's Joan, inspired maiden, makes the good life seem more than a mere possibility, but she is ruthlessly sacrificed by the jealous authorities of her day. The book that shows most dramatically the depths of Twain's despair is *The Mysterious Stranger*, published posthumously. This is a story about boys, but it is sadly unlike *Tom Sawyer* in almost every other respect. Its youngsters are ominously passive and hopeless; there is no virtue in them. They have not even the power to report what they see and hear, but must stand helplessly by and watch while their village world suffers an endless nightmare of pain and degradation. No Robin Hood is here; no bold, rebellious Tom to set things right. Mark Twain at last had lost his faith in youth. The tick had triumphed.

But *Tom Sawyer* is a better book, a truer book, than *The Mysterious Stranger*. It is Mark Twain's happiest and most hopeful novel. It is "a hymn put into prose to give it a worldly air."

Notes

1. *The Adventures of Tom Sawyer* (New York: Washington Square Press, 1960), p. 61. Subsequent references to the novel are to this edition.
2. Milton Meltzer, *Mark Twain Himself* (New York, 1960), p. 162.
3. *Ibid.*
4. *Ibid.*
5. Joseph Ritson, *Robin Hood: A Collection of Poems, Songs, and Ballads Relative to that Celebrated English Outlaw* (London, 1884), p. 234.
6. Ritson, p. 439.
7. Ritson, p. 7.
8. Ritson, p. 9.

The Sanctioned Rebel

Judith Fetterley

One of the major rhythms of *The Adventures of Tom Sawyer* is established in its opening lines: " 'Tom!' No answer. 'Tom!' No answer. 'What's gone with that boy, I wonder? You, TOM!' "[1] Much of the action of the novel is a variation on this theme of looking for Tom, for in the world of St. Petersburg the boy, Tom, is central. It is he who creates the major occasions for the town, and the emotional arcs of the book are described by his being lost or found. When Tom is thought lost, the town is in dismay; when he is found, it rejoices:

> The alarm swept from lip to lip, from group to group, from street to street, and within five minutes the bells were wildly clanging and the whole town was up! The Cardiff Hill episode sank into instant insignificance, the burglars were forgotten, horses were saddled, skiffs were manned, the ferryboat ordered out, and before the horror was half an hour old two hundred men were pouring down highroad and river toward the cave (p. 248).
>
> . . . .
>
> Away in the middle of the night a wild peal burst from the village bells and in a moment the streets were swarming with frantic half-clad people, who shouted, "Turn out! turn out! they're found! they're found!" Tin pans and horns were added to the din, the population massed itself and moved toward the river, met the children coming in an open carriage drawn by shouting citizens, thronged around it, joined its homeward march, and swept magnificently up the main street roaring huzzah after huzzah! (pp. 263–64).

The world of St. Petersburg is dull and sleepy, and its arch enemy is the boredom which lies at its heart, making it so sensation-hungry that everything that happens is greeted as an entertainment. Thus the discovery of Dr. Robinson's murder constitutes a local holiday for which school is dismissed. Thus the town turns out to fill the church as never before for the spectacle of a triple funeral. Thus the trial of Muff Potter is the biggest entertainment of the summer; and when Tom finally decides to testify at the trial, he does so as much out of a sense of what is dramatically appropriate and will improve the show as he does out of a tormented conscience.

Reprinted from *Studies in the Novel* 3 (Fall 1971): 293–304. Copyright 1971 by North Texas State University. Reprinted by permission of the publisher.

The boredom which lies at the heart of St. Petersburg is most fully pictured in the scenes which take place in the Sunday school and church the first Sunday of the novel. The dreadful monotony of Sunday school text, of prayer and sermon, the painful rigidity of never-varying rituals, symbolized by the superintendent's clothes—"a fence that compelled a straight lookout ahead, and a turning of the whole body when a side view was required" (p. 35)—is relieved only by a few paper wads, an occasional scuffle, a fly to be caught. The world of St. Petersburg is trapped into boredom by its own hypocrisy, by its refusal to admit how dull and uninteresting the things which it professes to value really are. It is against this background that Tom's centrality to St. Petersburg can be understood. He provides life, interest, amusement; he is a master entertainer with a bug for every occasion. No wonder St. Petersburg is always looking for Tom.

One of the central scenes which defines this aspect of the interrelation of Tom and his society is the moment in church when Tom discovers and releases his pinch bug. Tom's boredom has reached painful proportions; the momentary flicker of interest aroused by the image of the little child leading the lion and lamb before the hosts at Judgment Day has faded. Then he remembers his pinch bug, a "treasure" of the first order. He takes it out, it bites him, and he flips it on the floor. Immediately the congregation stirs itself; at last something is happening. A few minutes later a poodle which is the very image of the congregation, bored and sleepy, comes along and, like the congregation, begins to take an interest in the bug and to play with it. But after awhile he forgets about the bug and in starting to go to sleep, sits on it, whereupon it promptly bites him and sends him tearing around the church and ultimately out a window. "Tom Sawyer went home quite cheerful, thinking to himself that there was some satisfaction about divine service when there was a bit of variety in it" (p. 49). He has provided a brilliant entertainment and won the thanks of the congregation, for his act has not only amused them but has made it impossible for church to continue.

The other center of boredom in this world is school, and once again Tom has a bug to relieve him. Tom is bored to a point almost beyond endurance when he sticks his hand in his pocket and discovers the tick he has just purchased from Huck Finn: "his face lit up with a glow of gratitude that was prayer" (p. 65). His comrade, Joe Harper, as painfully bored as Tom, greets the tick and its promise of pleasure "deeply and gratefully" (p. 66). The language which describes the discovery of the tick is an impressive index of the boredom of school. But again the boys are not the only ones bored. The schoolmaster, Mr. Dobbins, is asleep when Tom comes in and only wakes up long enough to switch him. Tom's tick and his play with it become equally the source of the schoolmaster's interest: "He had contemplated a good part of the performance before he contributed his bit of variety to it" (p. 67). The switching is part of the complex game which the boys and adults play in order to make school bearable. It is the mode by which the teacher is allowed to save face and keep on professing his interest in school. It in no way prevents Tom from continuing to create interest through his pranks, for, unlike the world of Dickens, the switching in Tom's world leaves neither psychological nor physical scars. It is, indeed, the mark of the boys' success in gaining attention and creating interest; it is a modest form of showing off for both boys and teacher. The relationship between the adults and children in this novel is deeply symbiotic.

Tom's interactions with Aunt Polly develop another dimension of this relationship. Aunt Polly, like the rest of St. Petersburg, loves Tom, because he makes her laugh and gives variety to her life. But Aunt Polly expresses her affection for Tom by constantly rapping him on the head with her thimble, setting traps to catch him in lies, carping at him for being bad and breaking her heart, and enforcing labor on his holidays. She never comes out and openly says what Tom means to her until she thinks he is dead. In part, Aunt Polly is a victim of her own hypocrisy and unreality. She refuses to take account of the split which she everywhere expresses between her heart and her conscience, with its conception of duty. Thus she is never free to say what she truly feels. But this is really a very small part of the psychology behind Aunt Polly's actions. Tom knows that Aunt Polly's thimble on his head, like Dobbins's switching, is an index of the place he holds in her heart; thus he worries only when she does not rap him. But much more important, Tom knows that it is her resistance, her posture of disapproval, which creates his pleasure.

The fact that the boys' world of pranks is no fun without the existence of an adult world to prohibit them is made clear in a number of scenes in the story. When school is finally over and vacation finally comes, there is nothing Tom wants to do. What has happened to the lure of Cardiff Hill, which called to him so irresistibly through the schoolroom window? Clearly "hooky" is one thing and vacation another. When the boys run off to Jackson's Island everything is bully for the first day or so, but pretty soon they lose interest in going naked and sleeping out in the open and swimming whenever they want, because, as Joe says, "Swimming's no good. I don't seem to care for it, somehow, when there ain't anybody to say I shan't go in" (p. 138). But perhaps the most famous instance of this principle is the whitewashing episode, which casts Tom in the role of discovering it as a great law of human nature. The success of Tom's strategy rests on his intuitive discovery that people want to do what they are forbidden to. In order to change whitewashing from hard labor into the one thing the boys are mad to do Tom has only to present it as something he cannot allow them to do, an art requiring special skill which only he possesses, a task which he is under strict orders to perform only himself without help from anyone else. By means of this tactic Tom not only gets the boys to do the whitewashing for him; he gets them to pay him for the privilege.

The Adventures of Tom Sawyer is steeped in the rhythm of this relationship between adults and children. The delight of midnight trips is in creeping out of the window in answer to a secret signal and in defiance of an adult stricture. The pleasure of Huck Finn's society, like the attractiveness of his state, lies in its being forbidden. When Huck first enters the book, it is this angle from which he is viewed. Thus he is described as a "romantic outcast," a phrase which defines the point of view on him as Tom's. There is at this point no hint of what Huck's life might be like either from his point of view or the narrator's. The strong implication, however, is that the joys of his existence are imaginary, a product of prohibition. Huck is introduced in the book in great part as an element in Mark Twain's creation of the dynamic between pleasure and prohibition in the mind of Tom Sawyer. And Mark Twain's achievement in creating this dynamic in *The Adventures of Tom Sawyer* prepares us for Tom's passion for creating obstacles at the end of *Huckleberry Finn*. It is part and parcel of his conception of pleasure. If the adults have failed to fulfill their part of the game and provide difficulties for Tom to overcome, then he will simply have to play both parts and create the obstacles himself. That a new mode of pleasure has been discovered to the reader in the process of Huck's adventures is not Tom's fault; he is doing only what he thinks is expected of him.

II

Tom entertains his world and in return it provides the structures which make his pleasure possible and heaps on him all the attention he could possibly desire. The relationship between Tom and his community is remarkably positive and indeed it is so throughout the book. There are, however, aspects to this relationship which are a little darker than those so far discussed and which bring us to a further understanding of Tom's character, an understanding which begins to explain what happens to Tom in *Adventures of Huckleberry Finn*.

Tom's actions in the first half of *Tom Sawyer* are a series of entertainments, but they are also a series of exposures which reveal the absurdity and hypocrisy of his world. One of the basic hypocrisies which Tom exposes early in the book is that which lies behind the phrase "virtue rewarded." By "virtue" the community means hard, dull, stupid work and by "reward" it means a sense of pleasure and achievement in doing this hard, dull, stupid work. The exposure begins when Tom, having completed his whitewashing assignment, presents himself to Aunt Polly and reports that he is done. When she has assured herself that he is not lying, she proceeds to reward him with a choice apple and a "lecture upon the added value and flavor a treat took to itself when it came without sin through virtuous effort" (p. 21). The scene which precedes Aunt Polly's lecture has, of course, made a shambles of her premise. People do not enjoy what they work for; they enjoy what they play at. The "added value and flavor" of a treat come not through "virtuous effort" but through being told you cannot have it. But Aunt Polly herself no more acts on the basis of her scripture than Tom, for what she is now calling "virtuous effort" was just a few pages before hard work and punishment, something she would have to force Tom to do. The explosion of Aunt Polly's myth of human behavior, however, is built right into this scene: "And while she closed with a happy Scriptural flourish, he 'hooked' a doughnut" (p. 21).

The exposure of the hypocrisy of "virtue rewarded" continues in the scene in Sunday school in chapter 4. A certain kind of virtue is indeed rewarded in this incident but not exactly the kind the authorities pretend they wish to recognize. Outside the church on Sunday morning, Tom trades all the wealth he has gotten from selling whitewashing privileges the previous afternoon for Bible tickets. The exchange is certainly justified in Tom's eyes, for the opportunity to be called up in front of the entire Sunday school world to receive a Bible fulfills his ever-present dream of being the center of attention. But the tactic by which Tom wins his way to the Bible marks the absurdity of the terms of Judge Thatcher's presentation and expresses the absurdity of the "virtue rewarded" premise behind it:

> "That's it! That's a good boy. Fine boy. Fine, manly little fellow. Two thousand verses is a great many—very, very great many. And you never can be sorry for the trouble you took to learn them; for knowledge is worth more than anything there is in the world; it's what makes great men and good men; you'll be a great man and a good man yourself, someday, Thomas. . . . And you wouldn't take any money for those two thousand verses—no indeed you wouldn't" (pp. 40–41).

But Tom's exposure is made possible by the hypocrisy built into the situation and reflected in Judge Thatcher's speech. If the knowledge was its own reward, a thing which one would not take any money for, there would be no need for the bait of tickets yellow, red, and blue, and the Bible whose purchase they add up to. The very existence of these tickets defines the fact that no one would learn those verses without at least the dim possibility of having a moment of glory for it. All Tom does is to carry the implications of St. Petersburg Christianity to their logical conclusion, and thus there is a certain justice in his particular virtue being rewarded.

Tom's most dramatic exposure, however, occurs when he stages his own funeral and resurrection, for the situation he creates invites the adults to indulge in the hypocrisy of remorse:

> "But it's *so* hard—oh, it's so hard! Only last Saturday my Joe busted a firecracker right under my nose and I knocked him sprawling. Little did I know then how soon—Oh, if it was to do over again I'd hug him and bless him for it."

"Yes, yes, yes, I know just how you feel, Mrs. Harper, I know just exactly how you feel. No longer than yesterday noon, my Tom took and filled the cat full of Pain-killer, and I did think the cretur would tear the house down. And God forgive me, I cracked Tom's head with my thimble, poor boy, poor dead boy" (pp. 131–32).

The situations which Aunt Polly and Mrs. Harper remember are such as to make clear the nature of their remorse. The absurdity of claiming you would hug a boy who has just set off a firecracker under your nose is patent. It could only happen if one had knowledge at the time of something that was to happen later. As this is impossible, so the formulations are absurd and unreal, a fact made quite clear when the boys return and thimble crackings and cuffings continue. The remorse is an emotional indulgence which ultimately has the effect of making the mourners feel good about themselves, because it implies that their actions are no real index of their hearts.

Tom's appearance at his own funeral exposes the hypocrisy at the heart of the adult's lament. His entrance is perfectly timed to accomplish this exposure with maximum effect. At just the moment when the minister has moved the entire congregation to tears and is himself openly weeping over the angelic picture he has created of the boys, Tom appears in all his bedraggled and mischievous reality. The illusion that the minister has created and the congregation conspired in is exploded and the unreality at the heart of the funeral exposed. As James Cox has noted, "Tom's joke, his play funeral, provides the ultimate definition of what the 'sincere' funeral was to have been for the town in the first place—an entertainment! A tearful, lugubrious, and hackneyed production in which each of the participants was fully working up his part—but an entertainment nonetheless."[2]

The adults are sufficiently happy to get the boys back that they do not mind being exposed as ridiculous. The potential humiliation of the scene is averted by the singing of "Old Hundred" and the final note is one of reconciliation and joy. But it has been a tight situation for a moment. Tom's series of exposures has culminated in something particularly egregious, for it is far harder to be exposed as an emotional hypocrite than a moral one. What is it that allows Tom to get away with this exposure? The answer lies in the discovery of a further dimension to the symbiotic relationship between Tom and the adults of St. Petersburg.

A number of critics who have written on *The Adventures of Tom Sawyer* have discussed the book in terms of its relation to the convention of Bad Boy literature which appeared in the United States, particularly after the Civil War.[3] Books built around the character of the Bad Boy sprang up as a reaction against an inundation of highly moralistic juvenile fiction. This fiction pictured and exalted an unreal creature who was totally good and spent all his time in memorizing the Bible and going to church and taking care of his mother, and who reaped the rewards of this earth and then those of heaven. It also pictured an evil child who stole apples, lied to his mother, played hooky, and was eventually hanged. It was against the background of this absurdity that the Bad Boy books arose. Their hero, while called a Bad Boy to make clear that he is not the Good Boy of the moralistic fiction, is in fact just a real human boy, whose pranks, jokes, and rascalities are the natural result of his energy and healthiness. The Bad Boy is not really bad, only "mischievous," and it is clear that when he grows up he will be a pillar of the community. The implication behind this literature is clear: socially useful adults develop only from real boys who have shown some life as children. The rascality of such children is not negative; rather it is understood and affirmed as a stage they must go through on their way to becoming useful adults; it is indeed the indication that they will, in fact, become useful adults.

The Adventures of Tom Sawyer is a paradigm of the Bad Boy convention, and its structure and hero can be most clearly understood in its terms. There has been considerable critical debate on the structure of *Tom Sawyer* since Walter Blair published, in 1939, his article, "On the Structure of *Tom Sawyer*."[4] His thesis, most recently supported by Hamlin Hill, Robert Regan, and Albert Stone,[5] claims that the book enacts Tom's growth from callow, unworthy childhood to worthy maturity. Blair defined four major narrative strands in the story: "the story of Tom and Becky, the story of Tom and Muff Potter, the Jackson's Island episode, and the series of happenings (which might be called the Injun Joe story) leading to the discovery of the treasure."[6] Each of these strands, according to Blair, "is initiated by a characteristic and typically boyish action. The love story begins with Tom's childishly fickle desertion of his fiancée, Amy Lawrence; the Potter narrative with the superstitious trip to the graveyard; the Jackson's Island episode with the adolescent revolt of the boy against Aunt Polly, and Tom's youthful ambition to be a pirate; the Injun Joe story with the juvenile search for buried treasure."[7]

Three of these strands, however, "are climaxed by a characteristic and mature sort of action, a sort of action, moreover, directly opposed to the initial action. Tom chivalrously takes Becky's punishment and faithfully helps her in the cave; he defies boyish superstition and courageously testifies for Muff Potter; he forgets a childish antipathy and shows mature concern for his aunt's uneasiness about him."[8] The Injun Joe story for Blair was "the least useful of the four so far as showing Tom's maturing is concerned."[9] But surely there is no need for this reservation, for in Blair's terms Tom's pity on discovering Injun Joe's death is a mature act, replacing his self-centered and seemingly callous earlier response. But, of course, the problem with Blair's analysis is precisely in the terms, for while he has accurately described a pattern in the book he has, I feel, inaccurately evaluated its meaning. Blair assumes certain actions to be "mature" and positive and other actions to be "immature" and negative without ever establishing the grounds for his classification and valuation. The closest he comes is to say that Tom's actions are mature because each of them "eventuates in an expression of adult approval."[10] In fact, the basis of Blair's thesis, and of the essays of those who support him, lies in the claim that Tom's progress in the book is a movement from bad to good and that this movement is defined as such by the changing reaction of the adult community to him. But clearly the adults in *Tom Sawyer* are in all essentials like the children: "Mr. Walters fell to 'showing off'. . . . The librarian 'showed off'. . . . The young lady teachers 'showed off'. . . . The little girl 'showed off' and the little boys 'showed off'. . . . And above it all the great man sat and beamed a majestic judicial smile upon all the house, and warmed himself in the sun of his own grandeur—for he was 'showing off,' too" (p. 38). Indeed, the very "search for buried treasure," which Blair labels as "juvenile," is, upon Tom's success, taken up by every adult in St. Petersburg. If, in fact, the adults are in any way different from the children, the difference does not make them more positive than the children but more negative. The children admit, after all, that they are showing off to gain attention but the adults have to pretend that they are doing something else. The children are honest; the adults are hypocrites, a point which Tom's actions make again and again. Thus it hardly makes sense to assume that they provide the yardstick which charts a growth from something negative to something positive. In fact, it hardly seems accurate to describe Tom's change in the book as one of growth in this sense at all. One has only to compare the tone of the end of the book with that of the beginning to feel this. Indeed, in commenting on this ending, Blair does an about-face and finds that Tom's "adult" behavior in talking to Huck Finn means that he has "gone over to the side of the enemy."[11]

What Blair is responding to at the end of his article is Mark Twain's vision of the meaning of Bad Boy fiction as dramatized in *The Adventures of Tom Sawyer*. The structure of *Tom Sawyer* is at once an embodiment and an exposure of this convention and it takes its shape from the dynamics of the interaction between child and adult which lie behind the convention. Since the Bad Boy is just a natural child marked for the future as a solid, respectable citizen, he is the agent through whom the community can gain a temporary release from the boredom and rigidly of their codes and beliefs, a release which is dramatized in the conventional scene in which the Bad Boy licks the overly pious, unnatural Good Boy. But the Bad Boy does not hold any values which are at root different from those of the community, nor does he really intend to expose the hypocrisy of the values which the community holds and which the Good Boy is simply exaggerating. The Bad Boy is a rebel in that he temporarily flaunts and outrages the community, but he is a sanctioned rebel, because his rebellion is limited in time and intention; his rebellion is a stage which has respectability at its other end. The community wants, in fact demands, this rebellion, because it provides excitement and release, and because the ultimate assimilation of the rebellion constitutes a powerful affirmation of their values. The convention of the Bad Boy and the books that express it represent the form of rebellion without the reality, titillation without threat. They channel rebellion by confining it to a stage and sanctioning that stage, and ultimately they transform rebellion into affirmation.

The structure of *Tom Sawyer* is a perfect embodiment of this pattern. In the early part of the book Tom is consistently outrageous. He lies and steals and plays hooky as a matter of course. He hobnobs with Huck Finn against the express prohibition of the adults. He sneaks out at midnight to join the outcast in his adventure to the graveyard. There he watches a murder and makes no move to reveal the murderer. His early actions constitute a series of exposures, which culminates in his appearance at his own funeral. This is the height of Tom's rebellion and outrageousness, for in threatening to make the congregation look ridiculous in front of each other, in threatening to humiliate them, he pushes against the limits of what is sanctioned. Dignity is salvaged by the singing of "Old Hundred" but Tom's rebellion has reached its peak and from this point on his pattern of action changes.

In the first major scene after the resurrection episode, Tom is discovered in the ultimately approvable role, one which embodies to the highest possible degree the values of the community: he saves Becky not simply from the public humiliation of a whipping but from having to admit to herself or anyone else an interest in sex. He is here cast in the role of the true Southern gentleman. Such action clearly neutralizes the threat posed by his funeral and makes clear which side he is on. From this point on Tom adopts conventional values more and more explicitly. He becomes society's detective and exposes its murderer; indirectly he brings the murderer to bay and ultimately he kills him. He gets money and makes clear that he intends to invest it and make capital. In an extension of his role toward Becky, he saves her life and thus further adopts the conventional masculine role of protector of womanhood. In the final scene of the book, Tom, who began by longing for Huck's outcast state and by cordially hating along with him the confinements of clothes and schools, becomes the advocate of civilization, the adult who seeks to channel and transform the rebellion which threatens the community. As Henry Nash Smith has observed, "Mark Twain has written the Sunday-school story about the Good Little Boy Who Succeeded all over again with only a slight change in the hero's make-up and costume."[12] Thus Smith succinctly defines the essential similarity of the Bad Boy convention to the Good Boy literature which it was presumably attacking. And thus he succinctly defines the nature of Tom Sawyer's character and rebellion and the source of Mark Twain's final attitude toward Tom.

III

In spite of the negative undercurrents of the action and structure of *The Adventures of Tom Sawyer*, negative in terms both of Tom's relation to his community and of the narrator's and reader's attitude toward Tom, the tone of the novel is essentially genial and the character of Tom Sawyer emerges as essentially positive. Thus Robert Regan is moved to call *Tom Sawyer* "the most amiable of all Mark Twain's novels,"[13] and Kenneth Lynn remarks, "Of all Twain's major fictions, *Tom Sawyer* is the only one in which an initiation ends neither in flight nor in catastrophe, but in serene and joyous acceptance."[14] For indeed the focus of *The Adventures of Tom Sawyer* is on the harmony between Tom and his community and on the satisfactions of the symbiotic relationship between them. Further, all Tom's characteristics are ultimately placed within this context and are made positive by it. Thus Tom's egotism, his overriding passion to be the center of attention, and his insistence on masterminding every action constitute the mode by which he both provides pleasure for the community and becomes useful to them. It is his egotism, his desire to be the center of attention, which leads him to create the situations which entertain and release them; it is equally these characteristics which in great part move him to testify for Muff Potter at the trial and to take Becky's whipping.

Of course, there are negative overtones to his character. His self-pity with its undercurrent of revenge and aggression, issuing in the desire to make people suffer for what they have done to him; his capacity to subordinate his sense of others' feelings to his desire for an effect; his insistence on things being done according to the rules—a characteristic which links him to the hypocrisy and rigidity which he is otherwise engaged in exploding and looks forward to what he will become in *Huckleberry Finn*; his genius in manipulating people—all of these qualities are present in Tom in *The Adventures of Tom Sawyer*. But they are either secondary and muted or they are transformed by the way they operate in the particular situation of this book. For, again, the focus of *The Adventures of Tom Sawyer* is on the pleasures of the relationship between Tom and his community, which is in essence the relationship between the entertainer and his audience. And in this study of the entertainer, his genius is the joy of his audience, and the necessary egotism, selfishness, and aggressiveness of his character are exculpated by this fact.

It is only at the very end of the book that the tone toward Tom becomes noticeably negative and we feel the presence of some new attitude, some new perspective. What we feel, of course, is the birth of *Adventures of Huckleberry Finn*, for the change in attitude toward Tom is intimately connected with the discovery of Huck Finn. It is only very late in *Tom Sawyer*, when Huck is separated from Tom by the necessities of the plot, that the possibilities of his character are discovered. It is only then that Huck is discovered as a voice, and a mask, and a point of view, one which will define Tom Sawyer differently and crystallize the perceptions about him which dominate the end of the book. What is wrong with the ending of *The Adventures of Tom Sawyer* is that it is the beginning of *Adventures of Huckleberry Finn* and *Huckleberry Finn* is a quite different book and in it Tom Sawyer is a quite different character.

Notes

1. Samuel L. Clemens, *The Adventures of Tom Sawyer* in *The Writings of Mark Twain,* Definitive Edition (New York: Gabriel Wells, 1922–25), VIII, 1. Subsequent references will be to this edition of *Tom Sawyer* and will be included in parentheses in the text.

2. *Mark Twain: The Fate of Humor* (Princeton: Princeton Univ. Press, 1966), p. 140.

3. The following are most important: Walter Blair, "On the Structure of *Tom Sawyer,*" *MP,* 37 (1939), 75–88; John Hinz, "Huck and Pluck: 'Bad' Boys in American Fiction," *SAQ,* 51 (1952), 120–29; Jim Hunter, "Mark Twain and the Boy-Book in 19th-Century America," *CE,* 24 (1963), 430–38; Albert E. Stone, *The Innocent Eye: Childhood in Mark Twain's Imagination* (New Haven: Yale Univ. Press, 1961), pp. 58–90.

4. *MP,* 37 (1939), 75–88.

5. Hamlin Hill, "The Composition and the Structure of *Tom Sawyer,*" *AL,* 32 (1961), 379–92; Robert Regan, *Unpromising Heroes: Mark Twain and His Characters* (Berkeley: Univ. of California Press, 1966), pp. 117–21; Stone, pp. 78–89.

6. Blair, p. 84.

7. Ibid.

8. Ibid., pp. 84–85.

9. Ibid., p. 85.

10. Ibid.

11. Ibid., p. 88.

12. *Mark Twain: The Development of a Writer* (Cambridge, Mass: Harvard Univ. Press, 1962), p. 89.

13. Regan, p. 116.

14. *Mark Twain and Southwestern Humor* (Boston: Little, Brown, 1959), p. 196.

"I Never Thought We Might Want to Come Back": Strategies of Transcendence in *Tom Sawyer*

TOM H. TOWERS

While Huck Finn is now universally received as one of the principal achievements of American literature, *The Adventures of Tom Sawyer* has remained for most readers at worst a children's book, at best a nostalgic evocation of lost childhood, or, in Bernard De Voto's phrase, "the supreme American idyll."[1] Those who have found larger meanings in the book have usually concentrated on what they regard as Tom's maturation—his abandonment of childish self-pity and dime-novel posturing in favor of a morally responsible role in the community.[2] Even Leslie Fiedler, although troubled by the story's gothic undercurrents, has concluded that the novel is finally an evasion because in its world "violence doesn't count."[3]

All these views of *Tom Sawyer* suggest that it is positive and optimistic, or at least harmless, in its vision of man and the world; yet the action of the book seems at odds with that conclusion. The pranks and flirtations of the opening chapters soon give place to the midnight murder of Dr. Robinson. The escape into the beatific nature of Jackson's Island ends with the destructiveness of the great storm and, of course, with the supposed death of the boys. Even after his triumphant return to Aunt Polly, Tom suffers as the "dreadful secret of the murder" becomes to him "a chronic misery" (p. 143).[4] Nor does public confession free Tom from his visions of terror and death. Boyishly searching for treasure, he becomes involved in Injun Joe's murderous scheme against the Widow Douglas, and Becky's birthday party ends in the nightmare ordeal in the cave and the final confrontation with Joe. Despite the book's popular reputation, horror is very real in *Tom Sawyer*, and it is the horror and Tom's reaction to it that lie at the core of meaning in the novel and connect it to the dark unity of Twain's later work.

The structure of *Tom Sawyer* is defined by Tom's efforts to exchange the deadening actuality of his everyday life for a more intense, spiritually informed reality which he seeks in the graveyard, on the island, in his quest

Reprinted from *Modern Fiction Studies* 21 (Winter 1975–76): 509–20. Copyright 1976, by Purdue Research Foundation, West Lafayette, Indiana 47907. Reprinted with permission.

for secret treasure and with Becky in the cave. Opposed to that sought-for world is the town, which represents everything that inhibits the realization of freedom and selfhood. The townspeople, for example, are uniformly mired in vanity and hypocrisy. In a travesty of Christian humility, the Sunday-school teachers preen themselves before Judge Thatcher. Just as he hides his baldness beneath a wig, Dobbins, the schoolmaster, conceals a nasty prurience behind his apparent respectability—after he has bullied the children into submission, he slavers over the illustrations in his anatomy text. Not even Aunt Polly is free from vanity. Her glasses are for appearance only, and after Tom has tricked and defied her in the Jackson's Island adventure, she is angry with him only because he has allowed her to make a fool of herself before Mrs. Harper.

Worse than such pretense is the systematic denial of freedom in St. Petersburg, whose very name suggests authoritarian repression. Without doubt, Aunt Polly loves Tom, yet she conceives of her love chiefly as a duty to bend him to the customs of a spiritually dead society. As in the episode of the painkiller and the cat, her first rule for Tom is that he must be forbidden whatever he seems to desire. While she contemplates making Tom whitewash the fence, she muses, " 'It's mighty hard to make him work Saturdays, when all the boys is having holiday, but he hates work more than he hates anything else, and I've *got* to do some of my duty by him, or I'll be the ruination of the child' " (p. 12). Later, when she unjustly scolds Tom after Sid has broken the sugar bowl, she suffers in her conscience, but she cannot retract her harsh words because "she judged that this would be construed into a confession that she had been in the wrong, and discipline forbade that" (p. 26).

So far as Tom and the other children are concerned, the whole of society consists in restrictive, often humiliating rules and institutions. On weekdays there is school with its floggings, and on Sundays there is the confining propriety of church. There is, of course, neither learning in the school nor salvation in the church; both institutions seem to exist only to deny spontaneous humanity. Shoes and baths are the unnatural uses of unnatural society, and there are rules against swimming and playing and talking to Huck Finn. Still worse, the life of St. Petersburg is charged with cruelty and violence that result logically from the frustrations accompanying such ubiquitous repression. The first major incident in the novel is the murder of Dr. Robinson by Injun Joe, and the last third of the book is concerned largely with Joe's intended assault upon the Widow Douglas. But in some ways Joe seems no more than an embodiment of the unconscious desire of St. Petersburg generally. Like the landsmen in *Huck Finn* or the royal court in *Connecticut Yankee*, the townspeople of this novel regard death and suffering mainly as welcome diversion. They can be stirred from their lethargy only by the prospect of lurid death—the planned lynching of Muff Potter, the supposed drowning of Tom and Huck, or the children's ordeal in the cave. Even Aunt

Polly harbors a secret fascination with violence; she confesses, " 'I dream about [the murder] most every night myself. Sometimes I dream it's me that done it' " (p. 81).

In this environment, Tom's most elemental strategy for asserting his selfhood is a kind of guerrilla warfare against the town. The famous pranks—the fence painting, the gilding of Dobbins' head, the Sunday-school swindle—constitute a rebellion against the dishonesty and injustice of the adult world. Tom's targets are almost always authorities like the Sunday-school superintendent or the schoolmaster, or most frequently Aunt Polly; he attacks other children only when, like Sid, they are the willing agents of society. Moreover, Tom and his friends have formed a tacit alliance with the other victims and outcasts of the community, not only Huck, but also Muff Potter and the slaves. But, simply because they are children and thus powerless, the boys cannot ultimately succeed in their "revenge." Tom turns from rebellion and seeks freedom by trying, through a variety of strategies, to escape from or to transcend the stultification of St. Petersburg.

In nature the children intuit a spiritually vital world which seems to oppose that of adult society at every point. The town means restrictive rules and onerous tasks, but nature is the scene of games and leisure and, above all, freedom. The town is literally as well as symbolically sterile—all the women are middle-aged widows or prepubescent girls, and male sexuality is represented by Dobbins' prurience and Injun Joe's sadism. In contrast, the imagined world of the children is peopled by virile robbers and pirates, so beloved by their female captives that " 'after they've been in the cave a week or two weeks they stop crying and after that. . . . if you drove them out they'd turn right around and come back' " (p. 205). Similarly, death, which in town is at best a welcome relief from life's misery, is, in the boys' world, the prelude to new and fuller life, as when Tom and Huck seek in the graveyard symbolic renewal in the cleansing of their warts.

The disjunction between St. Petersburg and the boys' world of the hills and the river is recognized in the self-conscious repudiation of the values and uses of the town when the children enter spiritualized nature. First come the ritualistic meowings and bird whistles. Then the boys must cast off their clothes, the outward signs of their social roles. (The repressive function of clothes is demonstrated in Aunt Polly's practice of sewing Tom into his shirt; conversely, it is significant that the boys must become naked not only to swim or play at Indians, but even to become robbers or circus clowns.) Finally, the boys enter into wholly new identities as they cease to be Tom or Joe and become instead Robin Hood or The Black Avenger of the Spanish Main. With their new identities comes a new impunity; thus, Tom acknowledges that his "respectable" name, Thomas, is " 'the name they lick me by' " (p. 52), but as Robin Hood he boasts, " 'I can't fall; that ain't the way it is in the book' " (p. 64).

The chief episodic complexes in the novel—the murder plot, the Jackson's Island scenes, the treasure hunt, and the MacDougal's Cave adventure— are unified by Tom's efforts to enter permanently this world of vitality and freedom and to escape forever the dehumanizing life of St. Petersburg. To this extent *Tom Sawyer* anticipates *Huck Finn*, but there is a major and decisive difference between Tom's search for transcendence and Huck's. Each time Huck escapes from the greed and violence of society, he is reborn on the river and draws closer to the realization of the natural morality that is eventually his salvation. With Tom the process is almost exactly inverted. Each of his withdrawals brings Tom to a fresh sense of destructive isolation and death. Huck presumably sustains his new self as he "lights out for the territory," but Tom ultimately renounces the equivalent of Huck's "territory" in favor of the very community he has tried to escape throughout the book.

The adventure in the graveyard is Tom's first real attempt at full participation in the world of his intuitions, and in both its intentions and its effects the episode establishes the larger patterns of the novel. As I have suggested earlier, Tom and Huck come to the cemetery to invoke the spirits of the dead in a ritual of healing and renewal.[5] But instead of new life they discover irredeemable death in the form of Dr. Robinson's murder, and the implications as well as the facts of the incident are ruinous to the boys' aspirations.

First, Robinson himself has also come to the graveyard seeking in death—the corpse of Hoss Williams—the magical secrets of life, and his murder is a grisly warning of the end such quests must come to in the book. Second, in the figure of Injun Joe, Tom confronts a prophetic type of himself. Joe's murder of Robinson is a horrible magnification of Tom's own vengeful pranks against the town authorities. For example, Joe explains to Robinson just before he kills him,

"Five years ago you drove me away from your father's kitchen one night, when I come to ask for something to eat, and you said I warn't there for any good; and when I swore I'd get even with you if it took a hundred years, your father had me jailed for a vagrant. Did you think I'd forget? The Injun blood ain't in me 'for nothing. And now I've *got* you, and you got to *settle*, you know!" (pp. 68–69)

Later, with the Widow, his motive is again vengeance for past wrongs and humiliations:

". . . her husband was rough on me—many times he was rough on me—and mainly he was the justice of the peace that jugged me for a vagrant. And that ain't all. It ain't a millionth part of it! He had me *horsewhipped!*—horsewhipped in front of the jail, like a nigger—with all the town looking on!" (p. 179)

The abuses cataloged by Joe are clear echoes of the confinements, beatings, and embarrassments Tom himself suffers at home and in the town.

Twain continues the identification of Tom and Joe as he shows Tom and his friends transformed to murderous Indians who "killed and scalped each other by thousands" (p. 113). And he masks hero and villain in strikingly similar disguises—Tom as the Black Avenger of the Spanish Main and Joe as "the old deaf-and-dumb Spaniard" (p. 162). (The symbolic significance of Joe's masquerade becomes the more apparent for its otherwise inexplicable absurdity. At the level of "reality" Joe's Spanish disguise would surely attract rather than discourage the unwanted attention of the town.) In addition, both Tom and Joe disdain the acceptable ways to wealth and seek instead for buried treasure—perhaps more important, they are both successful in their quest. Unregenerate to the end, Joe dies with the treasure, and Tom survives to claim it only because he at last renounces what Joe stands for.

So far as the graveyard scene is concerned, the correspondence between Tom and Joe stands as a terrifying warning against both the urge to primitivism and the taste for vengeance. Just as the pathetic dereliction of Muff Potter prophesies the end of Huck's shiftlessness, Joe's viciousness, his "Injun blood," suggests the innate savagery of "natural" man. What has been revealed to Tom, though he cannot yet comprehend it, is the universal human impulse to violence and death, and, what is even more dismaying, through his surrogate self Joe, Tom's own capacity for evil.[6]

Reserved for the last is the greatest horror of all, the sense of absolute and unrelievable loneliness. Traditionally, the Romantic breakthrough to spiritual reality brings a vision of new life and with it a sense of new, transcendent unity with all men. I have explained that Tom and Huck, in an inversion of the usual pattern, find murder instead of rebirth in their spiritual excursion. In the same way, they are brought to isolation instead of community. Their secret knowledge separates the boys from the rest of mankind, and they take an oath in blood never to speak, in effect never to rejoin the community of men. Tom suffers isolation not only from the other children and the town generally, but even from his family. He must tie his jaws shut at night lest he confess to Sid in his sleep, and that sleep is troubled by nightmares of blood and death. Weeks later the secret remains "a very cancer," and Tom feels he is "a prisoner, dead to the world and its happenings" (p. 143). At last he passes into a long illness, from which he arises, not renewed in selfhood, but more persuaded than ever "that he alone of all the town was lost, forever and forever" (p. 144).

The ordeal of his guilty isolation points Tom towards the resolution that prevails in the book at large. Nothing really works to alleviate the horrible vision of evil and violence, but the isolation can be overcome, at least partially. When he can stand the burden of the secret no longer, Tom repudiates the religion of the graveyard and the blood oath and confesses to the district attorney. His action has not diminished the vices of society, much less those of human nature, but he has escaped his terrible loneliness, and, somewhat like a Melville character, he has re-entered the community, even if it is the doubtful community of St. Petersburg.

The Jackson's Island adventure follows the pattern already established in the murder plot. The boys flee from a devitalized, oppressive society and seek out the Romantic harmony of nature—and with it the buried treasure that will be the means of freedom and fulfillment. Initially they seem successful, and nature seems to conform to the Romantic myths. Everything is organically united and alive, and the boys themselves seem a necessary part of the total scheme.

> It was the cool gray dawn, and there was a delicious sense of repose and peace in the deep pervading calm and silence of the woods. Not a leaf stirred; not a sound obtruded upon great Nature's meditation. . . .
> Now, far away in the woods a bird called; another answered; presently the hammering of a woodpecker was heard. Gradually the cool dim gray of the morning whitened, and as gradually sounds multiplied and life manifested itself. . . . A catbird, the northern mocker, lit in a tree over Tom's head, and trilled out her imitations of her neighbors in a rapture of enjoyment; then a shrill jay swept down, a flash of blue flame, and stopped on a twig almost within the boy's reach, cocked his head to one side and eyed the strangers with a consuming curiosity; a gray squirrel and a big fellow of the "fox" kind came scurrying along, sitting up at intervals to inspect and chatter at the boys, for the wild things had probably never seen a human being before and scarcely knew whether to be afraid or not. All Nature was wide awake and stirring, now; long lances of sunlight pierced down through the dense foliage far and near, and a few butterflies came fluttering upon the scene. (pp. 95–96)

But there is no buried treasure—that is finally found not in nature but in the haunted house. And the longer the boys remain on the island, the more they are oppressed by the same forces they discovered in the cemetery. Most obviously, they suffer from a sense of lostness and isolation. Joe Harper speaks for all of them when he says, " 'I want to go home. It's so lonesome.' " Huck agrees, " 'it was getting so lonesome,' " and even to Tom "it was become very lonely" (pp. 107, 108). Besides the loneliness there is the consciousness that nature itself is more complicated than the idyllic daybreak passage suggests. The boys' last night on the island is interrupted by a great storm, which "seemed likely to tear the island to pieces, burn it up, drown it to the treetops, blow it away, and deafen every creature on it" (p. 112). The ancient sycamore, under whose seemingly protective branches the boys had pitched their tent, is one of the victims of the storm, and it is only good luck the boys are not killed when the falling tree demolishes their camp. Finally, the savage primitivism of Injun Joe is echoed in the boys' island games. They begin playing innocently in the river and on the beach, but in the end they become wild Indians, lurking in ambush to kill one another.

The darkest part of the Jackson's Island adventure is, of course, the boys' presumed death. In the graveyard, Robinson's murder shows them the necessary end of transcendent aspiration. The point is made even more emphatically here as it is the boys themselves who "die." Once more the quest after transcendence has brought Tom to the awareness of violence, loneliness, and death. Tom's real triumph in the Jackson's Island adventure is not the intended escape from repressive society to natural freedom, but rather his rebirth, ironically played out at his own funeral, into the very community from which he had fled.

The treasure hunt conforms to the same pattern. The boys begin with innocent dreams of freedom from the dreariness of St. Petersburg: Huck speculates, " 'I'll have a piece of pie and a glass of soda every day, and I'll go to every circus that comes along' "; Tom promises " 'to buy a new drum, and a sure-'nough sword, and a red necktie and a bull pup, and get married' " (p. 155). Earlier, seeking magical rebirth in the cemetery, the boys had witnessed murder, this time seeking liberating gold, they are drawn deeper and deeper into that region where Twain, unconsciously echoing Melville, says "the blackness of darkness reigned" (p. 171). Huck overhears the plan to rob and mutilate the Widow Douglas (Tom has gone off to Becky's birthday party), and in the few moments at the Welshman's cabin he experiences all the terror and isolation Tom knew earlier, and, like Tom, at last confesses his guilty knowledge. Tom's ordeal of conscience and isolation had issued in the symbolic death of his long fever and the rebirth into the community following his confession. The same motif, slightly altered, prevails here as Huck first informs on Injun Joe and then passes into a feverish coma from which he finally wakes into full membership in the community— the Widow first nurses him, and then adopts him, and he at last knows that combed respectability which, in this novel at least, is the only refuge from the savagery born in man. Correspondingly, the treasure, so Romantically dreamed of, turns out to be the loot of "Murrel's gang" (p. 165), and, like the boys themselves, it is eventually restored to society as Judge Thatcher puts it out at a safe six percent.

The descent with Becky into MacDougal's Cave is Tom's final venture into the world of his Romantic intuitions, and it is at once the richest, the most revealing, and the most devastating of the major episodes. From the outset the relationship between Tom and Becky is fraught with the same implications of rebellion, isolation, and death which are so evident in the earlier adventures. Tom first tries to attract Becky's notice in church by "cuffing boys, pulling hair, making faces" (p. 34). Later, at school, he again plays the role of rebel and lawbreaker in order to draw closer to Becky. The schoolmaster has questioned Tom about his tardiness, and when he sees Becky in the classroom, Tom decides against the expected lie and instead boasts, " 'I STOPPED TO TALK WITH HUCKLEBERRY FINN' "

(p. 50). As he had hoped, Tom receives a severe whipping and is sent to sit with the girls. Although the scene is permeated by the condescension of the mature, sophisticated narrator, the fact remains that just like the pirates who win the beautiful ladies in the boys' fantasies, Tom, by defying both law and decorum, has gained a place by Becky's side.

The progress of the courtship is consistent both with its beginnings and with the patterns developed in the cemetery, on the island, and in the haunted house. Their first private meeting proceeds from deception and secrecy, and it ends in what seems to be the "lovers' " blissful isolation from the commonplace world. Ostensibly innocent as the meeting is, Tom undertakes it in the spirit of his forbidden midnight trysts with Huck. He whispers to Becky, " 'Put on your bonnet and let on you're going home [for lunch]; and when you get to the corner, give the rest of 'em the slip, and turn down through the lane and come back. I'll go the other way and come it over 'em the same way' " (p. 56). When the rendezvous is accomplished, Tom forces Becky to become "engaged," and, although his notion of betrothal is rather vague, certain elements are clear enough. There must be whispered pledges, and, as those given in the graveyard are sealed in blood, these must be confirmed by a kiss—a kiss which on Tom's part has overtones of rape. The end of the ritual is an apparently happier version of the isolation which proceeds from the blood oath. Tom explains to the somewhat bewildered Becky, " 'Now it's all done, Becky. And always after this, you know, you ain't ever to love anybody but me, and you ain't ever to marry anybody but me, never never and forever' " (p. 58).

The anatomy book scene reemphasizes the isolating exclusiveness of the "engagement," and at the same time reveals more clearly the guilt and desperation of the schoolyard scene. It is customary to observe that when Tom rises to take the blame for tearing the book, he exhibits a new maturity as he sacrifices himself for his beloved.[7] But the nature of Becky's offense is, I think, more important than Tom's acceptance of her punishment. Dobbins' book is torn when Tom surprises Becky looking at "a human figure, stark naked" (p. 131). In her first outburst of "shame and vexation," Becky makes it quite clear that she expects to be punished not so much for tearing the page as for her sexual curiosity—she never mentions damaging the book, but she does tell Tom, " 'You are just as mean as you can be, to sneak up on a person and look at what they're looking at' " (p. 131). When Tom takes Becky's whipping, they are bound together in criminality and secret sexual knowledge.

The picnic adventure is the final working out of the "engagement" and of Tom's Romantic dreams generally. The episode begins, like so many others in the book, with deceit—and in this case seduction. Becky's mother has arranged for the girl to spend the night following the picnic with Susy Harper, but Tom promises her ice cream if, instead, she will come with him to the Widow's house on Cardiff Hill—the same hill that is the scene of Tom's Robin Hood masquerade and of Joe's aborted assault on the Widow. Before that plan can be put into effect, however, Tom, in the spirit of the Black Avenger, leads Becky into the cave. They wander away from the other children and are led on by the twisting corridors to a secret world appropriately hidden behind a lime-crusted waterfall. Here, isolated in their love from the tiresome, oppressive town, they plan to consummate the "engagement" by sharing what Becky calls their "wedding cake" (p. 194).

However, Tom's adventure in "true love" ends, as his other Romantic quests have ended, in unexpected terror and loneliness. Like the mine in *Roughing It*, MacDougal's Cave becomes a symbol of ultimate reality, and, as in *Roughing It*, that reality proves to be mysterious and terrible.

> It was said that one might wander days and nights together through its intricate tangle of rifts and chasms, and never find the end of the cave; and that he might go down, and down, and still down, into the earth, and it was just the same—labyrinth underneath labyrinth, and no end to any of them. No man "knew" the cave. That was an impossible thing. Most of the young men knew a portion of it, and it was not customary to venture much beyond this known portion. (p. 176)

In their quest for absolute unity and selfhood, Tom and Becky go far beyond the "known portion," and for a time they seem successful in their escape. After they pass through the magic curtain of the waterfall, they come to a "spacious cavern" phallically decorated with "a multitude of shining stalactites of the length and circumference of a man's leg" (pp. 190–191). Obviously, the cavern suggests the fulfilling sexuality implicit in the pirate fantasies and the secret of the anatomy book. But when the children move on to what appears to be a setting appropriate for the final breakthrough to new life—"a bewitching spring, whose basin was encrusted with a frostwork of glittering crystals" (p. 191)—they are nearly swallowed up by a horrible darkness. Thousands of bats, disturbed by the children, swoop at them and threaten to extinguish their candles.

Now the enchanted exploration becomes desperate flight, and the "intricate tangle" which had brought them to the "spacious cavern" and the "bewitching spring" leads them to a dark abyss, which has, Tom tell us, "no bottom" (p. 196). Their own voices have become frightening to them, so that Becky begs Tom not to call again for help because " 'it is too horrid' " (p. 192). At last they collapse to eat the "wedding cake," which they both now realize may be their last meal, and to talk tearfully of the town and families they left behind. Worst of all, at the very heart of the cave, at the end of their symbolic journey, they once more encounter Injun Joe, Tom's savage alter-ego and the embodiment of inescapable human depravity. Irrecoverably lost, Tom at last renounces his Romantic aspirations and his equally

Romantic defiance. He confesses to Becky, " 'I was such a fool! Such a fool! I never thought we might want to come back' " (p. 192).

In the end, coming back is the only life possible in the novel, and Tom's renunciation of transcendence is the culmination of the process begun in his exoneration of Muff Potter and continued in the return from Jackson's Island and in Huck's confession to the Welshman. However, Tom's retreat from Romanticism is in no way an endorsement of St. Petersburg. The adults are as dishonest and uncomprehending at the end of the book as at the beginning. Tom has only effected a necessary accommodation, not a true reconciliation. Having experienced the fierce energy of humanity's savage heart, Tom will, in the future, stick to the "known portion" of life. And though he may continue to play at robbers, it will now be self-consciously a game and therefore safe—to escape the horror he will forsake the magic.

The events of the novel, I believe, make it plain that this resolution is anything but the idyllic solution so often imputed to the book. In his own story, Huck renounces society and flees to the territory in order to preserve the selfhood he has found on the river. Tom, on the other hand, surrenders his version of the territory—the island and the cave—and returns to St. Petersburg. Neither "solution" really solves anything. Huck accepts isolation as the price of freedom, and we know from the Grangerford and Wilkes episodes, as well as from his relationship with Jim, how painful isolation will be for Huck. Tom sacrifices freedom to gain community, even though it is the deeply flawed community of St. Petersburg, the desperate community of the "damned human race." In neither book are freedom and community or love really compatible, and that melancholy fact reveals more clearly than anything else the profound despair that dominates Twain's artistic vision— not only in late works like *Pudd'nhead Wilson* or *The Mysterious Stranger*, but from virtually the outset of his career.

Notes

1. Bernard De Voto, *Mark Twain's America* (Cambridge, MA: Houghton Mifflin Company, 1932), p. 304. James M. Cox, *Mark Twain: The Fate of Humor* (Princeton, NJ: Princeton University Press, 1966), pp. 127–149, elaborates on the novel's idyllic qualities and argues that Twain criticizes adult society by creating a world in which "play is the reality principle" (p. 147).

2. See most notably Walter Blair, "On the Structure of *Tom Sawyer*," *Modern Philology*, 37 (1939), 75–88, and Barry A. Marks, "Mark Twain's Hymn of Praise," *English Journal*, 48 (November 1959), 443–449.

3. Leslie A. Fiedler, *Love and Death in the American Novel* (New York: Criterion Books, 1960), p. 563. Somewhat similarly, Thomas Blues, *Mark Twain and the Community* (Lexington: University of Kentucky Press, 1970), pp. 5–10, holds that Twain protects Tom from the ordeal of alienation by the "transformation of an adult community into one very much resembling a world of children" (p. 5).

4. All quotations from *Tom Sawyer* are taken from the following edition: Mark Twain,

The Adventures of Tom Sawyer (New York: The New American Library, 1959). Page references appear in parentheses.

5. Robert Tracy, "Myth and Reality in *The Adventures of Tom Sawyer*," *Southern Review*, 4 (Spring 1968), 530–541, has also suggested this motive in the graveyard expedition and has pointed out the correspondence between Robinson and Tom alluded to below. Tracy's study is the most thorough treatment to date of the mythic elements in the novel.

6. For a more specifically Freudian interpretation of the relationship between Tom and Joe, see Fiedler, p. 570.

7. Blair, 84.

A Hannibal Summer: The Framework of
The Adventures of Tom Sawyer

JOHN R. BYERS, JR.

When, in 1870–71, Mark Twain wrote what is now called the "Boy's Manuscript,"[1] he related the adventures of a lad named Billy Rogers in school and town and in the desperate throes of his love for one Amy Johnson. Told in the first person and cast as the diary of Billy, the work is essential to an understanding of the composition of *The Adventures of Tom Sawyer*, not only for the content which was to find its way into the novel of 1876 but also, and perhaps more importantly to the finished work, for the form, however brief. First, in choosing to record Billy's often awkward and even intimately amorous moments with Amy through the boy's own words, Twain obviously saw the disadvantages in attempting to recapture the nostalgia of young love through the immediacy of childhood language. The distance required for creating such a nostalgic work demanded the less personal and more removed third person and an older narrator delighted with the follies of boyish love and life. Twain later, in *Huckleberry Finn*, gave Huck no sexual yearnings possibly because of the almost embarrassing moments of the "Boy's Manuscript" and because of his choice of first person narration for the later novel. Second, in setting up the "Boy's Manuscript" as a diary with the day of the week preceding each entry, Twain foreshadowed the form of *Tom Sawyer*. In even a cursory examination of the novel, the reader is aware of the author's almost obsessive notation of the passage of time. Events happen in relation to other events with such time citations as for "forty-eight hours," "during three days," "for a week," "two long weeks," or "all of Wednesday and Thursday."

Because of the seemingly rambling nature of *Tom Sawyer*, several critics have observed that the Missouri summer of Hannibal is unduly long without attempting to apply a specific time frame to the novel. For example, Robert Spiller observes that *"Tom Sawyer*'s time span is one Missouri summer . . ."* but that "Twain arrests or syncopates the march of time as he pleases."[2] Bernard De Voto notes that "Tom's enchanted summer is similarly elastic. . . ," that "autumn should be well along" by the end of the novel, and that summer in Missouri "may indeed begin in April but it cannot last so long

Reprinted from *Studies in American Fiction* 8 (Spring 1980): 81–88.

as it is made to here."[3] Kenneth Andrews complains that the "improvisatory progress [of the novel] skips . . . improbabilities of time. . . ,"[4] and Leslie Fiedler comments that "*Huckleberry Finn* begins in the same idyllic summer of which *Tom Sawyer* had already consumed more than the normal number of weeks. . . ."[5] Without explanation of his method of tally, Harry Warfel does present some specific, though often unfounded, dates. He says "the time is from June to October sometime in the mid-nineteenth century." He continues with the speculation that the novel begins "about June 14," that the murder of Dr. Robinson occurs "on June 17," that the Examination Evening is "on June 24," that "after July 4" Tom is struck by measles, that Muff Potter's trial is held "about August 8," that Tom and Huck begin their treasure hunt "about August 21," that "ten days later" Huck intervenes for the Widow Douglas and Tom and Becky become lost in the cave, that Tom and Huck find the cave treasure "about September 17 . . . ," "as well as the body of Injun Joe" [sic], and that the tale ends "in October," in early October since Huck has been at the Widow's "for three weeks."[6]

Because so little careful work has been done with the time frame of *Tom Sawyer*, and because Warfel's dates are often open to question, it is essential to begin an examination of the dating in the novel by noting Twain's time references as they affect the progression of events. Since Twain records only two specific dates in *Tom Sawyer* (the night of Monday, June 17, the night of the murder of Dr. Robinson, and July 4), and other calculations must hinge on those two dates.

When, during the trial of Muff Potter, Muff's lawyer inquires of his surprise witness " 'Thomas Sawyer, where were you on the seventeenth of June, about the hour of midnight?,' "[7] the framework of the novel begins. Because the graveyard scene takes place on Monday night, the time of Aunt Polly's famous opening line, " 'Tom!' " is obviously Friday, June 14, for Tom fights the new boy, well-dressed and shod, on a Friday (p. 21), and the weekend is occupied by the whitewashing on Saturday and the church services on Sunday. On his way to school on Monday, Tom meets Huck Finn, who agrees to allow his friend to accompany him on that night to the graveyard with the dead cat. Following a full school day, Tom escapes his room, and he and Huck travel to the graveyard, where they await the witching hour and finally witness the murder of Dr. Robinson by Injun Joe.

The crime is known by 12:00 noon on Tuesday (p. 119), June 18, and Muff Potter is apprehended shortly after that hour. If, therefore, Tom's sleep is disturbed "for as much as a week after" the removal of Dr. Robinson's body (p. 123), during which time he ties his jaws "for a week" (p. 123) because of a supposed toothache to keep from revealing his secret to Sid, then the novel moves to Tuesday, June 25. A few days previous to June 25, however, Tom falls into a lethargy over Becky Thatcher, and Aunt Polly exposes him to her various cures, including her infamous "Painkiller," good for boys and cats. Because of his mistreatment on Tuesday by both Aunt

Polly and Becky, Tom, Joe Harper, who has also been mistreated, and Huck, who is game for any profession, leave St. Petersburg on Tuesday night (p. 135) for pirating on Jackson's Island, three miles below the town. The first full day on Jackson's Island is Wednesday, June 26, and the idyllic episode lasts until "dusk on Saturday" (p. 178), June 29, at which time the boys steal home in preparation for the funeral of Sunday, June 30. On Monday, Tom is back in school content with his mark on the town, but again disturbed by Becky and attentive toward Amy Lawrence. He is so incensed by Becky's ignoring of him and by Amy's prattle that he leaves school at noon for home. Although Aunt Polly awaits him with her up-braiding over the dream episode, the two are reconciled, and Tom returns to school for the afternoon, when he gallantly takes Becky's punishment over the anatomy book.

Between the end of Chapter 20 (Monday, July 1), his reconciliation with Becky, and the beginning of Chapter 22, Twain may have dismissed his time frame as unimportant or he may simply have had a lapse in his control. Chapter 21 opens with the statement "Vacation was approaching" (p. 202). But since vacation time begins in the novel before July 4, the "Examination Evening" must occur at 8:00 on either Tuesday, July 2, or Wednesday, July 3. Tuesday seems the better day because early in Chapter 22 Twain notes that "fourth of July was coming . . ." (p. 211). Thus, although Wednesday leaves only one day before July 4, that would be sufficient time for Tom to join the Cadets of Temperance. However, Tom's association with the group destroys the time frame, for apparently the only reward that prevents his leaving the cadets is the expectation of wearing his red sash during the approaching festivities of July 4. But Tom cannot endure the wait and so, after "forty-eight hours" (p. 211), gives up that dream. "During three days" (p. 211) Tom attaches his hope of parading with the Cadets to the possible funeral of Judge Frazer, but that dream too vanishes when the judge recovers from his illness, precipitating Tom's resignation. However, much to the chagrin of the boy, the judge dies that night. Follow-ing the funeral, for "three days" (p. 212) Tom keeps a diary, enjoys a traveling minstrel show, and for "two days" (p. 212) joins Joe Harper for their own performing group. Then comes the fourth of July (p. 212).

Consequently, between Tom's joining the Cadets and July 4, there is a span of approximately one week. It would be convenient to be able to account for that week, but since, by Twain's own reckoning, the murder is announced on Tuesday, June 18, since, by Twain's own reckoning, the boys leave for Jackson's Island on Tuesday, June 25, and since the Examination Evening is probably on Tuesday, July 2, one must conclude that Twain faltered by adding a week between the gilded dome of the schoolmaster and the disappointing Senator Benton of July 4. Its seems best, therefore, in spite of the additional week, to place July 4 on the Thursday following the Examination Evening and the beginning of the summer vacation.

After the "Glorious Fourth," then, a series of events occurs in the sleepy river town, where any excitement is good for several days' talk. First, a circus comes to town, and the boys play at their own circus "for three days" (p. 213). Then "a phrenologist and a mesmerizer"—apparently traveling together, but possibly arriving at different times—enlighten and entertain the townspeople possibly for several days (p. 213). Also a few "boys-and-girls' parties" (p. 213) are given. One suspects that these gatherings, like the Saturday cave picnic later in the novel, have been held on successive Saturdays. Becky Thatcher goes to Constantinople, and over the whole town hangs the pall of the murder of Dr. Robinson (p. 213).

Since apparently approximately two weeks elapse during the summer excitement and before Tom falls victim to measles, the time has moved to roughly Wednesday, July 17. Tom's first bout with measles lasts "two long weeks" (p. 213) or until Thursday, August 1. His first day of walking about the town sends him back to bed, "on his back" this time for "three weeks" (p. 214), which advances the novel to the time around the end of the week of Friday, August 23. Twain's decision to incapacitate Tom for five weeks in the middle of the summer adds nothing to the development of Tom or of the plot of the novel (the five-week episode occupies only two pages); it simply prolongs the summer.

What remains following Tom's recovery near the end of the week of August 23 is Muff Potter's trial and the escape of Injun Joe, the search for buried treasure, the cave adventure and the death of Injun Joe, and finally Huck's reconciliation with society. Since Twain has so often determined the days of the week when some incidents occur, it is not difficult to calculate the dating of other events. For example, with Tom's measles out of the way by August 23, one needs to advance past the trial of Muff Potter and the aftermath (Chapters 23–24) to the search for buried treasure by Tom and Huck in Chapters 25–26. The day on which the boys first choose to search the haunted house is a Friday (p. 237); both, however, agree that a Friday is not a good day for beginning a task and so return on Saturday to the house, where they are trapped in the loft by Injun Joe and his companion. Since the treasure hunt has begun on Thursday, a crucial day in that it determines the days of the week on which immediately preceding events occur, it seems probable that the aftermath of Muff Potter's trial—the adulation of Tom as he struts about town, the terrifying nights when he fears Injun Joe, the offers of rewards, the search for the escaped murderer, the securing of the St. Louis detective, his investigations, his leaving town, and finally the return of normalcy to St. Petersburg—all (pp. 225–26) occupy perhaps a week of the summer, that is, the week before Tom and Huck go on their treasure hunt. The aftermath apparently begins, then, on the Thursday before the hunt. And because the trial lasts three successive days, it probably begins on Monday.

Therefore, if Tom is still "on his back" with measles on Friday, August

23, he needs time to regain his strength for strolling about the town. That recovery time must occupy the week of Saturday, August 24, through Sunday, September 1, for by the time of the trial he is completely recovered. Thus, the trial takes place on Monday, September 2, through Wednesday, September 4. The aftermath must last from Thursday, September 5, through Wednesday, September 11. The treasure hunt begins on Thursday, September 12, and lasts through Saturday, September 14.

Although Twain is generally very careful with his sequential days of the week, Sunday, September 15, seems to have vanished. On the morning following the Saturday night (p. 249) after Tom's and Huck's horrifying experience in the haunted house, Tom lies abed pondering the gold that has escaped them and finally, after a quick breakfast, he seeks out Huck for a discussion of the whereabouts of " 'Number Two—under the cross' " without a thought of Sunday services. Later (p. 278), Twain notes that during the summer vacations there was no Sunday school, but he in no way accounts for the omission of the regular preaching hour. Sunday simply disappears, and Monday follows Saturday.

Beginning on Monday, September 16, then, Tom and Huck keep watch at the tavern where they hope to find "No.2" and the treasure. The watch continues on Tuesday, Wednesday, and Thursday (p. 254), cultimating in Tom's flight from the drunken Injun Joe in room No. 2 on Thursday night. Friday (p. 259), September 20, finds Becky Thatcher back in town, having arrived the night before. She and her mother make plans immediately for the picnic of the following day (p. 259). On Saturday night (pp. 263–64), then, there begins, for the first time in the novel, a divided stream of action with Tom and Becky becoming lost in the cave and Huck rescuing the Widow Douglas. Tom and Becky remain in the cave for "three days and nights" (p. 298) or until the afternoon hours of Tuesday, September 24, and are brought back to the town on that night. Meanwhile, Huck returns to the Welshman's house on Sunday morning (p. 270) to learn the details of his alarm of the previous night. After the Sunday church service (p. 279), word spreads of the missing Tom and Becky, and the Welshman immediately offers his help only to return from the cave on Monday morning to find Huck in bed delirious with a fever (p. 280). Tom recuperates from his cave experience on Wednesday and Thursday (p. 298) and finally attempts to visit Huck on Friday, September 27, but is denied entry to the sick room. He returns on Saturday and Sunday and finally sees Huck for the first time on Monday, September 30 (p. 299).

"About a fortnight" (p. 299) after Tom's escape from the cave on Tuesday, September 24, that is, about Tuesday, October 8, Tom learns that the opening to the cave has been closed with boiler iron. Injun Joe's burial probably takes place on the following day. On the morning following the funeral (p. 304) or on the morning of Thursday, October 10, Tom and Huck return to the cave, find " 'Number Two—under the cross' " and the

$12,000, and "shortly after dark" (p. 312) make their way to the Widow Douglas' woodshed, where they plan to hide their loot, only to be surprised by a party in their honor.

Following the celebration, the Widow takes Huck under her wing and generously, though unthinkingly, attempts to civilize him. He endures the agony of clean sheets and plates and combing for three weeks (p. 322) or until Thursday, October 31, at which time he disappears for two days (p. 322). Tom, ever the detective, finds his friend in an empty hogshead on the third day (p. 322), Sunday, November 3.[8] Huck pours forth his complaints, including " 'school's going to open, and I'd 'a' had to go to it . . .' " (p. 324), but finally vows " 'I'll stick to the widder till I rot . . .' " (p. 327). And so the novel closes.

Thus, *Tom Sawyer* covers, rightly or wrongly, the time span from Friday, June 14, when Tom is reprimanded for stealing jam, probably through Sunday, November 3, when he cons Huck into remaining with the Widow Douglas with the argument that respectability is necessary for entry into their recently created robber band. If Twain did attempt to use any controlling scheme in the novel, it is the often slow but steady progression of the days of the weeks and the weeks of the months of a very long Hannibal summer.[9] In only two instances in his usually meticulous attention to the passage of time does Twain err: in the collapsed week between the Examination Evening and July 4 and in the dismissed Sunday of September 15— minor flaws at worst. A far more serious fault lies in his decision to relegate five weeks of the novel, during which time nothing happens, to Tom's indisposition with measles. That the ailment is a typical childhood disease which logically fits into the pattern of boyhood experiences is no excuse for the imbalance in time devoted to the two-page episode.[10] Moreover, if Twain had not afflicted Tom with measles and had thus removed the five-week span from the time framework, the novel would have lasted only until approximately the end of September, a far more reasonable date for the ending of a summer's enchantment. However, in view of the prolongation of the time, it is not difficult to believe that Twain simply did not wish to bring to a conclusion the nostalgic record of his relived Hannibal summer in the mid-years of the nineteenth century. To end a novel is one thing; to end one's own childhood is quite another.

Notes

1.   So named by Albert Bigelow Paine, Twain's first literary executor. See Bernard De Voto, *Mark Twain at Work* (Cambridge: Harvard Univ. Press, 1942), pp. 3–44, for a full presentation and examination of the document.

2.   Spiller, et al., eds., *Literary History of the United States*, 3rd ed. (New York: Macmillan, 1963), p. 931.

3.   De Voto, pp. 10, 20.

4. *Nook Farm: Mark Twain's Hartford Circle* (Cambridge: Harvard Univ. Press, 1950), p. 207.

5. "Duplicitous Mark Twain," *Commentary*, 29 (March, 1960), 245.

6. "Introduction" to *The Adventures of Tom Sawyer* (New York: Harper and Row, 1965), pp. xii–xiii.

7. *The Adventures of Tom Sawyer* (New York: Harper & Brothers, 1903), p. 223. Subsequent references to volume XII of the Author's National Edition of *The Writings of Mark Twain* will be incorporated into the body of the paper.

8. In the latter part of the novel, Twain seldom alludes to weather conditions or to natural surroundings, either of which might indicate, however vaguely, the time of the year. At the beginning of the cave episode (September 21), he does refer to the greenness of the valley below (p. 262), and he camouflages the cave hole, through which Tom and Becky escape, with such thick sumac foliage (p. 307) that Huck, in the boys' attempt to find the treasure (October 10), cannot, although only a few feet away, see the opening.

9. Walter Blair, "On the Structure of *Tom Sawyer*," MP, 37 (August, 1930), 86n, on the other hand, observes: "The fact that the action of the book requires only a few months seems irrelevant since fictional rather than actual time is involved." One cannot, however, ignore Twain's constant references to the passage of specific lengths of time.

10. Twain's own case of measles (and the manner in which he was exposed) in the summer of 1845 may have remained so vivid in his memory that he felt compelled to include it in the novel. See Charles Neider, ed., *The Autobiography of Mark Twain* (New York: Harper & Brothers, 1959), pp. 77–78.

The Adventures of Tom Sawyer:
A Nightmare Vision of American Boyhood

CYNTHIA GRIFFIN WOLFF

Twain's second book of boyhood has more or less cornered one segment of the American Dream. Read with admiration (read during the long years when *Moby Dick* was relegated to obscurity), it captured both our lofty goals and our tragic weaknesses; and if it is not "the" American epic, it has epic dimensions. By comparison, its predecessor seems unworthy of serious attention (a "comic idyll of boyhood," says Leo Marx dismissively, on his way to a lengthy analysis of *The Adventures of Huckleberry Finn*)—no more than idealized reminiscences, pulp fantasies of an "Everyboy." Yet Huck himself is more particular about his antecedents: "You don't know about me," he says at the beginning of his story, "without you have read a book by the name of 'The Adventures of Tom Sawyer,' but that ain't no matter. That book was made by Mr. Mark Twain, and he told the truth, mainly." In the first instance, *this* is where he has "been before"—the world of this other fiction—and one explanation for the questing need that fills Huck's own tale must be found here, in the fabricated town of St. Petersburg on the Mississippi.

We are certainly correct to see Huck as heroic—an American Odysseus (or Hamlet); but if, for the sake of contrast, we diminish the complexity of Tom Sawyer's world—relegating it to the simplistic category of "All-American Boyhood"—we will find ourselves led seriously astray.

It is no easy thing for an adult American reader to get at the "real" world of this novel. Our culture has provided us with too many colorful, fleshed-out reproductions of it: a bicentennial stamp depicting Tom and the whitewashed fence; commemorative plates and pictures; and countless stage and film productions—each one full of life and merriment, each exuding the security of childhood-as-it-ought-to-be in small-town America. And every one of these sentimental evocations is false to the original.

In fact, Tom's world would be difficult to capture faithfully on film—impossible, perhaps, on stage: it is a phantom town inhabited largely by

Reprinted from the *Massachusetts Review* 21 (Winter 1980): 637–52. Copyright 1981, by permission of the Massachusetts Review, Inc.

ghostly presences. Consider, for example, the buildings that actually appear in the novel; consider *all* of them. To begin with, there are private dwellings: Aunt Polly's house, Jeff Thatcher's house (where Becky visits), the Douglas mansion, the Welshman's farm, and the "haunted" house where Tom and Huck so nearly lose their lives. Then there are institutional buildings designed specifically to bedevil an active boy: the church and the schoolhouse. However, all of these—houses, church, school—are places from which an average, energetic male youth is expected to flee: "his" world, the world to be explored and conquered, lies beyond—in lush Edenic woods, a river, and (presumably) a healthy, industrious town of tolerable size. And here the shadow world begins. There is a river; there are woods. But of the town, only menacing fragments await. Two taverns (one housing criminals), a courthouse, a jail, and a deserted slaughterhouse. Nothing more.

Let us be more specific. No stores are mentioned in the novel. No blacksmiths. No livery stable. No bank. Mark Twain, who renders the steamboat's arrival so vibrantly in *Life on the Mississippi*, put no busy wharf in the world of this fiction—no commercial steamboat traffic at all. Every bit of the bustling business that an impressionable reader might impute to Tom Sawyer's world is, in fact, notably absent from the novel; the only downtown buildings that actually do appear in the St. Petersburg of Twain's creation are those few grisly emblems of crime and punishment. Two taverns, a courthouse a jail, and a deserted slaughterhouse.

Placed against this somber background is a complex society of children, so tightly knit and so emotionally engaging that it tends to dominate the reader's attention. Ben Rogers and Billy Fisher and Joe Harper and Amy Lawrence and Jeff Thatcher: such names in this novel attach to people with specific histories and relationships, friendships and enmities, all of the subtle qualities that make them seem distinctive and "real." The slow accretion of this children's world renders Tom's and Huck's activities with a kind of palpable, three-dimensional plausibility.

> "Say—what is dead cats good for, Huck?"
> "Good for? Cure warts with."
> "No! Is that so? I know something that's better."
> "I bet you don't. What is it?"
> "Why spunk-water."
> "Spunk-water! I wouldn't give a dern for spunk-water."
> "You wouldn't, wouldn't you? D'you ever try it?"
> "No, I hain't. But Bob Tanner did."
> "Who told you so?"
> "Why he told Jeff Thatcher, and Jeff told Johnny Baker, and Johnny told Jim Hollis, and Jim told Ben Rogers and Ben told a nigger, and the nigger told me. There now!"

The very vividness of these children, then, makes all the more remarkable the peculiar air of vagueness, of faceless generality, that permeates Twain's evocations of most adult gatherings.

Consider these paragraphs describing Muff Potter's capture:

> Close upon the hour of noon the whole village was suddenly electrified with the ghastly news. No need of the as yet undreamed-of telegraph; the tale flew from man to man, from group to group, from house to house, with little less than telegraphic speed. . . . Horsemen had departed down all the roads in every direction and the Sheriff "was confident" that he would be captured before night.
>
> All the town was drifting toward the graveyard. Tom's heartbreak vanished and he joined the procession. . . . Arrived at the dreadful place, he wormed his small body through the crowd and saw the dismal spectacle. . . . He turned, and his eyes met Huckleberry's. Then both looked elsewhere at once, and wondered if anybody had noticed anything in their mutual glance. But everybody was talking. . . .
>
> "Poor fellow!" . . . "Muff Potter'll hang for this if they catch him!" This was the drift of the remark; and the minister said, "It was a judgment; His hand is here."
>
> Now Tom shivered from head to heel; for his eye fell upon the stolid face of Injun Joe. At this moment the crowd began to sway and struggle, and voices shouted, "It's him! it's him! he's coming himself!"
>
> "Who? Who?" from twenty voices.
>
> "Muff Potter!" . . .
>
> People in the branches of the trees over Tom's head said he wasn't trying to get away—he only looked doubtful and perplexed.
>
> "Infernal impudence!" said a bystander.

Here we have a convocation of most of the townsfolk. Yet not one is given a name (only the "outsiders"—Muff Potter and Injun Joe). Instead, there is a torrent of collective nouns: whole village, man to man, group to group, horsemen, all the town, the crowd, anybody, everybody, the crowd, voices, people, a bystander. Even the dignitaries remain nameless; they are merely "the Sheriff" and "the minister." When it is compared with the density of the scenes depicting children, this collection of citizens becomes vaporous: as "people" within the novel, they can scarcely be said to exist. No more than anonymous shadows—appropriate, indeed, to the illusory town of which they are citizens. Small wonder, then, that films and pictures falsify. Of necessity they give substance to entities—buildings and business and hurrying, excited people—that either do not exist at all within this fictional world or are, at best, only partially realized.

Since this is a boy's story, it is only fair to ask what a boy in such a world might make of himself. Given the character of the town Twain has created, given the social possibilities of St. Petersburg as we know it through this novel, what will Tom Sawyer become when he is a man? The question cannot be answered.

Initially Twain had intended the novel to be a kind of *bildungsroman*: as Justin Kaplan reports, it was to have had four parts—" '1, Boyhood & youth; 2 y & early manh; 3 the Battle of Life in many lands; 4 (age 37 to [40?]). . . .' " Yet the finished novel shows no sign of this early intention. In fact, Twain writes his "conclusion" with a kind of defensive bravado: "So endeth this chronicle. It being strictly a history of a *boy*, it must stop here; the story could not go much further without becoming the history of a *man*." At least one reason for the author's decision may be found in the very nature of the world he was moved to create. There are no available men in it—no men whom Tom can fancy himself imitating—no newspaper office with a garrulous editor, no general store owner to purvey gossip and candy, no lawyer lounging in an office buzzing with flies and heavy with the odor of musty books. Of course there *is* Judge Thatcher, "a fine, portly, middle-aged gentleman with iron-gray hair." But Judge Thatcher presides in the county seat, twelve miles away; he enters the novel only very briefly in chapter iv (to witness Tom's triumph-turned-humiliation in Bible class) and thereafter disappears entirely until chapter xxxii, when he is summoned to rejoice in the safe return of the children from the cave. Many adults who have not read *Tom Sawyer* since the days of their youth are apt to recall Judge Thatcher as a rather more vivid personage than he truly is in the novel. Perhaps we are recollecting cinematic images, or perhaps our own imaginations supply his presence because we feel compelled to remedy the novel's deficiencies and "normalize" the town. But the stubborn fact remains. The town is not normal, certainly not congenial to a boy's coming of age.

It is, of course, a matriarchy (and in this respect, contrasts markedly with the various patriarchal systems that Huck encounters in his journey down the river), a world that holds small boys in bondage. The town that we are shown in this book is saturated with gentility, that is, with women's notions. A man may dispense Bible tickets or conduct the ceremony on Sundays; but the church service, the Sunday School exercises, the daily ritual of family prayers—these are all clearly defined as fundamental components of something that Aunt Polly (and other women like her) have defined as "duty" or "morality." Similarly, the mayor himself may judge the elocution contest; but this masculine salute to "culture" merely reinforces already established female allegiances to the melancholy and banally "eloquent" in literature. The very opening word of the novel establishes the situation. " 'Tom!' " The boy's name called by his impatient aunt. " 'Tom!' " The demanding tone permeates the novel, no other voice so penetrating or intrusive. What is a male child to do against this diminutive drill master? Surrender is out of the question: the dismal results of capitulation greet him in mournful, not quite masculine figures. Mr. Walters, the superintendent of the Sunday School, "a slim creature of thirty-five, with a sandy goatee and short sandy hair; he wore a stiff standing-collar . . . a fence that compelled a straight lookout ahead, and a turning of the whole body when a side view was required." And, more contemptible, "the Model Boy, Willie Mufferson [who took] as heedful care of his mother as if she were cut glass. He always brought his mother to church, and was the pride of all the matrons. The boys all hated him, he was so good."

Rebellion, however, is no easy thing to manage. Tom cannot bring himself to dislike Aunt Polly. Occasionally, he admits to loving her; and when he genuinely saddens her (as during his disappearance to the island), he discovers that "his heart [is] full of pity for her." Pity and its cousin guilt: these are Aunt Polly's most formidable weapons (no less so for being used without guile). " 'She never licks anybody,' " Tom complains as he sets about beginning to whitewash the fence. " 'She talks awful, but talk don't hurt—anyways it don't if she don't cry.' " Tom might be able to contend with open anger, but he receives only reproaches that insinuate themselves into that budding thing called "conscience." Discovered after a stealthy trip abroad at night, "Tom almost brightened in the hope that he was going to be flogged; but it was not so. His aunt wept over him and asked him how he could go and break her old heart so; and finally told him to go on, and ruin himself and bring her gray hairs with sorrow to the grave, for it was no use for her to try any more. This was worse than a thousand whippings, and Tom's heart was sorer now than his body. He cried, he pleaded for forgiveness, promised to reform over and over again." In Tom's world, female children are no easier to deal with than their adult models. Becky Thatcher rules him by alternating tears with lofty reproaches; and although Tom's angry feelings toward her are a good deal more available to him than any genuinely hostile feelings he might have toward the generation of mothers, he nonetheless continues to wish for a more direct and "manly" emotional code. "He was in a fine rage. . . . He moped into the schoolyard wishing she were a boy, and imagining how he would trounce her if she were."

With no acceptable model of "free" adult masculinity available, Tom does his best to cope with the prevailing feminine system without being irretrievably contaminated by it. His principal recourse is an entire repertoire of games and pranks and superstitions, the unifying motif of which is a struggle for control. Control over his relationship with Aunt Polly is a major area of warfare. Thus the first scene in the book is but one type of behavior that is repeated in ritual form throughout the book. Tom, caught with his hands in the jam jar—about to be switched. " 'My! Look behind you, aunt!' The old lady whirled round, and snatched her skirts out of danger. The lad fled, on the instant, scrambled up the high board fence, and disappeared over it. His Aunt Polly stood surprised a moment, and then broke into a gentle laugh. 'Hang the boy, can't I never learn anything? Ain't he played

me tricks enough like that for me to be looking out for him by this time?' "
Crawling out his bedroom window at night is another type of such behavior,
not important because it permits this or that specific act, but significant as
a general assertion of the right to govern his own comings and goings.
Bartering is still another type of this behavior. Trading for blue Bible coupons
or tricking his playmates into painting the fence—these are superb inventions
to win the prizes of a genteel society without ever genuinely submitting
to it.

The logical continuation of such stratagems would be actual defiance:
the rebellion of authentic adolescence to be followed by a manhood in which
Tom and his peers might define the rules by which society is to be governed.
But manhood never comes to Tom; anger and defiance remain disguised in
the games of childhood.

Twain offers these pranks to us as if they were no more than humorous
anecdotes; Aunt Polly is always more disposed to smile at them than to take
them seriously. However, an acquiescence to the merely comic in this fiction
will blind us to its darker side. A boy who seeks to control himself and his
world so thoroughly is a boy deeply and constantly aware of danger—
justifiably so, it would seem, for an ominous air of violence hangs over the
entire tale. It erupts even into the apparently safe domestic sphere.

When the children depart from their schoolmaster in chapter xxi to
begin the lazy summer recess, they leave him disgraced—his gilded, bald
pate blazing as the ultimate spectacle in the school's pageant. "The boys
were avenged. Vacation had come." Mr. Dobbin (even his name invites
laughter) is hilariously humiliated, and he is apt to linger in our memories
primarily as the butt of a good joke. Yet for most of the children most of
the time, he is a source of genuine terror.

The one "respectable" man whom Tom sees regularly, Mr. Dobbin, is
a sadist. Having reached maturity with the unsatisfied ambition to be a
doctor, he spends his free time perusing a book of "anatomy" (that is, a book
with pictures of naked people in it). His principal active pleasure is lashing
the children, and the preparations for the approaching commencement exercises merely provide an excuse to be "severer and more exacting than
ever. . . . His rod and his ferule were seldom idle now—at least among the
smaller pupils. . . . Mr. Dobbin's lashings were very vigorous ones, too; for
although he carried, under his wig, a perfectly bald and shiny head, he had
only reached middle age and there was no sign of feebleness in his muscle.
As the great day approached, all the tyranny that was in him came to
the surface; he seemed to take a vindictive pleasure in punishing the least
shortcomings." If the village itself (with taverns, courthouse, jail, and deserted slaughterhouse) is composed of the elements of crime and punishment,
then Mr. Dobbin might be construed as one of the executioners—disarmed
at only the final moment by the boys' "revenge" and exiting to catcalls and

laughter. The joke is a fine exercise in imaginative power, but it does not fully succeed in countering the potency of the masculine "muscle" that is used with such consistent vindictiveness and violence.

Violence is everywhere in Tom's world. Escape to the island does not answer: random, pitiless destruction can find a frightened boy just as lightning, by chance, can blast a great sycamore to fall on the children's camp and signify that catastrophe is never far away.

Clearly, Tom is a major figure in the play of violence, yet his part is not clear. Is he victim or perpetrator? Is the violence outside of him, or is it a cosmic reflection of something that is fundamental to his own nature?

His games, for example, have a most idiosyncratic quality; the rebellion and rage that never fully surface in his dealings with Aunt Polly and the other figures of authority in this matriarchal world find splendid ventilation in fantasy. Richly invigorated by his imagination, Tom can blend the elements of violence and control exactly to suit his fancy. Acquiescent to society's tenets in real life, in day-dreams Tom is always a rebel.

> The idea of being a clown recurred to him now, only to fill him with disgust. For frivolity and jokes and spotted tights were an offense, when they intruded themselves upon a spirit that was exalted into the vague and august realm of the romantic. No, he would be a soldier. . . . No—better still, he would join the Indians, and hunt buffaloes and go on the warpath in the mountain ranges and the trackless great plains of the Far West, and away in the future come back a great chief, bristling with feathers, hideous with paint, and prance into Sunday-school, some drowsy summer morning, with a blood-curdling war-whoop, and sear the eyeballs of all his companions with unappeasable envy.

Safe in his own fictional world, Tom participates in carefully constructed rituals of devastation. He and his cohorts may be outlaws of any kind; however, whatever roles they choose, there are always careful sets of regulations to be followed. In games, control reigns supreme: " 'Guy of Guisborne wants no man's pass. Who are thou that—that—' 'Dares to hold such language,' said Tom prompting—for they talked 'by the book,' from memory."

The real import of these rules—this rigid regimentation of boyish fantasy—becomes clear several times in the novel as the children play. "Huck said: 'What does pirates have to do?' Tom said: 'Oh, they have just a bully time—take ships and burn them, and get the money and bury it in awful places in their island. . . .' 'And they carry the women to the island,' said Joe; 'they don't kill the women.' 'No,' assented Tom, 'they don't kill the women—they're too noble.' " And at the conclusion:

> "Tom Sawyer's Gang—it sounds splendid, don't it Huck?"
> "Well, it just does, Tom. And who'll we rob?"

"Oh, most anybody. Waylay people—that's mostly the way."

"And kill them?"

"No, not always. Hide them in the cave till they raise a ransom."

"What's a ransom?"

"Money. You make them raise all they can. . . . That's the general way. Only you don't kill the women. You shut up the women, but you don't kill them . . . It's so in all the books."

Pirates and robbers and Indians. Such are the figures of Tom's creation; and so long as they remain merely imaginary, governed by the "code" of play, they are clearly harmless. "You don't kill women. . . . It's so in all the books."

Given the precarious balancing of control and violence in Tom's fantasies, we can easily comprehend his terrified fascination with Injun Joe's incursions into the "safety" of St. Petersburg. Accidentally witness to Injun Joe's murderous attack, Tom's first response is characteristic: he writes an oath in blood, pledging secrecy. "Huck Finn and Tom Sawyer swears they will keep mum about this and they wish they may Drop down dead in Their tracks if they ever tell and Rot." It is an essentially "literary" maneuver, and Tom's superstitious faith in its efficacy is of a piece with the "rules" he has conned from books about outlaws. However, Injun Joe cannot easily be relegated to the realm of such villains. It is as if one element in Tom's fantasy world has torn loose and broken away from him, roaming restlessly—a ruthless predator—genuinely and mortally dangerous.

He has murdered a man, but perversely, he does not flee. Instead, he loiters about the town in disguise, waiting for the moment to arrive when he can take "revenge." Humiliated once by the Widow Douglas's husband (no longer available to the Indian's rage), Joe plans to work his will upon the surviving mate. " 'Oh, don't kill her! Don't do that!' " his nameless companion implores.

"Kill? Who said anything about killing? I would kill *him* if he was here; but not her. When you want to get revenge on a woman you don't kill her— bosh! you go for her looks. You slit her nostrils—you notch her ears like a sow! . . . I'll tie her to the bed. If she bleeds to death, is that my fault? I'll not cry, if she does."

It is almost a parody of Tom's concocted "rules" for outlaws; even Injun Joe flinches from killing a woman. Sadistic torture (of a clearly sexual nature) is sufficient.

His grievance is twofold: against the absence of the man who would be his natural antagonist; and then against the woman who has inherited the man's property and authority. Seen in this light, his condition is not unlike the hero's. Tom, denied the example of mature men whom he might emulate, left with no model to define an adult nature of his own. Tom, adrift in a matriarchal world—paying the continuous "punishment" of guilt for the "crime" of his resentment at genteel restraints, conceiving carefully measured fantasies within which to voice (and mute) his feelings. Injun Joe is Tom's shadow self, a potential for retrogression and destructiveness that cannot be permitted abroad.

Yet genuine vanquishment is no easy task. No other adult male plays so dominant a role in the novel as Injun Joe. Indeed, no other male's name save Huck's and Tom's is uttered so often. The only contender for adult masculine prominence is that other angry man, Mr. Dobbin. But the schoolmaster's vicious instincts are, in the end, susceptible to control through humor: he can be humiliated and disarmed by means of a practical joke. After all is said and done, he is an "acceptable" male, that is, a domesticated creature. The Indian, an outcast and a savage, is unpredictable; he may turn fury upon the villagers or act as ultimate executioner for Tom. When Tom's tentative literary gestures prove insufficient, desperate remedies are necessary. Twain invokes the ultimate adventure. Death.

Death has several meanings for Tom. On the one hand, it is the final loss of self—a relinquishment of control that is both attractive and frightening. Confronted with reverses, Tom sometimes longs for the blissful passivity of death, deterred primarily by the sneaking fear that "guilt" might be "punishable" even in the unknown land to which he would travel. "It seemed to him that life was but a trouble, at best, and he more than half envied Jimmy Hodges, so lately released; it must be very peaceful, he thought, to lie and slumber and dream forever and ever, with the wind whispering through the tree and caressing the grass and the flowers over the grave, and nothing to bother and grieve about, ever any more. If he only had a clean Sunday-school record he could be willing to go, and be done with it all."

On the other hand, properly managed, "death" might be the ultimate assertion of control, the means a boy might use in this puzzling female world to win a satisfactory "self" after all. "Ah," Tom's fantasy runs, "if he could only die *temporarily*!"

The triumph of "temporary death" and the fulfillment of that universal fantasy—to attend one's own funeral and hear the tearful eulogies and then to parade boldly down the aisle (patently and impudently alive)—is the central event in the novel. The escapade is not without its trials: a terrible lonesomeness during the self-imposed banishment and a general sense of emptiness whenever Tom falls to "gazing longingly across the wide river to where the village lay drowsing in the sun." Yet the victory is more than worth the pain. Temporarily, at least, Tom's fondest ambitions for himself have come true. "What a hero Tom was become, now! He did not go skipping and prancing, but moved with a dignified swagger as became a pirate who felt that the public eye was on him." He has definitely become "somebody" for a while—and he has achieved the identity entirely upon his own terms.

Yet this central miracle of resurrection is merely a rehearsal. Its results are not permanent, and Tom must once again submit to death and rebirth in order to dispatch the specter of Injun Joe forever.

The escapade begins light-heartedly enough: a party and a picnic up river into the countryside. Yet this moderated excursion into wilderness turns nightmare in the depths of the cave. "It was said that one might wander days and nights together through its intricate tangle of rifts and chasms, and never find the end of the cave. . . . No man 'knew' the cave. That was an impossible thing." Existing out of time, the cave is a remnant of man's prehistory— a dark and savage place, both fascinating and deadly. Once lost in the cave, Tom and Becky must face their elemental needs—hunger, thirst, and the horror, very quite real, of extinction. For Tom alone, he stumbles upon Injun Joe, who has on. The temptation to despair is very dness rise superior to fears in the long un Joe and all other terrors." Thus he length of a string lest he be separated then another, then "a third to the out to turn back when he glimpsed roped the line and groped toward a small hole and saw the broad is beloved river, Tom has earned

ures to an admiring audience, ro of his own adventure story. ried treasure; Judge Thatcher ays that he hopes "to see Tom a day." Endowed with an excess of accept- e been conferred upon him as the result of his , certainly, about the particulars of the adult male roles , but nonetheless christened, as it were, into the "rightful" m), Tom seems to have surmounted the deficiencies of his

hollow victory after all. Just as Tom must take on faith the pronouncement of his future as a "great lawyer" or a "great soldier" (having no first-hand information about these occupations), so we must accept the validity of his "triumph." The necessary condition for Tom's final peace of mind (and for his acquisition of the fortune) is the elimination of Injun Joe. And this event occurs quite accidentally. Taking the children's peril as a warning, the villagers have shut the big door to the cave and triple-bolted it, trapping Injun Joe inside. When the full consequences of the act are discovered, it is too late; the outcast has died. "Injun Joe lay stretched upon the ground, dead, with his face close to the crack of the door. . . . Tom was touched, for he knew by his own experience how this wretch had suffered. . . . Nevertheless he felt an abounding sense of relief and security, now."

Tom's final identification with the savage, valid as it certainly is, gives the lie to the conclusion of this tale. What do they share? Something irrational and atavistic, something ineradicable in human nature. Anger, perhaps; violence, perhaps. Some unnamed, timeless element.

> The poor unfortunate had starved to death. In one place near at hand, a stalagmite had been slowly growing up from the ground for ages, builded by the water-drip from a stalactite overhead. The captive had broken off the stalagmite, and upon the stump had placed a stone, wherein he had scooped a shallow hollow to catch the precious drop that fell once in every three minutes with the dreary regularity of a clock-tick—a dessert-spoonful once in four-and-twenty hours. That drop was falling when the Pyramids were new; when Troy fell; when the foundations of Rome were laid; when Christ was crucified; when the Conqueror created the British empire; when Columbus sailed; when the massacre at Lexington was "news." It is falling now; it will still be falling when all these things shall have sunk down the afternoon of history and the twilight of tradition and been swallowed up in the thick night of oblivion. . . . It is many and many a year since the hapless half-breed scooped out the stone to catch the priceless drops, but to this day the tourist stares longest at that pathetic stone and that slow-dropping water when he comes to see the wonders of McDougal's Cave. Injun Joe's cup stands first in the list of the cavern's marvels; even "Aladin's Palace" cannot rival it.

Whatever Injun Joe represents in this fiction—whatever his complex relationship may be to Tom—he cannot be dealt with by summary banishment. Shut up by fiat; locked away. It is an ending with no resolution at all.

Taken seriously as a psychological recommendation, the ultimate disposition of the problem of Injun Joe offers no solution but that of denial. Lock away the small boy's anger; lock away his anti-social impulses; shut up his resentments at this totally feminine world; stifle rebellion; ignore adult male hostility: they are all too dangerous to traffic with.

Thus Tom's final "self" as we see it in this novel is a tragic capitulation: he has accommodated himself to the oddities of his environment and given over resistance. A resolution to the story is established not by changing the bizarre quality of the fictional world (not even by confronting it), but by contorting the small hero into compliance. He becomes that worst of all possible things—a "Model Boy"—the voice of conformity in a genteel society. Huck complains. " 'The widder eats by a bell. . . . Everybody's so awful reg'lar a body can't stand it.' " And Tom responds. " 'Well, everybody does that way, Huck. . . . If you'll try this thing just awhile longer you'll come to like it. . . . Huck, we can't let you into the gang if you ain't respectable you know.' "

He has even lost his sense of humor.

The fault is Twain's, of course. Tom has earned the right to "be somebody"; but his creator's vision has faltered. Twain averts his attention from the struggle that should be central and shrinks from uncivilized inclinations. In the end, his hero must settle for security in a world that will always be run by its women.

However, Huck continues doubtful. And in his own book, he pursues the quest for fathers. Fully to understand his needs, we must know—exactly—where he has been before. Here, in *The Adventures of Tom Sawyer*.

Social Play and Bad Faith in
The Adventures of Tom Sawyer

FORREST G. ROBINSON

Though it is generally granted a place among Mark Twain's "major" works, *Tom Sawyer* has not attracted critical attention commensurate with its high canonical station. Indeed, it is not unusual to find professional students of American history and literature who admit that they have not gone back to *Tom Sawyer* since they first read it—or since it was first read to them—as children. Such benign neglect is not altogether surprising. Though they should know better, many readers have been influenced by Mark Twain's caveat that his "book is intended mainly for the entertainment of boys and girls."[1] Undoubtedly, many others have acquiesced in the view, advanced for decades in survey courses around the country, that despite its interest as a formal departure, and its chronological significance as Mark Twain's first sustained meditation on "the matter of Hannibal," *Tom Sawyer* is nonetheless a mere foretaste of greater things to come. For some, the book is read as an adjunct to *Huckleberry Finn*; and such readers are perhaps understandably predisposed to regard Tom as a conventional, rather mindless proto-entrepreneur. For the most part, however, *Tom Sawyer* has been widely accepted as a minor juvenile classic—"the supreme American idyll," in Bernard De Voto's familiar characterization.[2]

De Voto's brief but very suggestive qualifying remarks on the novel are probably less well known. Though he viewed *Tom Sawyer* as "a book eternally true about children," he was careful to add: "The pastoral landscape, however, is a part not of cloudland but of America. It is capable of violence and terror." Hinting perhaps that the culture which it portrays, idyll and violence and all, has been rather childlike, if not childish, De Voto concludes:

> The St. Petersburg of Tom Sawyer is a final embodiment of an American experience many layers deep, from the surface to whatever depths one may care to examine, each layer true. What finds expression here is an America which everyone knows to be thus finally transmuted into literature. . . . In the presence of such a finality, technical defects, here freely acknowledged,

Reprinted from *Nineteenth Century Fiction* 39 (June 1984): 1–24, by permission of the Regents of the University of California.

are trivialities. It does not matter much that some of the artist's inventions are weak, that some of the situations and dialogue fail rather dismally, or that, by some canon of abstract form, the book lacks a perfect adjustment of part to part. It does matter that here something formed from America lives as it lives nowhere else.[3]

    Subsequent critics have been slow to explore the layers of meaning and truth that De Voto first hinted at a half century ago. Walter Blair has written exhaustively on the history of the novel's composition, on the real-life models for its main characters, and on Mark Twain's literary sources. Critically speaking, however, he finds *Tom Sawyer* "a light book suitable for children and for adults satisfied with a funny story."[4] Henry Nash Smith, having reviewed a similar array of background materials, argues that grave weaknesses in the structure and style of *Tom Sawyer* were obstacles to an effective treatment of "the problem of values to which Mark Twain had devoted so much attention in his early work."[5] In effect, Blair and Smith make much more of the alleged flaws in *Tom Sawyer* than De Voto does, and they have helped to promote the rather common opinion that the novel is either inconsequential, or confused, or both, and that it is to be valued primarily for the way it anticipates *Huckleberry Finn*.

    Rather more recently, James M. Cox has implicitly accepted the critical challenge laid down by De Voto two generations ago. Taking the novel seriously on its own terms, Cox dismisses the charge of flimsy plot construction on the grounds that "the reality of the adventures lies not so much in their order as in their relation to Tom." Centered on its juvenile protagonist, the action of the story is defined by Tom's unwavering commitment to a dream of himself as hero in a world of play. With the discovery that coherence resides in a dominant character rather than plot, Cox insists that "every episode of *Tom Sawyer* enacts . . . the conversion of all 'serious' community activity—all duty, pain, grief, and work—into pleasure and play. Tom Sawyer himself is the agent of this conversion."[6]

    The appeal of Cox's argument has several dimensions. His analysis and implicitly positive assessment of *Tom Sawyer* arise from principles and standards generated from close critical attention to the text. Cox is aware of history and biography and chronology, but he is not blinded by them. More specifically to my present purposes, his application of the pleasure principle and the notion of play strikes us as apt, for it describes Tom's behavior quite plausibly and at the same time serves admirably to illuminate his motivation and his relationship to the community. In what follows I take Cox's lead in regarding *Tom Sawyer* as a novel of social analysis and in using the notion of play as a window on that world. At the same time, however, I differ quite significantly from Cox in the form of play that I discover in St. Petersburg and in my characterization of the social framework in which the playing occurs. Along the way I also offer evidence to suggest that the special brand of social play to be found in *Tom Sawyer* gives rise to a more intricate—if rather more submerged—plot organization than has so far been observed.

From that moment at the very beginning of *Tom Sawyer* when aunt Polly looks over rather than through her spectacles, because "they were her state pair, the pride of her heart, and were built for 'style,' not service" (p. 39), we are alerted to the importance of social appearances in St. Petersburg. All of the important phases of village life are governed by ordinarily unspoken but evidently rigid rules and conventions. Domestic affairs, school, church, the political and legal establishments, the status hierarchy—in all of these areas a strict code works to enforce order and the maintenance of degree. For the most part, the members of the community have learned to accept and even to take pleasure in shaping themselves to the severely angular construction of their reality. The adults know their places in church, just as the children know theirs in school. All take parts, and play them, accepting apparent inconvenience and discomfort in the dutiful adherence to proper form. The young men of the community, for example, are willing to endure "sitting with their toes pressed against a wall for hours together" in order to achieve "the fashion of the day," boot toes turned sharply up "like sleigh-runners" (p. 61). Though the social regimen of the little society may strike us as comically extreme, our reaction is certainly to some degree the result of our failure—one we share with the residents of St. Petersburg—to recognize the constraints, objectively numerous and rather bizarre, that we bend to in our own daily lives. In larger part we respond as we do because the novel directs our attention with unremitting persistence to the potent rigor of convention in the village society. Quite evidently, amidst his fretting about whether he was writing for adults or children, in *Tom Sawyer* Mark Twain yielded to a deep, though incompletely acknowledged, impulse to write a novel of social analysis.

Though the status hierarchy in St. Petersburg is rather rigidly fixed, the social ladder stretches generously from "the aged and needy postmaster, who had seen better days," through a broad range of middling families like the Sawyers and Harpers, to "the widow Douglas, fair, smart and forty" (p.66), with her amiably aristocratic ways, and to such eminences as the "fine, portly, middleaged gentleman with iron-gray hair . . . the great Judge Thatcher, brother of their own lawyer" (p. 62). The outcasts are surprisingly few. Huck Finn and Muff Potter are tolerated and are even granted condescending sympathy so long as they keep their places on the margin. Only Injun Joe, half-breed and suspected felon, is forced completely outside the capacious orbit of local society. The great majority of the villagers accept their assigned ranks unreflectingly, without any apparent desire to resist the codes that order and limit their lives. Rather, they assert themselves through public display of conspicuous mastery of their roles. The necessity for spelling and spectacles and hymns is never questioned; thus the clear objective is to be the best speller, to wear the most fashionable spectacles, and, with the Rev. Mr. Sprague, to recite hymns "with a relish, in a peculiar style which was much admired in that part of the country" (p. 67). To be sure, the desire for approval occasionally reaches lunatic proportions. Consider the lamentable example of the young biblical enthusiast who once vaingloriously "spread himself" before the congregation by reciting from memory "three thousand verses without stopping." Unfortunately, "the strain upon his mental faculties was too great, and he was little better than an idiot from that day forth" (p. 60). In spite of such hazards, however, all St. Petersburg joins in the scramble for public acclaim. This is especially the case at church, where rituals of devotion and edification readily give way to an orgy of showing off. The superintendent, the librarian, the young men, the teachers, the boys and girls—members of every age and rank vie for attention. "And above it all" Judge Thatcher "sat and beamed a majestic judicial smile upon all the house, and warmed himself in the sun of his own grandeur—for he was 'showing off,' too" (p. 63).

Despite appearances, such wholesale self-indulgence reinforces rather than threatens the social order, for the ostentation is an expression of pride of place, not the ambition to subvert or climb. The showing off merely confirms the status quo. Following the urbanely superior narrator, the reader will undoubtedly be amused by the inflated posturings of the villagers; but he will be wrong if he supposes, as Cox does, that "the adult rituals" of St. Petersburg "are nothing but dull play."[7] We may find them dull, but only after we have enjoyed the show. More to the point, the villagers themselves take manifest pleasure in their relatively artless affectations. Hopelessly encumbered as they may appear, the members of the little community adhere to rigidly structured roles and routines with evident gusto. Our assessment of his style notwithstanding, the Rev. Mr. Sprague

> was regarded as a wonderful reader. At church "sociables" he was always called upon to read poetry; and when he was through, the ladies would lift up their hands and let them fall helplessly in their laps, and "wall" their eyes, and shake their heads, as much as to say, "Words cannot express it; it is too beautiful, *too* beautiful for this mortal earth." (p. 67)

In fact, the villagers have an enviable latitude and ingenuity when it comes to pleasure. Is it dull in the schoolmaster that he responds to news of a murder by declaring a "holiday for that afternoon"? Not in the view of his neighbors. Indeed, "the town would have thought strangely of him if he had not" (p. 105).

Cox's characterization of St. Petersburg features an extreme contrast between the real play of Tom Sawyer and the somehow inauthentic play of the adults. He equates Tom with the "world of boyhood . . . where play, make-believe, and adventure are the living realities defining the false pieties and platitudes which constitute the dull pleasure of the adult world."[8] In addition to his misapprehension of adult amusements, Cox errs in both the breadth and the extremity of his definition of the "world of boyhood." The definition is too broad in that it ignores the vast majority of children in St. Petersburg who conform without protest to the values and behavior patterns prescribed by grown-ups. When we observe them at play, we find the children of St. Petersburg imitating their elders, holding "a juvenile court that was trying a cat for murder, in the presence of her victim, a bird" (p. 166). And if we remind ourselves of Sid and Mary Sawyer, of the Thatcher children and Amy Lawrence, of the impeccably dressed newcomer whom Tom scuffles with in chapter 1, of "the Model Boy, Willie Mufferson, taking as heedful care of his mother as if she were cut glass" (p. 66), of the scriptural prodigy who damages himself, and of the nameless, obedient juvenile assemblage at school and church, then the "world of boyhood" shrinks dramatically.

Cox's contrast is also too extreme in its clear suggestion that Tom inhabits a world of imagination and action that is radically different in degree, and possibly in kind, from the world of the grown-ups. The error here derives in good part, I believe, from limitations inherent in Cox's notion of play. He construes the term in the theatrical sense, with Tom cast as the central character who performs before a receding audience composed of townspeople, the narrator (who handles props and draws the curtain), and a multitude of adoring readers. The advantages of this approach are very considerable, especially in opening up the pervasive theatricality of the novel's action and mode of presentation. But the method is misleading when it draws attention away from the fundamental realism of Mark Twain's social analysis, and when it leads to audience-response measurements of the alleged dullness of adult performances. In fact, Tom shows off like everyone else in town, and he does so for the same reasons, according to the same rules, and with the usual amount of zest and pleasure. Tom is willing, for example, to strive for excellence in spelling; but he extends himself at school principally because success earns him a "pewter medal which he had worn with ostentation for months" (p. 80). Moreover, there is abundant evidence that Tom advocates the strict observance of orderly, established procedures. "After the hymn had been sung," we learn, it was the convention for the minister to turn "himself into a bulletin board and read off 'notices' of meetings and societies and things till it seemed that the list would stretch out to the crack of doom." The narrator's amusement betrays a rather sharper edge when he observes, "Often, the less there is to justify a traditional custom, the harder it is to get rid of it." As if to add insult to injury, the minister goes on to his regular, and regularly interminable, prayer "for the church, and the little children of the church . . . for the oppressed millions groaning under the heel of European monarchies and Oriental despotisms" and "the heathen in the far islands of the sea." We are hardly surprised to find that Tom "did not enjoy the prayer, he only endured it—if he even did that much" (pp. 67, 68). But despite the fact that he "was restive, all through it," Tom

> kept tally of the details of the prayer, unconsciously—for he was not listening, but he knew the ground of old, and the clergyman's regular route over it— and when a little trifle of new matter was interlarded, his ear detected it and his whole nature resented it; he considered additions unfair, and scoundrelly. (p. 68)

The reader may be inclined to share the narrator's evident view that the prayer is mechanically prolix and therefore, like the recital of "notices," somehow unjustified. For Tom, however, the prayer is justified simply because it is "a traditional custom," and he objects to the slightest departure from its familiar, outward dullness. In this light Tom's scrupulous adherence to literary "authorities" in his adventures, and his urging of Huck to submit to the widow's civilizing influence—"we can't let you into the gang if you ain't respectable, you know" (p. 235)—point to the unmistakably adult models which inform his values and conduct.[9]

We can move toward an even clearer sense of Tom's behavior if we shift briefly from the theatrical frame of reference to a notion of play as spontaneous activity taking rise from the relatively unencumbered promptings of the imagination.[10] The nearest approach to such "free" play occurs at the beginning of the famous whitewashing episode, when Ben Rogers appears on the scene.

> He was eating an apple, and giving a long, melodious whoop, at intervals, followed by a deep-toned ding-dong-dong, ding-dong-dong, for he was personating a steamboat. As he drew near, he slackened speed, took the middle of the street, leaned far over to starboard and rounded to ponderously and with laborious pomp and circumstance—for he was personating the "Big Missouri," and considered himself to be drawing nine feet of water. He was boat and captain and engine-bells combined, so he had to imagine himself standing on his own hurricane deck giving the orders and executing them.
> "Stop her, sir! Ting-a-ling-ling!" The headway ran almost out and he drew up slowly toward the side-walk.
> "Ship up to back! Ting-a-ling-ling!" His arms straightened and stiffened down his sides.
> "Set her back on the stabboard! Ting-a-ling-ling! Chow! ch-chow-wow! Chow!" His right hand, meantime, describing stately circles,—for it was representing a forty-foot wheel. (pp. 47–48)

Meanwhile, apparently absorbed in his own activity, Tom goes on with the whitewashing and pays "no attention to the steamboat" (p. 48). In fact, however, and in contrast to Ben's total oblivion to his actual surroundings, Tom is alive to the possibilities of the objective circumstances. While Ben plays at being a steamboat, Tom plays—in a very different way—at seeming not to notice. On one side, we have virtually unselfconscious make-believe; on the other, alert, self-conscious and purposive dissimulation. While Ben plays, Tom schemes. In the upshot, of course, artless plays succumbs to artful plotting.

In following the inevitable logic of the child-play versus adult-play argument, Cox is inclined to minimize what he calls the "embryo business-man" in Tom, and focuses instead on "the essential criticism the episode . . . makes of the original chore." Viewed from this angle, the whitewashing incident exposes the poverty of adult initiative—aunt Polly's demands are a "dull-witted stratagem for getting work done at low pay in the name of duty"—and the concomitant superiority of a juvenile rejoinder in which "Tom shows off his handiwork" while completing the task "in the name of pleasure."[11] In order to preserve this line of thought, however, we must ignore the force of the contrast between Tom and Ben and seriously overstate the contrast between the behavior of aunt Polly and Tom. If we acknowl-edge—as I think we must—that the episode demonstrates Tom's prodigious mastery of deception and the strategies of self-interest, then we must go on to observe that his conduct, unlike Ben's, is hardly spontaneous and free. In fact, if it is true that aunt Polly contrives to get "work done at low pay," then the same can be said of Tom, except that he gets it done at a considerable profit to himself and that the name of pleasure serves his purposes better than "duty."

There is at least one more critical liability in approaching the whitewash-ing episode as an example of play-as-performance in which "Tom shows off." While it is undeniable that Tom adopts a role in his dealings with his friends, it is wrong to assume that his role is abandoned and the action completed when the curtain closes on his aunt's freshly painted fence. Tom's fellows fall into this error, and they do so at the cost of becoming victims once again. For the very next day Tom capitalizes on an extremely depressed market when he trades the proceeds of his artistic enterprise for enough tickets to win a Bible. No one in the congregation is so foolish as to believe that Tom has actually memorized enough verses to earn the tickets, but there is no denying that he possesses the requisite number. Thus all doubts are carefully suppressed, and Tom is

elevated to a place with the Judge and the other elect, and the great news was announced from head-quarters. It was the most stunning surprise of the decade; and so profound was the sensation that it lifted the new hero up to the judicial one's altitude, and the school had two marvels to gaze upon in place of one. The boys were all eaten up with envy—but those that suffered the bitterest pangs were those who perceived too late that they themselves had contributed to this hated splendor by trading tickets to Tom for the wealth he had amassed in selling whitewashing privileges. These despised themselves, as being the dupes of a wily fraud, a guileful snake in the grass. (p. 63)

To a much greater extent than in the whitewashing incident, there is a conspicuous element of spectacle here; Tom is indeed the happy hero in a kind of performance. But there is a good deal more to be observed in his triumph. As I have already suggested, Tom's elevation is hardly an isolated episode; rather, it is the final step in a carefully orchestrated sequence of events that first took life when Tom spotted Joe (*Big Missouri*) Harper and decided to feign indifference. This opening move led, in turn, to the successful duping of Joe and a host of friends, the effortless completion of an onerous chore and the masterful evasion of punishment, the gathering of unearned treasure, the subsequent doubling of profit from the very advantageous conversion of capital (at the expense of the original and still unsuspecting victims), and the final, admittedly dramatic, cashing in. At one level the elegance and boldness of the scheme strongly suggest that Tom takes as much pleasure from the conception and prosecution of his elaborate plot as he does from its spectacular denouement. Much of the fun, it appears, is in the doing. At another level the complex attenuation of Tom's scheme is evidence of greater development and continuity between episodes than the isolated performance model recognizes. Events are related not merely because Tom is *in* them but also to a large extent because he *orders* them. Thus in this cluster of incidents, as in many others in the novel, Tom Sawyer's plotting serves to emplot *Tom Sawyer*.

In winning his way to the top, Tom outwits and exploits members from every age group and class in the community. The other children are twice taken in, and provide ready sources of free labor and capital. The adults are equally easy prey; for, as Tom shrewdly divines, their incredulity is not as deep as their craving for amusement. Along the way Tom makes a mockery of honesty and good faith, but he does so in a manner that is, paradoxically, easily detected and yet impervious to public disapproval. We can begin to unravel this paradox by observing that in moving toward his objectives, Tom has enjoyed the cooperation, both willing and unwilling, of the community. His victims either get what they asked for, or have themselves to blame for their undoing, or both. In effect, Tom has collaborated with his neighbors in what I will call "bad faith." As I use this term, it describes varieties of deception that may seem to violate law or custom but which in fact enjoy the tacit, often unconscious approval of the society as a whole. Thus acts of bad faith are social and cultural in nature; they depend for their successful performance on the acquiescence of their witnesses. A telling feature of such acts is their incorporation of silent prohibitions against the admission that they have occurred. For their part, Tom's neighbors can never fully acknowledge to themselves or others the full extent to which they have been deceived.

To do so would risk a humiliating revelation of their willingness to be misled. On Tom's part, full acknowledgment of bad faith would entail the potential for an unbearable assault of guilt, or the loss, through their public disclosure, of the social intuitions which form the basis of his power. This delicate equipoise of threats to the collective peace of mind would collapse were it not for the fact that bad faith—the reciprocal deception of self and other—is the ruling characteristic in the social dynamics of the village.

St. Petersburg society is a complex fabric of lies: of half-truths, of simulation, dissimulation, broken promises, exaggeration, and outright falsehoods. Tom is exceptional only in the sheer quantity of his showing off; Huck's faith is more than once betrayed; the local ladies are easy marks for vendors of quack cure-alls and exotic religions; the entire community turns a blind eye to Injun Joe's grave robbing and the presence of liquor in the Temperance Tavern; and the Judge himself is moved to deliver an encomium on lies of the generous, magnanimous stripe. Appearances notwithstanding, there is evidently something in bad faith for nearly everyone. How else account for the often quite eager flight or surrender to deception? One imagines, in fact, that St. Petersburg is hardly unusual in all this and that varieties of bad faith are universally a feature of human societies. They are the covert mechanisms of flexibility and resilience that work imperceptibly to mitigate rigid laws and customs, and thus provide a measure of latitude adequate to the accommodation of apparently incompatible demands for conformity and individual self-expression. This is, of course, to highlight the *good* in bad faith. To an extent at least, the good is inseparable from the bad, for the social advantages here described are the direct result of broad-based, generally blind complicity in departures from public commitments to such values as truthfulness and fairness. In excess, it seems obvious, such lapses from the social faith would figure prominently in varieties of cultural pathology. "Bad faith," in short, describes the spectrum of unacknowledged and sublimated deceits that a society resorts to in its quest for stability and equanimity. It is the "give" in the outwardly stiff St. Petersburg system. [12]

It must be obvious by now that if Tom is playing at all, he is playing a sustained, purposeful, relatively complex social game. A comprehensive examination of the ways and means of his bad faith would require several times the space available here. Still, one may safely generalize that Tom's rapid upward mobility in St. Petersburg is the index of his masterful mimicry of adult strategies of bad faith, and his possession, to an uncommon degree, of social intuition, audacity, and an arsenal of artifice. Their skillful use enables him to gain glittering notoriety and the pinnacle of the social ladder, and, at the same time, to avoid censure.

But if Tom is like Icarus in his mastery of artifice and in the swiftness and dizzying pitch of his ascent, he is Icarian as well in his precipitous vulnerabilities. Tom's genius for manipulation makes it possible for him to play at the perilous margins of social tolerance for bad faith. As we have seen, Tom takes full advantage of all opportunities for exploitation; but susceptible as he is to the pride of mastery, he is prone to the kind of false move that threatens a fall as abrupt as his climb. The radical extremes of Tom's potential are precisely, if somewhat obliquely, evident to those villagers "that believed he would be President, yet, if he escaped hanging" (p. 173).

Again, space does not permit a full survey of the perils that beset the adventurer in bad faith. But the characteristic pattern of such reversals is perfectly manifest when Tom, in his glittering climb from whitewasher to triumphant church hero, has a close and totally unforeseen brush with catastrophe. Having mounted the platform to join the local bon ton, Tom is encouraged to honor the audience with a brief demonstration of his pious learning. "Now I know you'll tell *me*," urges the Judge's perfectly ingenuous wife: "The names of the first two disciples were—" When Tom responds, "DAVID AND GOLIAH" the uppercase type is alone adequate to suggest the enormity of his lapse and the stunned surprise of the congregation. Sudden and steep though it is, however, the hero's fall does not end in disgraceful defeat. With the reader, the members of the community appear to be much more amused than offended by Tom's antics. The bubble of their pretensions has been pricked, but much of the potential for resentment has been dissipated in the embarrassment of the quondam celebrity. Moreover, there is an ample measure of triumph in Tom's apparent humiliation. For the adults, he has been the source of entertainment and the occasion for a gratifyingly spontaneous expression of communal high spirits. For his juvenile peers, Tom's egregious lapse serves to ameliorate feelings of envy and betrayal. Most important of all, even in defeat Tom is precisely where he wants to be, at the center of the stage, when the narrator good-humoredly draws "the curtain of charity over the rest of the scene" (p. 65).

The language and setting of Tom's flirtation with ignominy may serve as a reminder of the undeniable value of the play-as-performance approach to the novel. But the boy's embarrassing moment on the stage is also an important phase in his education as the leading gamesman in St. Petersburg. Superficially, the lesson of Tom's exposure is that schemes of deception are morally wrong and are therefore doomed to failure. In fact, Tom learns that strategies of self-aggrandizement on his ambitious scale must be complete to the last detail if they are to succeed. In plotting his course of action, he fails to anticipate developments—in this case, questions about apostles—that exceed his admittedly formidable resourcefulness and dexterity. Thus in entering and playing the game Tom's error is strategic rather than ethical.

In confirmation of this general lesson, and as a potential guide for the future, Tom is well placed to make observations on some of the finer points of the social game. First, it must be evident to him that his neighbors are perpetually ready to be deceived. In this case, the congregation's craving for amusement along with the superintendent's burning ambition to show off a prize pupil combine to envelop a transparent falsehood in a mantle of bland credibility. Thus the episode illustrates the axiom that community tolerance for lies is directly proportional to the service the deceit renders to the desires and vanities, almost always unacknowledged, of those who endure the deception. Given the right return on their gullibility, the villagers will swallow almost anything. As a corollary to this rule, there is an evident premium on falsehoods that are offered up in the name of some noble or educational cause. This feature lends a sort of pious plausibility to the decision to be deceived, and, should the deception be exposed, it provides the grounds for a gratifying outburst of righteous indignation.

Second, Tom learns that failure—outright exposure of the act of deception—can be turned to his personal advantage. This is so because the community investment in varieties of duplicity is so fundamental and far-reaching that the detection of group acquiescence in a single lie points by implication to the complex fabric of deceptions and half-truths that all have silently agreed to accept, and to ignore. The admission that one has been deceived threatens to trigger the awareness that one is perpetually deceived. Since this awareness is humiliating to the individual and threatening to the stability of the group, the most seasoned and successful deceivers will always be ready with new lies to veil old ones, or with smooth palliatives to ease the sting of the victim's anger and embarrassment. Tom's apparent failure at church works substantially to his advantage because it alleviates the anger of his juvenile victims, draws attention away from the foolish gullibility of the adults, and averts discord with the happy illusion that the episode is a harmless prank. Meanwhile, his success tarnished slightly but still intact, Tom remains the central attraction.

The exposition and the oblique analysis of the dynamics of village social behavior are the primary business of the early chapters of *Tom Sawyer* and a major theme and principle of organization in the novel as a whole. The narrator directly addresses this preoccupation when he pauses, in chapter 2, to observe that Tom "had discovered a great law of human action, without knowing it—namely, that in order to make a man or a boy covet a thing, it is only necessary to make the thing difficult to attain" (p. 50). Mark Twain's survey of the community is remarkably comprehensive and systematic, moving from the domestic scene to the peer group, through a host of institutional arrangements, and including along the way a glimpse of the relations between the sexes. This preliminary anatomy of village "sociology" forms the quite essential background to the understanding of subsequent developments. Notable throughout *Tom Sawyer* is the consistency with which the characters adhere to patterns of behavior set forth in the opening chapters of the text. The principal agent and structural focus of this unfolding analysis is, of course, Tom Sawyer. Tom's consistency derives in part from his sure intuitive grasp of the ruling cultural assumptions of St. Petersburg society.

As the narrator says, Tom masters these principles "of human action, without knowing it." It derives, too, from his prolonged exposure to, and astute mimicry of, the artful manipulative strategies of his aunt Polly. In the finer points of the social game, Tom's education begins right at home.

Though aunt Polly views herself, with some justice, as a fool in her relationship to Tom, and though she insists that "old fools is the biggest fools there is" (p. 40), she is in fact a worthy opponent and an able mentor in the fine art of St. Petersburg gamesmanship. A substantial strand of *Tom Sawyer* is given to the description of the running, apparently interminable battle between the good-hearted old woman and her nephew. Superficially, the contest pits aunt Polly's insistence on honesty, probity, obedience, propriety—in a word, respectability—against Tom's pursuit of freedom and the pleasure principle. To all appearances, it is the familiar conflict between youth and age, nature and civilization. In fact, however, the apparent terms of the struggle are merely a conventional pretext for what is at root a battle of wills. When aunt Polly rewards Tom for his good work on the fence, she forces him to endure "an improving lecture upon the added value and flavor a treat took to itself when it came without sin through virtuous effort. And while she closed with a happy Scriptural flourish, he 'hooked' a doughnut" (pp. 51–52). While the humor in this brief encounter springs in part from a perception of sprightly pleasure subverting leaden piety, there is a deeper human comedy in the spectacle of naked willfulness masquerading in the liveries of virtue and desire. Aunt Polly is much more in love with her own voice and with her power to hold her nephew captive than she is with virtue. And her nephew will relish his doughnut principally because it bears palpably sweet testimony to the triumphant autonomy of his own will. It is the comedy, then, of the devious ingenuity we humans bring to having things, even the most trivial things, our own way.

Tom is blessed by nature and training with ample resources for the domestic struggle. He is physically quick enough to scale a fence in the wink of an eye. And he is mentally quick as well. Aunt Polly complains that you "can't learn an old dog new tricks," but in the same breath she acknowledges that Tom "never plays them alike, two days, and how is a body to know what's coming?" Moreover, in laying his plans, Tom displays increasingly close attention to matters of detail. Improvement in this area is vital, for when his foresight falters—as it does when he neglects the apostles, or when he sews his collar closed with black instead of the original white thread—Tom becomes vulnerable to the consequences of discovery. But even in tight places Tom can rely on his sharp intuitive judgment of his aunt's limits. "He 'pears to know just how long he can torment me before I get my dander up," aunt Polly observes, "and he knows if he can make out to put me off for a minute or make me laugh, it's all down again and I can't hit him a lick" (p. 40). Finally, and most crucially, Tom is absolute in his control of his face. He views it as a weakness in Becky that her expression often betrays her feelings: "Girls' faces always tell on them. They ain't got any backbone" (p. 154). Muff Potter and Huck Finn are equally prone to give themselves away. But Tom has the ability to feign or dissimulate moods as his perceived self-interest would seem to require. He is a pillar of apparent indifference as he lays schemes for Joe Harper, and, though he knows he is late for school, "he strode in briskly, with the manner of one who had come with all honest speed" (p. 77). This consummate mastery of face is the clearest outward manifestation of the gamesman's inward self-control, and it aptly expresses his ruling ambition to give nothing away.[13]

The contest between Tom and his aunt appears to involve him in the effort to avoid the punishments meted out for the violation of her rules. To an extent this impression is accurate, though it should be emphasized that Tom errs not when he breaks rules, but only when he gets *caught* breaking rules. That aunt Polly is surprised to find the fence whitewashed betrays her assumption that Tom will defy her will whenever it conflicts with his own. Indeed, we may go even further in this direction and argue that the old woman's expectation that her nephew will break her rules is the indirect manifestation of the fact that she places great value on Tom's rebelliousness. To be sure, she is totally unaware of this contradictory wrinkle in her makeup. It is equally evident, however, that the rules are relatively unimportant except as occasions for the game and that the game cannot begin until a rule has been broken. Paradoxically, then, Tom serves his aunt best when he seeks to escape detection in the violation of her orders. Tom shares his aunt's blindness to this dimension of their relationship; yet he values the game as much as she does, and is perfectly happy to play along. In effect, the woman and the child unconsciously collaborate in the creation of a pleasurable contest of wills. As the following passage clearly illustrates, when the contest is finally joined, the issue of compliance with rules appears in its true colors as the merest pretext for an exhilarating round of artful deception and catlike pursuit.

> While Tom was eating his supper, and stealing sugar as opportunity offered, aunt Polly asked him questions that were full of guile, and very deep—for she wanted to trap him into damaging revealments. Like many other simple-hearted souls, it was her pet vanity to believe she was endowed with a talent for dark and mysterious diplomacy and she loved to contemplate her most transparent devices as marvels of low cunning. Said she:
> "Tom, it was middling warm in school, warn't it?"
> "Yes'm."
> "Powerful warm, warn't it?"
> "Yes'm."
> "Didn't you want to go in a-swimming, Tom?"
> A bit of a scare shot through Tom—a touch of uncomfortable suspicion. He searched aunt Polly's face, but it told him nothing. So he said:

"No'm—well, not very much."

The old lady reached out her hand and felt Tom's shirt, and said:

"But you ain't too warm now, though." And it flattered her to reflect that she had discovered that the shirt was dry without anybody knowing that that was what she had in her mind. But in spite of her, Tom knew where the wind lay, now. So he forestalled what might be the next move:

"Some of us pumped on our heads—mine's damp yet. See?"

Aunt Polly was vexed to think she had overlooked that bit of circumstantial evidence, and missed a trick. Then she had a new inspiration:

"Tom, you didn't have to undo your shirt collar where I sewed it to pump on your head, did you? Unbutton your jacket!"

The trouble vanished out of Tom's face. He opened his jacket. His shirt collar was securely sewed.

"Bother! Well, go 'long with you. I'd made sure you'd played hookey and been a-swimming. But I forgive ye, Tom. I reckon you're a kind of a singed cat, as the saying is—better'n you look. *This* time." (pp. 41–42).

Quite appropriately, when it begins to appear that Tom has in fact complied with her instructions, aunt Polly responds with a marked division of feeling. On one side, she is "half glad that Tom had stumbled into obedient conduct for once." "Stumbled" betrays her assumption that Tom's apparent obedience has been an unintentional accident and points to her submerged preference for disobedience and the preservation of the game. That she is "half sorry her sagacity had miscarried" complements this sentiment, for it is an expression of regret that her suspicions turned out to be groundless. Thus the sum of aunt Polly's response is rather grudging approval of Tom's seeming compliance and much more emphatic disappointment that his inadvertent obedience has spoiled the fun. In reality, of course, Tom has bested her in the game of cat-and-mouse, for her reluctant acknowledgment of his good behavior is ironically premature. But the match of wits is hardly revitalized when young Sid reminds his aunt that "you sewed his collar with white thread, but it's black" (p. 42). This intrusion of solid, irrefutable fact resolves the question of objective right and wrong, but it also levels the uncertainty which first gave the contest life. There can be no doubt that Tom would have preferred to avoid detection; the rewards of disobedience would have been immeasurably sweetened by the success of his subterfuge. As it is, victory is wrenched from his grasp, aunt Polly is spared the mild embarrassment of miscarried sagacity, and Tom rushes from the room vowing vengeance on Sid. But Tom's abrupt defeat is augmented by the loss, which he shares with aunt Polly, of the game which they have both so obviously and thoroughly enjoyed. It is, of course, richly paradoxical that in a debate ostensibly committed to the discovery of truth, the actual ingress of truth should spell the end of pleasure. Yet if we succeed in holding this episode at arm's length long enough to perceive that its peculiarities are at once quite distinctive and everywhere to be found in *Tom Sawyer*, then we may begin to recognize that such apparent inconsistencies mirror quite faithfully the deeper cultural logic of bad faith, St. Petersburg style.

Tom's education as a gamesman reaches its climactic fruition in the planning, execution, and aftermath of the mock resurrection that appears in chapter 17. For sheer virtuosity in boldness, anticipation of details, mastery of face, and the strategic scope of its engagement with St. Petersburg society, the episode is the finest flowering of Tom's youthful genius. The first seed of the elaborate plot is planted when Tom, recently rejected by Becky and feeling himself "a forsaken, friendless boy," decides to abandon the village for a life of crime. Characteristically, the plan is rooted in self-pity, and has the kindling of guilt in faithless hearts as its principal objective. "Nobody loved him; when they found out what they had driven him to, perhaps they would be sorry" (p. 114). Tom finds similarly long-suffering allies in Joe Harper and Huck Finn, who join him in an escape to Jackson's Island.

A much more elaborate scheme begins to germinate when a steamboat loaded with townspeople circles the island in search of the victims of a drowning accident. In a flash of insight Tom grasps the implication of the situation: "Boys, I know who's drowned—it's us!" Just as quickly, he recognizes that his fondest fantasy has come true and revels with his companions in the happy consequences of being imagined dead.

> They felt like heroes in an instant. Here was a gorgeous triumph; they were missed; they were mourned; hearts were breaking on their account; tears were being shed; accusing memories of unkindnesses to these poor lost lads were rising up, and unavailing regrets and remorse were being indulged; and best of all, the departed were the talk of the whole town, and the envy of all the boys, as far as this dazzling notoriety was concerned. This was fine. (pp. 124–25)

At the same time, however, Tom is initially uneasy that aunt Polly will suffer unnecessarily on his account, and so steals away from camp with a note, inscribed on a sycamore scroll, that he plans to deliver when she is asleep. He returns to the village, finds a secure hiding place in his aunt's sitting room, and listens in as Mrs. Harper and the members of his own family give way to their feelings. The women overflow with expressions of love for their good-hearted boys and bewail in unison the remorse that afflicts them for their cruel mistreatment of the dearly departed. Tom's vanity is thoroughly gratified by what he overhears—indeed, he is "more in pity of himself than anybody else"—and he can barely resist "the theatrical gorgeousness" of stepping forward to relieve his aunt's misery (p. 129). With instinctive anticipation of emergent opportunities, however, Tom holds back long enough to learn that the funeral will be held if the boys do not return by Sunday, four days hence. With this sad announcement the bereaved party breaks up for the night, and aunt Polly falls into a restless sleep. Moved by pity for her evident suffering, Tom approaches her bed, the saving message in hand: "But something occurred to him, and he lingered, considering. His face lighted with a happy solution of his thought; he put the bark hastily in his pocket. Then he bent over and kissed the faded lips, and straightway made his stealthy exit, latching the door behind him" (p. 130). So much for good intentions.

As we soon learn, Tom abandons his aunt to her guilty suffering because he fears that the disclosure of his actual circumstances will threaten the success of his grandest scheme yet. It is a matter, simply, of priorities; and Tom's first priority, the "happy solution of his thought," is to attend his own funeral. The scheme is admittedly irresistible in its audacity, and the timing of its execution is perfect. Tom restrains his companions until the assembled community has worked itself into a fever of grief: "At last the whole company broke down and joined the weeping mourners in a chorus of anguished sobs, the preacher himself giving way to his feelings, and crying in the pulpit." Then, while "the minister raised his streaming eyes above his handkerchief, and stood transfixed," Tom leads the small band into the church. "First one and then another pair of eyes followed the minister's, and then almost with one impulse the congregation rose and stared while the three dead boys came marching up the aisle" (p. 141). The community's initially breathless response has the quality, one imagines, of the stunned dazzlement that would accompany the glimpse of an avatar. The minister's text, "I am the resurrection and the life" (p. 140), is still fresh in the minds of his auditors as the boys enter the room, and the unfolding of the familiar religious mystery in palpable form must seem to verge on the miraculous. At the least, the young trickster is transcendent to the extent that his seeming return from the grave confers spiritual renewal and an affirmation of unity on the gathered congregation.

> Suddenly the minister shouted at the top of his voice:
> "Praise God from whom all blessings flow—SING—and put your hearts in it!"
> And they did. Old Hundred swelled up with a triumphant burst, and while it shook the rafters Tom Sawyer the Pirate looked around upon the envying juveniles about him and confessed in his heart that this was the proudest moment of his life.
> As the "sold" congregation trooped out they said they would almost be willing to be made ridiculous again to hear Old Hundred sung like that once more. (p. 141)

It is remarkable that the sudden descent from credulous wonderment does not leave the St. Petersburg citizenry in a mood of vengeful embarrassment. They have been "sold," and they know it. Yet they are amiably—

and for the moment, even consciously—disposed to be pleased with what amounts to an admission of their immersion in bad faith. This happy brand of hypocrisy is in fact a secular *credo quia absurdum est* in which the suspension of disbelief is proportional to the perceived social dividends of knowing gullibility. The most realistic measure of resurrections, it appears, is not their demonstrable proximity to truth, but their power to affirm and enhance the common life. No one is deceived by Tom, but no one fails to be moved by his timely reenactment of the ancient fable of rebirth and regeneration. The community's resentful embarrassment at the exposure of its credulity is thus rather readily dissipated in the deeper revelation of its capacity for hope, unity, fellow feeling, and the tolerance of harmless folly. As the bearer of such gratifying news, the consummate gamesman serves briefly as a kind of high priest in a ritual affirmation of the enabling paradoxes of quotidian social life. The master and the fullest embodiment of that complex social game, Tom is temporarily immune from ordinary justice because the exposure of his scheme serves to highlight the social benefits to be derived from bad faith. He "sells" his neighbors with impunity because he leads them to an apprehension of the fact that his strategy of deceit is in fact a replica, in high relief, of the cultural status quo. The gamesman's final victory is thus to give the game away—to show his victims, in terms that they can accept, what they are.

This is not suggest that the community reaction to Tom's exploit is unmingled approbation. Bad faith will permit in one mood what it will condemn in another, and Tom has transported his neighbors to the outermost limits of their tolerance for self-knowledge. It is the telling symptom of this ambivalence that "Tom got more cuffs and kisses that day—according to Aunt Polly's varying moods—than he had earned before in a year" (p. 141). Tom's neighbors are relieved that the boys are alive, uplifted by the timely confirmation of their religious prepossessions, and exhilarated by the apparently spontaneous overflow of communal high spirits and fellow feeling. These are the very handsome returns on their readiness to be deceived. But Tom's neighbors are also obliged by their bad faith to retreat to the illusion that they are above doubleness and gullibility. It follows that some resentment will settle on Tom's evident maneuvering. In the upshot, the tension between the poles of the situation persists unchanged, but the general awareness of its pervasiveness rapidly diminishes with the return to routine preoccupations. For a brief interval, however, the terms of the culture's bad faith surface in high relief. Then, quite rapidly, and for the obvious reason that such a spectacle of antinomies is unbearable for long, the game recedes to a level comfortably beneath conscious awareness.

Meanwhile, Tom may have arrived at an enhanced appreciation of the terms of his role as St. Petersburg's preeminent gamesman. He must be a bit baffled by the effortlessness with which he has come to dominate village social play, but he cannot fail to recognize and to be exhilarated by the dramatic expansion of his power and prestige. On the other hand, he is certainly much less aware of the fact that his authority springs directly from his intuitive mastery of the arts of deception. After all, Tom is what we would be inclined—in a righteous mood—to call a hypocrite. Full self-awareness on this score would be fatal to his gamesmanship, for it would be accompanied by the onset of guilt and the erosion of confidence and manipulative élan. But bad faith is Tom's best ally when it comes to deceiving himself, as it is his leading asset as he stands in triumph before the dazzled congregation. Thus sheltered in the illusion that he is free of the impulse to deceive, Tom will continue to occupy center stage before an audience of breathlessly attentive and willingly "sold" admirers.

Notes

1. *The Adventures of Tom Sawyer*, ed. John C. Gerber, Paul Baender, and Terry Firkins, Vol. 4 of *The Works of Mark Twain* (Berkeley: Univ. of California Press, 1980), p. 33 (Mark Twain's Preface). Hereafter references to this edition will be cited parenthetically in the text.

2. *Mark Twain's America* (Cambridge, Mass.: Houghton, 1932), p. 304.

3. *Mark Twain's America*, pp. 304, 306, 307.

4. *Mark Twain and Huck Finn* (Berkeley: Univ. of California, Mass.: Harvard Univ. Press, 1962), p. 75.

5. *Mark Twain: The Development of A Writer* (Cambridge, Mass.: Harvard Univ. Press, 1962), p. 91.

6. *Mark Twain: The Fate of Humor* (Princeton, N.J.: Princeton Univ. Press, 1966), pp. 131, 146.

7. *Mark Twain: The Fate of Humor*, p. 141.

8. *Mark Twain: The Fate of Humor*, p. 147.

9. Early on in his chapter on *Tom Sawyer* in *Mark Twain: The Fate of Humor*, Cox acknowledges that the children imitate the adults of St. Petersburg: "Tom Sawyer and his gang . . . are children at play—their world is a play world in which adult rituals of love, death, war, and justice are reenacted in essentially harmless patterns" (p. 131). In the same voice, however, Cox insists on a clear distinction between Tom's "pleasure" and the adults' "dull play" (p. 141). My general position on Tom's relationship to the community and some of its details are clearly anticipated in Judith Fetterley's fine essay, "The Sanctioned Rebel," *Studies in the Novel*, 3 (1971), 293–304. Though she follows Cox in settling on a dramatic model for the analysis of Tom's role in St. Petersburg, Fetterley stresses the similarities between the attitudes and behavior of adults and children (pp. 300–301) and argues that the townspeople endure Tom's egotism and aggressiveness because he amuses them and affirms their values: "For indeed the focus of *The Adventures of Tom Sawyer* is on the harmony between Tom and his community and on the satisfactions of the symbiotic relationship between them" (p. 303).

10. Cox seems to have something like this in mind when he asserts that "in Mark Twain's world of boyhood, the imagination represents the capacity for mimicry, impersonation, make-believe, and play" (*Mark Twain: The Fate of Humor*, p. 148).

11. *Mark Twain: The Fate of Humor*, p. 141.

12. My notions about the reciprocal deception of self and others emerged haltingly

from my study of *Tom Sawyer*; but they surfaced long before I had a term for them. Thus I settled on "bad faith" belatedly, and with some misgivings. It is not a formulation that Mark Twain would have warmed to. The term is frequently used as a translation of Sartre's term *mauvaise foi*, and readers of *L'Etre et le néant* will recognize very substantial similarities between my notions and the French philosopher's much more fully developed argument. This imposing background to my own comparatively modest designs has been useful in its ways: It has tended to confirm my impression that *Tom Sawyer* is a specific cultural installment on a universal human phenomenon; and it has helped me to clarify my own thinking. But, again, my definition of "bad faith" derives from *Tom Sawyer*, and it should not be measured alongside *mauvaise foi*. Bad faith as I find it in the novel is social and cultural in its origins and operations, while *mauvaise foi* is emphatically an individual phenomenon. This fundamental difference gives rise to others, notably in the balance and tone of moral assessments. My own thinking in these areas is much closer to what I find in the descriptions and discussion of collective world building in Peter L. Berger and Thomas Luckmann, *The Social Construction of Reality* (Garden City, N.Y.: Doubleday, 1966), and, more briefly, in Peter Berger and Stanley Pullberg, "Reification and the Sociological Critique of Consciousness," *History and Theory*, 4 (1965), 196–211. I am aware that my notions about bad faith may be cognate in certain respects with such Marxian concepts as "alienation" and "false consciousness." For a very useful overview and evaluation of recent contributions, see Patrick Gardner, "Error, Faith, and Self-Deception," *Proceedings of the Aristotelian Society*, N.S. 70 (1970), 221–43. Herbert Fingarette, *Self-Deception* (London: Routledge; New York: Humanities Press, 1969), is also helpful.

13.   The parallels between my characterization of Tom Sawyer and historian John Dizikes' more general portrait of the American gamesman are numerous enough to suggest that Mark Twain's young hero was patterned after a familiar Jacksonian type. Like Tom Sawyer, the gamesman "acknowledged the rules in order to circumvent them when it suited him. Getting around, bending, or undermining the rules, without clearly breaking them, was, for the gamesman, a fundamental part of the game." Dizikes goes on to note the gamesman's skill at calculation, his tendency to work by indirection, his gravitation to "situations of ambiguity and uncertainty," and his absolute commitment to victory. Finally, all successful gamesmen expressed their "nerveless self-control" and asserted their mastery of all situations by putting on a poker face. "The poker face," Dizikes argues, "was a game face in a land where all life was treated as a game, and it was never abandoned because the game never ended" (*Sportsmen and Gamesmen* [Boston: Houghton, 1981, pp. 38–39, 42, 287).

Tom Sawyer and Children's Literature

FRED G. SEE

"Mark Twain, learning to be a river pilot in the early days in the valley! What things he must have seen, felt, heard, thought! When he wrote a real book he had to put all aside, all he had learned, felt, thought, as a man, had to go back into childhood."

Sherwood Anderson, *Dark Laughter*

In spite of Tom Sawyer's brilliance, in spite of the perfectly central place he occupies in our national literature and consciousness, he posed an interesting problem for Clemens. Tom Sawyer could not well be cast in a sequel, though Clemens tried repeatedly. It is true of course that he reappears in *Adventures of Huckleberry Finn*, in order to provide the "evasions" necessary to save Huck and Jim from the logic of a story which, without Tom's peculiar energy, could only have a tragic ending. Something allowed Clemens to use him there, with risky and ludicrous results that neutralize Huck's helplessness and Jim's misery. But even so it is almost necessary in this sequent novel for Tom to die to the fictive world he animates and rescues with his frantic play.

Clemens' other attempts to write about Tom were uninspired. Both *Tom Sawyer Abroad* (1894) and "Tom Sawyer, Detective" (1896) insist on the priority of the original novel by looking backward toward its authority as they open; and even *Huck Finn* famously recalls Tom's debut: "You don't know about me, without . . . a book by the name of 'The Adventures of Tom Sawyer.' " This is true too of the fragments "Huck Finn and Tom Sawyer Among the Indians" (1894) and "Tom Sawyer's Conspiracy" (1897–1899). Tom is an original with very uncertain future. The sequent novels depending on his energy remain satellites of their own beginning elsewhere, in a text that can be cited but never recuperated. And even *The Adventures of Tom Sawyer* itself, though it does not open reminiscently, begins by putting Tom under the power of a precedent authoritative voice, that of Aunt Polly, who loudly calls him from his mischief to a reckoning that he only just manages to evade.[1] Here too, in other words, something comes before him to constrain the experience that he struggles to determine with his will. For Tom Sawyer, personal action is always a signature; yet he always seems oddly subordinate to something else. If we conflate the gestures that

Reprinted from *Essays in Literature* 12 (Fall 1985): 251–71, copyright Western Illinois University.

inaugurate each of these texts we can identify an important aspect of their subject: none begins independently; each reacts to the precedent authority from which it struggles, but not always successfully, to free itself.

And yet these texts are also filled with the authority that is so dramatically Tom's own. Thus they always seem conflicted, the trace of some division that is not fully clear. On the one hand, Tom insists upon the exciting apparatus of action. On the other hand, we are always kept aware of the superior power set against his strenuous fantasy. Another authority always comes first, whatever he is doing. Sometimes this is Aunt Polly's summons to come and be punished; sometimes it is the logic according to which adult judgment tends to frame itself: the division of time into arbitrary periods; the need to remember rules and patterns; the rigid limits and taboos of life in St. Petersburg. Call this the power of sequence, a power which Tom is at first unable to assume convincingly and which indeed he seems to suffer both as a child and as the occasion of Clemens' writing. This is a power that counts seconds and minutes, parses social space, and articulates the burdensome social numbers and intervals which Tom sees as threatening in various degrees. It seeks to enclose him in categories and lock him into place, to bar the door to the polymorphous freedom which he expresses in his fantasies. It puzzles and opposes him by insisting on sequences that his will cannot reorder and whose beginning lies beyond him, in an authority that remains beyond his reach.[2]

Huck confronts these limits too, and so does Jim, in terrible episodes along the corrupt shores of the river, but the confrontations really begin with Tom in his adventures, and focus there in the subplot of Injun Joe and in the magnificent scenes in McDougal's Cave. Such limits often suggest numbers or amounts—Number Two, which is Injun Joe's secret meeting place; or the division of the week into days, which both prohibits (on Fridays, say) and allows (on all other days) certain kinds of adventures; or the measurement of hours and candle-stubs and bits of food that count down toward nothing as Tom and Becky languish in the darkness. This logic of sequence and measurement abuts Tom's fantastic evasiveness and is its rival in his experience, perhaps in the experience of all children. It is a measurement which means to imply that freedom and pleasure are finite, if not forbidden. There is a contradiction in Clemens' work between the self caught in sequence and measurement and the self freely expressed in fantasy and play. These are the two linked and opposing ways of ordering reality that lay claim to Tom Sawyer, and he is the border between them.

This opposition is not simple, since it constitutes a structure thanks to which rules and energies are transmitted from one generation to the next. This cultural structure understands both the need for sequence and for independent choice, and children's literature is one of the places where their bordering is revealed to us as an experience of our own lives. As a child caught between two powerful and conflicting claims on consciousness, then,

Tom represents an especially important juncture, one that we all share. His motives and his struggles along this border represent the process by which cultural patterns of meaning are signified. In America this has generally been figured as the frontier, a place that marks the difference between civilized laws and natural freedom to choose for oneself. But in Tom's case this frontier is something rather different, something not entirely geographical: it is the condition of childhood, the place where the child's power is measured against its will by the limits of adulthood. I want to go on to discuss Tom Sawyer as an instance of the literary child, and to suggest a very broad way in which he, like all such children, reflects the arduous coherence of culture. In doing this I will begin by putting some considerable stress on Tom's innocent character. But in the end, never fear, Tom will evade this weight, just as he does all the others that seek to oppress him. Determine him as we may, Tom Sawyer is a border that remains open.

For a moment, however, I want to translate Tom's dilemma into theoretical terms, in order to suggest the broadest possible application of that dilemma and to generalize briefly about children's literature. According to recent theories of meaning (and of culture), the algorithm $\frac{S}{s}$ allows signification (say, the process of literary representation) to be understood as the systematic result of mutually related opposites.[3] This algorithm allows us to compute the variously differing pressures and events of our universe, which can thereby resolve into a limited number of patterns within any culture, subjectivity, or text. Thus for instance the complex relationships between children and adults, or for that matter in any coupling of differences, can be calculated thanks to the rule which meaning follows as it seeks out form.

The peculiarly American confrontation of wilderness and civilization across the frontier that separates and joins them is an instance of this algorithm. On one side is the power which tends to become monolithic as it reproduces itself in the coordinates and grammars that allow us to find our way into and through culture. On the other side is the powerful tendency which holds the question of value open to a variety of possibilities. The frontier between these two is tense, whether it is wilderness and chart or Signified and signifier that meet at the point of juncture. And moreover it is a condition of any such frontier that it should fray and change, constantly shift and relax before pressures of many kinds. Yet it is always there. It separates mutually exclusive and remorselessly different ways of judging or knowing, which can nevertheless be expressed and related by means of this structure of meaning. Contemporary theoretical approaches to meaning ask us to accept this algorithm as irreducible.

But can such a place of transformation ever be considered as being irreducible? There is perhaps nothing more primal in human culture; but does the algorithm adequately express the complex activity that goes on at the place of the frontier within the sign? Or, to put it another way, if we examine the structure of the algorithm itself ("Any mechanical or repetitive computational procedure," is the way *The American Heritage Dictionary* simplifies the term), can we see more complex components to the opposition which occurs just at the rim of either's capacity? The *barre* or barrier, for instance, which limits the roles of Signified and signifier, seems to contain the force of either. Yet the algorithm suggests anything but an energetic relationship. It does not represent the sign as a meeting of mutual energies. It seems instead to be monolithic: for Saussure, as Jacques Lacan says, that line between S and s is "an impassable gap,"[4] and the algorithm reveals the extent to which the thematics of modern linguistics is "suspended . . . at the primordial position of the signifier and the signified as being distinct orders separated initially by a barrier resisting signification."[5]

Lacan more than any other structuralist thinker has come to terms with the border which resists signification, and his sense of what occurs at this juncture within the sign is remarkably far-ranging. It has essentially to do with psychoanalysis rather than with literature *per se*. Nevertheless, his understanding of the *barre* illuminates basic literary questions and generalizes structures with which literature also concerns itself, in particular (for my argument here) the development of the child's personality and the nature of subjectivity. The idea that the *barre* divides different modes of knowing as radically opposed as representation and reality, or adult and child, develops from the more obvious conclusion that the barrier between Signifier and signified can also be understood as the line between conscious and unconscious thinking. It has also been suggested that the *barre* represents repression: the alienation of desire, or its censorship by law; or the division between the real and the symbolic; or between thought and that which signifies thought. If so it is an essentially mythic joining and division, the place where mythic narratives focus to explain the fundamental split in our reality; a place—the place—within man's consciousness and language where our distance from our own instincts is inscribed.[6] Thus it is we ourselves who are both divided and unified by this apparently irreducible mark of our doubleness. This division therefore indicates the differences, and the relationship, between the order of law and the force of private will. It is the point at which we choose without knowing it a life not ordered but broken by calendars and statutes; and gain a language ruled by grammatical combinations rather than by the overbearing clarity of the child's first vocabulary, urgent single words to suit immediate needs and desires. All such mystified conditions of wholeness (one might almost call them the conditions of childhood) are made impossible or irrecoverable along this border, at the line of division between the exemptions we first offer to the child, and only later proscribe.

But more exactly, how or where does this struggle of differences take place? Can they be given a narrative form as well as an algorithmic one? Lacan argues that "signifier and signified are two networks of relations which do not overlap," though something called a "multiple interplay" takes place between these two aspects of the sign—which nonetheless remain autonomous.[7] It is this interplay I wish to explore, in the sense that any sign consists of the relationship between a value which makes it part of a system of rules, and a different value which allows instinct to express itself without regard to logical rule. We might well call these the order of the adult and the order of the child, which coexist in our personalities and in many of our literary texts. Neither can yield fully to the other, that is not in their natures. But as with any two bound opposites, a signifying field is created between their energies; and here they negotiate the result of their differences from one another. This result is what we recognize as a sign. It expresses, among other things, the opposition between culture and instinct—the border where childhood becomes aware of itself as different and separate from adult power.

Take for instance the texts we call children's literature, texts which privilege the child as a central subject. This literature ranges from poems as simple as "Ring Around the Rosie" to novels as sophisticated as *What Maisie Knew*. Where in either would one look to find the "multiple interplay" that the child—the subject at the *barre*, the border where meaning or value begins to assume a structure—represents? Where do instinct and law conjoin in the literary child, and how, to signify the importance of their own coupling? In Maisie herself, no doubt. She is first the ward of a court decree, and then the audience of sexual license, so that a "wretched infant" becomes a figure "around about whom the complexity of life would . . . turn to fineness, to richness."[8] Maisie registers the forces poised on either side of the *barre*, law and instinct, by "drawing some stray fragrance of an ideal across the scent of selfishness, by sowing on barren strands, through the mere fact of presence, the seed of moral life" (p. viii). She is all opposites—one of James's signs for the interplay of natural and cultural energies, consciousness on a border which will dissolve only with "the death of her childhood," when inevitably, James says, "her situation will change and become another affair, subject to other measurements and with a new centre altogether" (p. xi).

"Ring Around the Rosie" encodes activity on this same border, though in a somewhat different way. According to Iona and Peter Opie the rhyme in unlikely to date from a time earlier than 1881, but they (though disapprovingly) hint at "origin-citers" who "say that the rhyme goes back to the days of the Great Plague. A rosy rash, they allege, was a symptom of the plague, posies of herbs were carried as protection, sneezing was a final fatal symptom, and 'all fall down' was exactly what happened." In fact this reading of the text seems more plausible than the Opies' bare suggestion that the rhyme is only a "dramatic singing game."[9] So it is indeed, but to what end? Something impelled it, made it general, handed it across generations, represented some popular choice both to invent and preserve—and this resides not in any conceivable content, since it seems on the surface to be gibberish, but rather in the fact that we keep it in custody for children to come; we love not only to play it as children but to teach it, and not because it serves any evident purpose. Its purpose has in fact almost been forgotten, as is the case with British hobby-horse games, which are traditional and cohesive formulas that signify communal bonding and ritual.[10] So too I suspect with "Ring Around the Rosie," which seems to me to show how children's texts encode and order certain threats. For example: we are told that plague deaths amounted to at least fifty per cent of the population of Europe, perhaps much more. The effect on survivors was unmistakably pronounced. G. G. Coulton mentions the "loosening of all social ties" and an extreme "hardness of heart," to which he adds the confusion and despair caused by an affliction that could neither be prevented nor cured nor even avoided: nothing about the Black Death, neither cause nor effect, could be rationalized; it caused the achievement of a culture's reasoning to suffer a general collapse.[11] Boccaccio writes of the fearful and superstitious flight of survivors: "Men and women without number abandoned the city, their houses and estates . . . in search of a country place," many of them sickened and died where they fell; "what is more serious and almost incredible, parents avoided visiting and nursing their own children."[12] In this terrible confusion "even the reverend authority of divine and human law had almost crumbled and fallen into decay. . . . As a result everyone had leave to do as he saw fit" (p. xxvi).

This widespread failure of institutions and social patterns, in fact of all law and rational order, must have reduced the law of meaning to its most desperate and divided rudiments. Under these conditions the order of language as well as culture might very likely fall into a terrible simplicity just proximate to instinct. Of course I am speculating, but what would be preserved until last might well have been the need to protect one's children: to ensure their survival from the specter of adult neglect, which according to Coulton was becoming general; or simply from the parents' disappearance in a landscape of pestilent and licentious horror, through which, Boccaccio reports, the population at large "ran wild . . . and there was no one to prevent them" (p. xxv), "giving themselves free rein in lewdness and debauchery" (p. xxvi): "Out of sheer necessity," he tells us, "quite different customs arose among the survivors from original laws" (p. xxvii). This was a cultural crisis which seemed before men's eyes to be undoing the pattern of laws, god-ordained and politically enforced, that distinguishes man from his own natural ferocity. Any such crisis might well return human behavior to the region of the *barre*, that hypothetical place where law first couples with instinct and where instinct always thereafter seeks release. At this point the logic of any culture would become brilliantly simple, would it not?

Here, thanks to the degradation of cultural patterns and the arousal of new license (since repression is beginning to weaken under the conditions of crisis which Boccaccio describes), we may sense the depth where the first rule of culture was enforced and is now being forgotten and perhaps reinscribed. What better place for the reinscription than the text of a game which puts the child's importance and pleasure together at the center of things?

and which encodes all the evidence of danger in the rhythm of a dance? And a text, moreover, which—our own experience has already shown—can never be lost to memory: the text represents the very structure of memory; in a sense, it is our memory. What then would the rhyme be saying to the future?—"If you see these things, rashes, violent coughing, bunches of herbs, piles of bodies, stay away. Remember this!"

But what do *we* instruct when we teach "Ring Around the Rosie" to our children? If not the danger of the plague, and of course not, then at least we teach the possibility of teaching, and of learning, the rule of knowledge which persists as a hedge against any such danger as Boccaccio describes. The game preserves the possibility of ordering and remembering knowledge, and this preserves the race; it keeps structure alive. The pattern of the game draws a circle that can shut death and misrule out. The circle and the dance and the doggerel are not only order and rule, they are the possibility of order and rule. On the other side, facing them, is the loss of all rhyme, and reason. This is an instance of what can happen at the *barre*, when the custodians of knowledge see their authority set at hazard, as instinct and randomness and annihilation are mysteriously released against them by some power outside of reason. Already we are seeking, under the authority of a federal agency, a mythic or folkloric "method to prevent human interference with repositories [of nuclear waste] during the first 10,000 years after their closure," which future generations (so distant that their language will be wholly alien to any we now know) might, had they forgotten its danger, tamper with; and release a deadlier plague.[13] We need to remember sometimes that the law of signs can sequester us in safety, as well as repress us.

So "Ring Around the Rosie" works, apart from its content (which is really mnemonic skill set against the loss of logical order) just as "The House That Jack Built" does. It teaches us the possibility of its own form, and thus of all formal order. It links together a related series which suggests the barest outline of social rule—an enchainment made up of a domestic place, a couple of institutions (marriage, a priesthood), an economy, and the possibility of hedging against predators like rats and stray dogs. Jack's text is scarcely rich in event, but it is inexhaustibly fascinating (the Opies cite versions in print for the last 150 years, but concede a much more substantial antiquity).[14]

This is one aspect of children's literature: the tendency of the text to represent its own order, to preserve and insist upon the grammar by which things can always combine. This is something we require to be taught. The alternate axis of children's literature reverses the polarity of the same structure, privileging instinct in the form of fantasies powerful enough to dissolve rational limits, at least temporarily, in order to escape confining (and sometimes lethal) logical categories. *A Thousand and One Nights* works like this; so do C. S. Lewis' Narnia Chronicles. Such texts put the order of logic under the power of dreams and wishes, things we know without learning. Sometimes the resistance to such fantasies comes in the personified form of adult law-givers, tyrants who represent the obsessive rule of rational thought: for instance the violent and lustful King Shahryar, who is beguiled by the inventions of Shahrazad; or any number of wicked kings and queens, aunts and great-aunts, beadles, headmasters, or uncomprehending parents. Or sometimes this force of law, which signifies without self-interrogation and therefore with no sense of its own logic or motive, is also present symbolically as the pressure of winter or drought, entropy or obstinate unyielding flow, figures of punishment or dread or death that bar the door to the ecstasy of risk and mark the limit to eccentric freedom.

"To Think That I Saw It On Mulberry Street," the first book published by Dr. Seuss, is a good example of a children's text which turns the other way to celebrate instinct over the order of logic. The young hero is interrogated by his stern father, who daily quizzes him about what he sees on the way home from school. Was it only a horse and a wagon on Mulberry Street? The father presses the boy to report more and more of what he sees, to keep his eyes open, to observe and remember, to define and justify his place in the world in terms of a detailed and sequential narrative. Nothing. A horse and a wagon. So he embroiders, initially to satisfy the law. His fantasy adds exotic animals, a chariot, a band, the city fathers, a police escort, airplanes, esoterica of all kinds. They are chained together loosely as a parade, but they come from an imagination which displaces whatever real people or events the boy might have seen. The paternal command to observe objectively is forgotten in the delight of an original response, and blinds the son to the logic the father insists that he find. Instinct enjoys its own power to construct an alternate world; it keeps the coldly judicial interrogation at a distance—for a while. When he returns home the rule of law, reduced here to a very simple image of paternal power, but strong enough to cancel the memory of play, obliterates his instinct for free invention. He forgets everything he has created in his own private space. But for a brief time, the child's freedom has escaped the logic of adult law into a place of ecstatic play.

I wonder if these opposing modes do not suggest an epistemological border which is embodied in children's literature, which strives both to insist on the order of law and to find ways around it. Children's literature serves a cultural necessity (if this is true) by teaching not only law, but the possibility of law; and a deep subjective necessity, by teaching not only the pleasure but the function of evasive fantasy. On either side the genre answers a need— of culture, and of the self; it lets us know where the wild things are, and the way back. As a genre it provides a frontier across which crucial negotiations take place. The law of logical chaining makes its case at the expense of imaginative play; the freedom of private fantasy displaces the enchainment of brute facts. In the extremest form fantasy exerts itself against law, or law moves to override imagination. But the lesson is never, or at least seldom, one or the other; more typically it is their response to one another's claim on consciousness. The border is therefore never a simple *barre*. It is not an irreducible line of confrontation or repression, or of merely pathological release. It is a depth of field where we experience in perspective the struggle that is the meaning and value of culture, and of the self. This struggle inheres in all signs, however apparently simple they may be, since without such an orderly exchange our experience of the universe would be hopelessly divided between ideas that could never be represented, and isolated facts beyond our comprehension. *The Adventures of Tom Sawyer* is an especially interesting children's book because it allows both of these tendencies to seek their limits, and then implies the result of their balance.

Take for instance the opening chapters, which sketch a tendency developed by the adventures to follow. Here we see Tom alternately encountering and evading an authority which is as absolute in this St. Petersburg as in the Czar's, for instance in the episode that concludes Chapter I and caps our first experience of him. This is his fight with a dandy, epitomizing Tom's own struggle with the demands of culture. Tom meets a mysterious stranger, "a boy a shade larger than himself" ("shade" implies both degree, and apparition) whose costume is "simply astounding":

> His cap was a dainty thing, his close-buttoned blue cloth roundabout was new and natty, and so were his pantaloons. He had shoes on—and it was only Friday. He even wore a necktie, a bright bit of ribbon. He had a citified air about him that ate into Tom's vitals. [15]

And yet this early and rudimentary version of Niklaus in *The Mysterious Stranger*, in whom Tom instinctively recognizes a rival, is precisely as obstinate and belligerent as Tom himself. Their confrontation begins with an exchange of threats and insults and proceeds to the business at hand, the establishment of a border—"Tom drew a line in the dust with his big toe" (p. 24)—which each instantly attempts to violate. The two of them stand face to face, "each with a foot placed at an angle as a brace, and both shoving with might and main, and glowering at each other with hate" (p. 23). Their motion reveals their relationship, and suggests the central relationships on which the novel is predicated: the opposition of equally energetic forces, conformity and instinct: "If one moved, the other moved—but only sidewise, in a circle" (p. 21).

If Tom wins the fight, and forces his dandified antagonist to " 'Holler 'nuf,' " it is only in order that the same struggle might shift to new places and repeat itself (in the confrontation where Tom plays one role and Injun Joe another, for example, in the cave). Driven off, this boy treacherously hits Tom with a stone prudently cast from a distance. Chased farther away, he continues his part in the opposition from the safety of his home. Tom "held a position at the gate for some time, daring the enemy to come outside, but the enemy only made faces at him through the window and declined," until the law of this border forces a suspension of the conflict: "the enemy's mother appeared, and called Tom a bad, vicious, vulgar child, and ordered him away." When Tom climbs through his own window late that night he is ambushed by his aunt, the same authority in another relationship to the subject child, and her power translates his freedom into servitude: "When she saw the state his clothes were in her resolution to turn his Saturday holiday into captivity at hard labor became adamantine in its firmness" (p. 25).

What (to paraphrase James) is life without windows? or without adamant? These are the opposing images whose implications bracket Tom's world as the book moves on to the portals and rock of the cave. Chapter II deals with his celebrated transformation of the fence in need of whitewashing. This border is conceptual as well as literal, an image representing the difference between the punitive duty imposed by adult law and time which would otherwise be spent freely, according to Tom's own sense of play. This border allows him to discover the necessary skill of the confidence man, and to turn a rich profit in the wealth of childhood—besides an apple, a kite, a dead rat and a piece of string, he acquires

> twelve marbles, part of a jews harp, a piece of blue bottle-glass to look through, a spool cannon, a key that wouldn't unlock anything, a fragment of chalk, a glass stopper of a decanter, a tin soldier, a couple of tadpoles, six fire-crackers, a kitten with only one eye, a brass door-knob, a dog-collar—but no dog—the handle of a knife, four pieces of orange-peel, and a dilapidated old window sash. (pp. 32–33)

Clemens draws one conclusion for us: "Work consists of whatever a body is *obliged* to do, and . . . play consists of whatever a body is not obliged to do" (p. 33). Tom has found the "great law of human action," Clemens says, "without knowing it." His manipulation of St. Petersburg youth is still innocent; the darker meaning of borders is not revealed until much later, when Tom discovers the genuine treasure that replaces this trash, and the place of real peril of which this border is only a white-washed version. But already he begins to understand that play is not only amusement, but also free movement, oscillation between opposing limits; and that borders can be places of opportunity as well as restriction.[16]

Meanwhile, something inheres in the rubble Tom has garnered. Most of it consists of the fragments of the adult power which these children have not yet achieved in its fullness, cast-off signs of the privileges forbidden to the young: a key, a door-knob, the handle (but not the blade) of a knife, and the stopper of a decanter. These suggest differences between what is and is not safe. The toy cannon and soldier and the fire-crackers point to the professional scale of violence which opens to Tom at the end of the novel, when West Point seems a likely academy for his training. Especially we see the currency of the window, here represented by a sash, appear over and over—the stranger with whom Tom fights retreats behind one, Tom slips in and out of them; ways in and out of enclosures abound in the novel, and it is no wonder that locks and door-knobs and window-sashes make up part of the symbolic wealth of the town's children. They stand for both the adult's power to control space and the child's fascination with escape. They are the barriers and apertures of the domestic and institutional structures of village life.[17] Later, in other forms, this lovely junk associates to more powerful events. A dead cat is instrumental in drawing Huck and Tom to the graveyard where they witness the murder; the knife and the liquor reappear there also. A length of string is of some use to Tom in the cave, and there are locked doors everywhere. The cast-off rubbish conveys a sense of the local borders between adult life, a region where power is immediate, and the life of the child, where it is only represented. For adults these tokens of authority are real. For children they are merely symbolic. Or say that these frayed and worthless scraps, payment by those who wish to approach a fence made attractive by the illusion of responsibility, are evidence of the erosive activity along the *barre*. The fence calls forth scraps of meaning, broken or partial signs of culture's power. Authority in St. Petersburg objectifies itself in these tokens violently separated from adult life. They reverse the expression of authority: here, approaching Tom's fence, they assume an opposite use— they dissolve duty as an experience of law. If one understands the law of borders, and Tom begins to, one may move either way across its field, and, for example, make play of the signs of duty and law.[18]

But gradually the novel discloses the power of logic, too, by transforming Tom's seemingly aimless career of fun into first-hand experience of the terrible and unmalleable limits at either end of any play; and the images of power, of weapons and of open and closed portals, become urgent rather than playful standards of measurement. Childhood is a condition where adult authority is not only made symbolic but comes real, that is to say. The duded-up boy is only a symbol of the adult persona. Injun Joe is the monstrous radical truth of adult power, an expression of the violence which the adult may, if he chooses, unleash.[19] Childhood itself is the bordering condition where the meaning of culture tends to break apart, as we see in the episode of the fence; but also to become brilliantly simple and powerful. Meaning can move either way. Tom and his friends translate adulthood into games which are metaphors of the culture they are not yet ready to accept as a pattern of restrictions and loss. But they are gradually being initiated into the meaning of what Aunt Polly delivers as a "grim chapter of Mosaic law, as from Sinai," that is, as graven in stone (p. 44), adamantine, authority so far beyond interrogation, and at the same time so inescapably stipulated, that it signifies adult experience as suffering under the dread of numbered commandments. This authority is chiefly given into the hands of institutions, families, the church, the school, and the judicial system; and individuals are typically reduced either to prisoners or to criminals—or to children—in these institutional places.

But individuals can also partake of such power and wield it. During Sunday worship Tom uses a fly, and then a beetle, to amuse himself; and in school he and Joe Harper, in order to "pass the dreary time" (p. 82), inflict the experience of bordering on a captive tick:

> . . . he put Joe's slate on the desk and drew a line down the middle of it from top to bottom.
>
> "Now," said he, "as long as he is on your side you can stir him up and I'll let him alone; but if you let him get away and get on my side, you're to leave him alone as long as I can keep him from crossing over."
>
> "All right, go ahead; start him up."
>
> The tick escaped Tom, presently, and crossed the equator. Joe harassed him a while, and then he got away and crossed back again. This change of base occurred often . . . the tick tried this, that, and the other course, and got as excited and anxious as the boys themselves. . . . (pp. 83–84)

Whatever freedom there seems to be on one side or the other of this border between the power of two children is only an illusion. Like adults, they only pass on their own burden of boredom or anxiety to the creature they bedevil; just as they receive an arbitrary experience of authority themselves and transform it into what they call their play, which seems to offer choice but does not. Their play is encircled by a power they can never escape, and always reflects this authority. Duty and freedom are thus not wholly distinct modes, as the boys first believe. They are opposites related by the energy of bordering, the process that drives all signs. (Later, for example in "The Great Dark," this traverse of an equatorial ground will take on a more clearly metaphysical meaning, when Clemens suggests that we labor under the scrutiny of an all-powerful divinity who watches us cross the illuminated circle of his microscope as we move out of and back into the shadows.)

All this is to say that Clemens is interested in the process of childhood, not a static representation. *The Adventures of Tom Sawyer* is an episodic work, to be sure. Still there is a development of themes going on. The same pattern reappears over and over; but it modifies according to a law.[20] The structure of the limitations which Tom learns begins as something inconsequential, and he can easily enough appropriate the rubble of its signs; but after the violations he and Huck witness in the graveyard—corpse-robbing, desecration, murder, blasphemy, betrayal, false oaths—their play increasingly yields to the adult pressures it has only been imitating, and time weighs as heavily all week long as it does during the sermons on Sunday.[21] This new and secret knowledge begins the end of their play with false wealth, the fragments of adult power. Clemens begins to draw them toward measureable, not imaginary, value, and in order that they may merit it, toward desperately real adventures which make the pleasure of their games of piracy and robbery fade. These adventures reveal the deep secret, hidden from children and from most adults, which Clemens means to make Tom encounter.

We can see this happening as Tom's play becomes more and more burdensome, shadowed by sickness as well as terror. His afflictions are numerous after the scene of violation. Rebuffed by Becky, he runs off with Joe and Huck, but that illusion quickly loses its appeal. On their return the boys witness their own funeral and rejoin the community in a kind of triumph, but this is no more an escape from the threats looming over them than is the interlude on Jackson's Island. In other words, Tom is not returned to a state of childhood, or reborn after the enactment of his death to a world essentially different from the one he sought to escape. Childhood fantasy is lost to Tom over the duration of this threat. He has become merely vulnerable; like the insect on the slate, he is only somewhere in-between. When summer recess arrives, then, that interlude between an end and a beginning of boredom and discipline, it offers problems rather than distractions. "The dreadful secret of the murder was a chronic misery [that is, an affliction in and of time]. It was a very cancer for permanency and pain" (p. 213). For two weeks Tom is sick, "dead to the world and its happenings" (p. 213). He recovers from this second enactment of death to find his childhood world much reformed by a revival, and "he alone of all the town . . . lost, forever and forever" (p. 214). Once again loss is not followed by a regeneration. The experiment with the tick is recalled specifically, perhaps, in his terror under the "terrific storm" which strikes while he is thus "lost" and convinces him that "he had taxed the forebearance of the powers above . . . It might have seemed to him a waste of pomp and ammunition to kill a bug with a battery of artillery, but there seemed nothing incongruous about the getting up such an expensive thunderstorm as this to knock the turf from under an insect like himself" (p. 214). And then he relapses again into yet another sickness, which precedes his greatest and most perilous adventure.

Much deadens Tom's capacity for pleasure during this awful summer, much contaminates his play. Episodes of weakness abound; the danger of adult crime and revenge and power everywhere encroaches on the dimension of childhood experience. Their responsibility for Muff Potter torments Tom and Huck. The menace of Injun Joe haunts them. Nothing seems simple, and Tom drifts away from his old capacity for play among the fragments of adulthood. Knowing what he knows, he moves directly away from the scenes of play into the next chapter, which concerns Muff's trial, a trial which threatens real consequences, for a murder the accused did not commit; and Tom finds that he has the sanctity of adult institutional power in his custody.

His heroic behavior at the trial and after it is part of his usual pattern of experience: alternating torment under adult law and childish glory as law is evaded and becomes play, freedom from extremes. His "days were days of splendor and exultation to him, but his nights were seasons of horror"

(p. 225). The logic of what must happen—the threat is the threat of death, measured by the avenger who defines and limits their fantasy—holds both boys "in the same state of wretchedness and terror" (p. 225). Death is becoming more and more real, play less and less consoling. All the adult knowledge of secret violence and sin afflicts them now, and is represented by the motifs associated to Injun Joe. Dread, worry, the weight and pressure of time that always seems to be running out or closing in, all these concerns impose themselves. We need to notice how typically Injun Joe suggests counting and the measured pattern of time, since such enchainment of the barest facts of perception and the inescapable logic of cause and effect constitutes their dread of his power as much as his violations do. Their horror, which is also his epistemology, takes on the form of the moments that pass and diminish the distance of his terrible advent. What he represents to them is not so much any particular reprisal as the realization that punishment and dread can be calculated, counted, and counted on as a base of experience, that the power of sequence can take precedence over the free time of their fantasy.

This calculation involves them in its own mode of linking and numbering the successive moments in their lives, which are no longer free of his awful vitality. And this awareness brings with it the understanding that the logic of adults can be more powerful than any strategies of evasion. It is not only the half-breed's association to primal license that makes him so formidable. It is also his relentless numbering, more terrible than Captain Hook's but of the same order, a destruction that signals and measures its own approach, passing second by second by second. It is this which turns him away from the simple vagrancy that is not so different from Huck's and gives him a place from which to plot numerically exact strategies of cruelty and punishment. Now he is the enemy upon whose calculus we all must wait, as Huck does, whether we follow him to spy or stay to suffer his violence. "Ten o'clock came. . . . Eleven o'clock came. . . . Huck waited what seemed a weary long time, but nothing happened" (p. 246). Then he follows the criminals, drawn by what he cannot resist, "allowing them to keep just far enough ahead." They "moved up the river street three blocks," and as Huck follows them he "closed up and shortened his distance . . . then slackened his pace, fearing he was gaining too fast." The "beating of his own heart" measures his terror, then "a man cleared his throat not four feet from him!" (p. 265). Huck shakes "as if a dozen agues had taken charge of him at once," but knows now exactly where he is in relation to his threat in the darkness that draws him on, "within five steps" (p. 266). And then he hears that Injun Joe has calculated his resentment and revenge:" 'It ain't a millionth part of it!' " that the widow's husband had him jailed—he had him horse-whipped too, like a slave.

Ten, eleven, a dozen, three four, five, millions and millions—Huck and Tom approach something other than youth along this series of episodes.

The sequence is a movement which is anything but "play." It concerns itself not only with the burden of time and numbers, but over and over again with an encroachment tallied in hours and steps and the fractions of a boy's pulse, so that even the most exciting adventure must be carried on under the shadow of fear and anxiety: "When they reached the haunted house [where they go to look for treasure] there was something so weird and grisly about the dead silence that reigned there . . . and something so depressing about the loneliness and desolation of the place, that they were afraid, for a moment" (p. 239). In another moment these fears will be exactly signified by that arithmetical monster, Injun Joe, and his companion.

Huck's involvement with Injun Joe culminates in a febrile delirium that echoes Tom's earlier illness, and also spreads outward to infect the entire village. St. Petersburg feels "sickening disappointment" (p. 281) each time Tom and Becky seem to have been found, and are not; "All the long afternoon the village seemed empty and dead" (p. 280), and the burden of time which Tom and Huck have kept secret begins to generalize as the power of brute logic threatens the power of play: "Three dreadful days and nights dragged their tedious hours along, and the village sank into a hopeless stupor. No one had heart for anything" (p. 281). The events which are nearly simultaneous in action, but which the narrative alternates—Huck's discovery of Injun Joe's plot and the immurement of Tom and Becky—unify St. Petersburg as nothing else, not even the revival or the trial, has been able to do. Whatever value these losses signify must be both more central and universally shared: something deep and serious is hazarded by the tense penultimate movement of the novel.

Meanwhile, with Becky's return from a journey "Both Injun Joe and the treasure sunk into secondary importance for a moment." The problem is still measured, but now it is under the influence of childish games which come briefly with her presence to provide "an exhausting good time" (p. 259). Tom balances his plans with her against the plan to spy on Injun Joe, which he and Huck have secretly plotted: "The sure fun of the evening outweighed the uncertain treasure; and boy like, he determined to yield to the stronger inclination" (p. 261)—certain against doubtful pleasure. And so the remarkable adventure of the cave begins, as play sets tactics aside and the inclination toward "sure fun" ignores the numbering of steps which Tom has delegated to Huck.

After their picnic, the children approach the cave and enter its "opening shaped like an A," like the entrance to the alphabet. The cave seems abecedarian; it seduces its visitors with the illusion of a beginning that is known and shared by all those who inhabit the place of culture. "Its massive oaken door stood unbarred" (p. 262); authority allows itself to lapse here at a border which has been traversed times without number, which allows itself both to imply and to limit the experience of unknown depths. Its effect is "romantic and mysterious" (p. 262); the children at play in this place "were astonished to find that they had been taking no note of time" (p. 263). Within, Tom and Becky visit "the familiar wonders of the cave . . . dubbed with rather over-descriptive names, such as 'The Drawing Room,' 'The Cathedral,' 'Aladdin's Place,' " and so on. The upper regions of the cave play on the illusion offered by the abecedarian portal. They are covered with a "tangled webwork of names, dates, post-office addresses and mottoes," all according to some logic the same scripture, written on the walls with candle-smoke. In this region time and space are appropriated by personality: the tangled web is historical and social; it coordinates an identity which is shared rather than secret. But it is the region below that matters more, that founds personality itself; though that is not yet clear.

Tom and Becky move on from this upper place, "drifting" (like Huck on the raft), and scarcely realize "that they were now in a part of the cave whose walls were not frescoed" (p. 283). Here they write their own names on the wall, and this marks a new limit; no one else has gone this far into the interior of the cave, which is, in spite of its inviting and familiar opening, "a vast labyrinth of crooked aisles that ran into each other and out again and led nowhere . . . [an] intricate tangle of rifts and chasms" which the "tangled webwork" of the upper region only represents, and inadequately at that: there is, there must be, a web below the web, a tangle beneath the tangle, something made accessible but also diminished by the public language that is only its upper region. One might, it is said, move endlessly in these depths, "go down, and down, and still down, into the earth . . . labyrinth underneath labyrinth, and no end to any of them." Parties of visitors are "unable to elude each other for the space of half an hour without going beyond the 'known' ground," but there is always another depth of this border which has not yet been crossed, somewhere beyond or below, which, like the cave itself, is inexhaustibly complex: "No man 'knew' the cave. That was an impossible thing . . . Tom Sawyer knew as much of the cave as anyone" (p. 263).

The disappearance of Tom and Becky into these depths draws the town after them, to a point but to no purpose. Tom is beyond their measurement in the place of his trial. He penetrates past the familiar and romantic portals of selfhood, beyond what can ever be communal, beyond the power of authority to claim and define, even beyond his own ability to chart. On one side of this frontier, once he finally confronts the perspective afforded by its depths, is what has always already been inscribed and made known, what is as familiar as the alphabet, what can be shared and judged. On the other side is a place that has not yet even been romanticized, beyond the most serious efforts of the village to locate: "remotenesses of the cavern were being ransacked that had never been visited before . . . every corner and crevice was going to be thoroughly searched" (pp. 280–281), but Tom is (as usual) somewhere else, outside the range of any such search, in the place of peril and discovery which his games and mischief have only imitated up to now.[22]

This is the deepest depth and extent of the border, " 'all a mixed-up crook-edness' " (p. 285) where days cannot be counted (p. 294) and nothing orga-nizes the mystery of an immense and immediate meaning: " 'Oh, Tom, you didn't make any marks!' " (p. 287). Time is beyond estimation here. So is direction. So are numbers.[23]

But Tom is energized here. This becomes his place. If he knows "as much of the cave as anyone" it is because the depth is congenial to him. It is the best possible scene for his evasions of adult power (a condition which we have already realized is only a metaphor of genuine wisdom and authority) because it is the best possible scene for a confrontation with adult logic. Here Tom finds the need for measurement arising out of fantasy, and evasion a means of learning to count on his own terms. He will manage to elude authority, after all. But in this deepest episode, where he encounters adult power at its grimmest and most beastly—where the feral depth of all behavior is revealed—his heroism and adventure are no reenactments. They have no precedent in his reading. They are spontaneous and all his own: they are play become real, play testing the limits of human endurance with human life at stake.

We all know what happens. No simple logic or fantasy helps him to escape. First Tom must show his skill at improvisation; that is, independence of action. Better an impromptu effort than to "bear the weight of the heavy time in idleness" (p. 293). In his pocket he finds a kite-string. (Is it the one he acquires in exchange for a chance to whitewash the fence?) With it he begins to explore. At first of course he finds not an escape but a limitation, most horribly Injun Joe, whose association with the passage of heavy time now becomes more clear: both limit Tom's freedom to evade. But he is "willing to risk Injun Joe and all other terrors" (p. 294) as well as the "bodings of coming doom" (p. 295) which so relentlessly close in to engulf him. Huck in his own darkness feels it too, this counting down of moments running out, their awful concatenation in a series which ends not in wealth but in zero and threatens to close out life.

But Tom finds a way around the problem. He can evade the logical privilege which mortifies Huck's freedom. The enchainment of rules and the reification of passing time are terrible: " 'The widder eats by a bell; she goes to bed by a bell; she gits up by a bell—everything's so awful reg'lar a body can't stand it' " (p. 323). This is precisely as terrible as the apathy that Tom feels in the cave; but Tom in that place shows us his ability to transcend enclosures. The cave becomes not a limit but a dimension of testing where Tom discovers and evades an absolute entrapment, the fullest and most grotesque aspect of adult law; and then he turns back toward a middle ground.

The entrance of McDougal's Cave comes under adult law, finally, if its depths do not. The law stipulates that not even Tom, who knows so much of it—now more than ever—is to be admitted to this place again, where something so precious has nearly been lost to brute chance, to drifting; but he has discovered a way around the law in its social as well its feral manifestation. The cave appals the custodians of boundaries, who bring Tom back from his dangerous freedom to a system of rules where patterns can be formally taught and learned. Judge Thatcher "hoped to see Tom a great lawyer or a great soldier some day. He said he meant to look to it that Tom should be admitted to the National Military Academy and afterward trained in the best law school in the country, in order that he might be ready for either career or both" (pp. 321–322). But Tom, resilient with his secret experience of the cave, allows he wouldn't mind going in again. The Judge knows (what adult does not?) that " 'there are others like you, Tom. . . . But. . . . Nobody will get lost in that cave any more.' " Law seeks to enforce itself with the most arbitrary of limits: " 'Because I had its big door sheathed with boiler iron two weeks ago, and triple-locked—and I've got the keys' " (p. 299–300).

Judge Thatcher's concern is clear enough, and he responds as power so typically does—with a prohibition like that laid down by Sleeping Beauty's father. But it is also, perhaps, the danger of Tom's ability to turn the cave inside out that provokes authority to signify itself as edict, rather than as an initiation into the secret places of nature sought out by the child (Becky's examination of the Schoolmaster's forbidden book is another case in point). What does the law against spinning wheels mean to the kingdom of the doting, all-powerful father? An end to spinning, and thus to weaving; therefore an end to renewal: entropy. Under this law everything must wear out. The preservation of tradition, and of power by those who already possess it, and with whom tradition and power must therefore die rather than be shared, is the real function of this law that blinds itself to the child's freedom to strive and to risk. Better death than your competence, this is partly what the father's edict implies.

But there is no bottom to Tom's place of transformation and evasion, where whatever happens remains hidden from these adults. He folds the power of law back on itself. This is his luck and his greatness. The Judge seeks to close a bordering place which Tom has mastered. He has dissolved its limitations by going to his own, to "the fullest stretch of the kite-line" where he is able to see, and just at the point of turning back, "a far-off speck that looked like daylight," and, when he reaches it, is able finally to enact not his own death, but his rebirth (as Huck does in escaping Pap's cabin, in the later novel): "pushed his head and shoulders through a small hole and saw the broad Mississippi rolling by!" (p. 297). The danger in Tom's knowledge is this miraculous exit, a secret possessed exclusively by him, by a child: his way out is always a way in too, a defiance of all portals under the rule of law: " 'It's about five mile into there the way anybody but me would go . . . but there's a mighty short cut that they don't anybody but me know about' "

(p. 306). This is the short cut around locks, around law, around the measurement of freedom by enclosures: the awareness of one's own beginning.

Tom's short cut is the route away from the strict rule of measurement, whether five miles or three days or any number of any quantity at all, to a place where choice is open to logic and to instinct too. It is not Tom's first evasion or his last, but it is his greatest. It gives him permanent access to a middle ground beyond the extremest law but short of chaos: the place where the treasure of the imagination turns real in experience and the most dreadful version of adult power can be overcome. Here one order mutually gives up its strength to the other. This is the function of the border region along which the two powers abut. It is here that Tom finds permanent access to the order of enchainment and logic. At Injun Joe's "Number Two" he discovers the fortune whose value he can divide, share, increase, and measure. Everything about number and sequence falls within his grasp here. If One is the number of the self, Two is the number at which one's social future begins to take shape. This means definition and hierarchy. It means that Tom can take the place which has become his own, to the confused delight of St. Petersburg, in the realm of law, above but founded on the trackless maze where improvised power, power as an art acquired through risk, begins: the place of underived discovery, of instinct free of time, rule, and sequence. If Tom finds the power of logic here, and he does, it is also the place to which he can return when he needs to escape it. He and Huck and the other boys will carry on their adventures endlessly now as "Tom Sawyer's Gang," with "guns, and a cave" (p. 325) and a blood initiation sworn on a coffin at midnight, " 'in the lonesomest, awfullest place you can find' " (p. 326). The cost of this thrilling freedom, which has been returned to them by Tom, in the illusion of respectability, a hard price for Huck to pay; but this is possible now, this lonesome awful oath, as play rather than as terror, because Tom has mastered the border where law and chaos turn toward one another and exchange the energies that make our language and balance our lives. His gift is the gift of balance which allows children a measure of independence. It does not perfect them, or the world of adults that they imagine they imitate; but it allows them to play rather than to suffer.

Still, Tom Sawyer was never able to fulfill his promise in another text. As late at 1898 he makes an appearance in Mark Twain's notebook, advising the son of Satan (the "Mysterious Stranger") how to behave in the hierarchy of St. Petersburg. Here Tom speaks the social logic of Missouri schoolchildren to a supernatural boy who stands outside logic, outside space and time and any constraints of grammar or superior strength; a boy who can master English, Latin, Greek and mathematics at a glance; whose clothes are new every day, though he brings no luggage with him to the village; who produces piles of gold and silver coins out of nothingness; who can speak the language of cats; who takes on human form and dismisses it at will; who comes from nowhere and disappears into a void when the text breaks off after 16,000 words. William Gibson asks himself why Clemens "let this story lapse after a moderately promising beginning when he had dozens of ideas for continuing it" (as the notebook entries show). We might ask this question of a number of Clemens' projects. In this case, Gibson suggests, it may have been that "certain inherent contradictions within the character . . . and in his projected action proved too great for Twain to resolve. Apparently he wanted to make his stranger both a boy and an angel. . . ."[24] Perhaps so; but this stranger is less a boy, in the sense that Mark Twain invented the species, than a mystified presence beyond the logical constraints that boys, and all children, resist and learn. With such a character as this at the center of a text there can be no place for Tom, whose own adventures with lessons and clothes and cats and gold and sudden disappearances and remanifestations and, for that matter, voids, are so precisely strenuous and signifying. He drops out of this manuscript after two very brief conversations with the limb of Satan. Tom has little to say to this superior uncomprehending image of the noumenal, this reprise of the dandified stranger standing in his way at the entrance to *The Adventures of Tom Sawyer*; and the dandy apparition displaces him altogether.

Whatever his plans for the mysterious stranger, it was Tom who Clemens wanted to be seen as a boy and an angel, struggling to claim and to resist each of the lessons that children's literature teaches. Tom was meant to incorporate the "multiple interplay" between law and instinct, sequence and inspiration. He unifies these two extremes, finally, and moves between them at will; but without erasing either. Tom finds the tension that motivates all balance. He confirms a dilemma by mediating the terms of its contradiction. Once this is successfully enacted it cannot with authenticity be foreclosed and need not be recuperated, because the threat it suggests is dissolved by the temptation it has resisted.

Thus Tom is not on one side or the other of his border, seeking to aggrandize an exclusive choice. He constitutes himself as the site of negotiation, represented at so sufficiently deep and complex a level that any new discoveries of this sort could only derive from their original instance. He has balanced the option of logical rule against the temptation of pure fantasy. No logic can ever overwhelm him now; no fantasy can ever isolate him beyond the reach of his reason. He is the possibility, not the stipulation, of logic and evasion both. He has worked free of the two dangers which children's literature seeks to warn against. He lives not in the absence of either but in the presence of both ways of knowing, along the *barre* where the energy of all signs is most intense and fruitful. Tom Sawyer is the perfectly achieved text of the child, and the perfectly mutual intercourse of the sign. Nothing of any literary interest will ever happen to situate him again along such a tense and interesting border—nothing apart from his role in *Adventures of Huckleberry Finn.* This requires that he come back again from the dead, take on the persona of the good boy, Sid, and, from behind this angelic mask (a place he has also learned to master in his own story), work to release the other aspect of his remarkable energy. This he does in order to explode the strict logic to which Huck and Jim are bound by the river's flow, which must carry the raft deeper and deeper into slave territory, deeper into the rule of law and away from the freedom they fantasize: like the cave, the river is not merely a sign of natural depth; it too has a logic (so do all natural powers) which men must realize and master before they can be free and easy.

But this service Tom performs for them, not for himself; and he accomplishes it in a fantastical episode which foreshadows the buffoonery of the later, pallid sequels. The greatness of the second book is Huck's; but not until it is ratified by Tom's ability to maneuver and transform. Huck is the sequel to Tom; he is the new figure of the child caught between crushing law and the exciting dream of escape, between the pain of confinement and the urge to light out. He finds his own and different border, along the shore, and its dangers are more bitter than any faced by Tom in the earlier book.. As Leslie Fielder says, *"Tom Sawyer* is a book about glory . . . while *Huck Finn* is an account of staying alive, which Tom cannot be persuaded to take seriously. Even as the bullet enters him, crossing the border between his world of idyllic make-believe and the adult world of slave-holding reality, he is already planning to wear that bullet on a string around his neck, swagger with it down the main street of Hannibal."[25] Tom saves *Huck Finn* from ruin, but he is only a borrowed moment in the finer sequent novel whose dilemma he dissolves so oddly, not only with his play but with his pain: his depth, his burden, the immense grace of his bordering begin and end in the text of his own childhood, *The Adventures of Tom Sawyer.*

Notes

1.   Aunt Polly's sternly matriarchal meaning is noticed by Cynthia Griffin Wolff in her fine essay *"The Adventures of Tom Sawyer:* A Nightmare Vision of American Boyhood," *The Massachusetts Review*, 21 (1980), 642.

2.   Wolff speaks of St. Petersburg as "a world which holds small boys in bondage," p. 641. Cf. Tom H. Towers, " 'I never thought we might want to come back': Strategies of Evasion in *Tom Sawyer,*" *Modern Fiction Studies*, 21 (1975–76), 510. And no study of Tom Sawyer as a child can ignore Albert E. Stone's *The Innocent Eye: Childhood in Mark Twain's Imagination* (New Haven: Yale Univ. Press, 1961), especially Chapter III, "Tom Sawyer and His Cousins." I am sometimes, and sometimes in important ways, at odds with this excellent work, but it remains the best of its kind.

3.   I discuss this relationship at length in my study *Desire and The Sign*, forthcoming from Louisiana State University Press.

4.   Anika Lemaire, *Jacques Lacan*, trans. David Macey (London: Routledge & Kegan Paul, 1977), p. xiii.

5. Jacques Lacan, *Ecrits: A Selection*, trans. Alan Sheridan (New York: Norton, 1977), p. 149; cf. Lemaire, p. 43.

6. Lemaire, pp. 45; 7, 106, 130; 117; 116, 118.

7. Lemaire, pp. 38–39.

8. Henry James, *What Maisie Knew* (New York: Charles Scribner's Sons, 1908), pp. v, vi. Subsequent references will be given parenthetically in the text.

9. *The Oxford Dictionary of Nursery Rhymes*, ed. Iona and Peter Opie (Oxford: Oxford Univ. Press, 1983), pp. 364–365.

10. E. C. Cawte, *Ritual Animal Disguise: A Historical and Geographical Study of Animal Disguise in the British Isles* (Cambridge: Rowman, 1978), pp. 208–227 and passim.

11. G. G. Coulton, *Medieval Panorama* (New York: Norton, 1957), pp. 495, 493.

12. Giovanni Boccaccio, *The Decameron*, trans. Frances Winwar (New York: Modern Library, 1955), "Preface," p. xxvii. Subsequent references will be given parenthetically in the text.

13. Thomas A. Sebeok, "Pandora's Box: How and Why to Communicate 10,000 Years into the Future," in Marshall Blonsky, ed., *On Signs* (Baltimore: Johns Hopkins Univ. Press, 1984), p. 450.

14. Iona and Peter Opie, p. 231.

15. Mark Twain, *The Adventures of Tom Sawyer* (New York: Harper & Brothers, 1903), p. 21. Subsequent references will be given parenthetically in the text.

16. On the idea of play in *Tom Sawyer* see Michael Oriard, *"From Tom Sawyer to Huck Finn:* Toward Godly Play," *Studies in American Fiction*, 8 (1980), 185, 187; and James M. Cox, *Mark Twain: The Fate of Humor* (Princeton: Princeton Univ. Press, 1966), pp. 132–148.

17. See Wolff, p. 643; Towers, p. 510; and Kenneth S. Lynn, *Mark Twain and Southwestern Humor* (Boston: Greenwood Press, 1959), p. 193.

18. See Oriard, pp. 185, 187.

19. See Wolff, p. 648.

20. See Lewis Leary, "Tom and Huck: Innocence on Trial," *The Virginia Quarterly Review*, 30 (1954). The purpose of the pattern beneath the novel's episodic organization, Leary argues, is "the recreation of boyish adventure. Its theme [is] the brave curiosity of the imaginative boy, [which] leads from innocence to knowledge of . . . the evil which is revealed to them and which will cloud and lengthen the whole summer for them . . . in no manner of their making" (p. 419).

21. See James M. Cox, "Remarks on the Sad Initiation of Huck Finn," *The Sewanee Review*, 62 (1954), 389–405.

22. See Thomas P. Riggio, "Mark Twain and Theodore Dreiser: Two Boys Lost in a Cave," *Mark Twain Journal*, 19 (Summer, 1978), 22.

23. See Lynn, pp. 195–196.

24. *Mark Twain's Mysterious Stranger Manuscripts*, ed. William M. Gibson, "Introduction," (Berkeley: Univ. of California Press, 1969), p. 9.

25. Leslie Fiedler, *Love and Death in The American Novel* (New York: Criterion Books, 1960), p. 574.

The Village in *Tom Sawyer*: Myth and Reality

THOMAS A. MAIK

Much has been written about Mark Twain's use of the town in his fiction. Generally, the towns, of his later fiction—Dawson's Landing of *Pudd'nhead Wilson*, Hadleyburg of "The Man that Corrupted Hadleyburg"—are associated with Twain's despair of the human race; those towns are symbolic of the smugness, hypocrisy, and cruelty of humanity. Although Bricksville and Pikesville of *Huck Finn* share the negative qualities of Dawson's Landing and Hadleyburg, usually readers and critics exclude St. Petersburg of the early *Adventures of Tom Sawyer* from such associations. I propose to reexamine the St. Petersburg idyll, challenge the myth, and, in doing so, expose the frequently harsh and unpleasant realities of the town in that novel.

We know from the standpoint of the developing writer that Mark Twain struck gold when he began drawing on what Henry Nash Smith refers to as the "Hannibal material." For Twain, that world of his childhood turned out to be a richly suggestive one, one that he never tired of using. Although he "mined" the material over and over again after discovering it in the mid-1870s, his most successful use of it belongs to the ten-year period immediately after the discovery.

In 1875, Twain first portrayed the river town in his richly evocative and autobiographical serialized pieces that he submitted from January to August in the *Atlantic Monthly* under the title "Old Times on the Mississippi." Even in this nostalgic reflection of his boyhood days and riverboating experiences, something was awry in the river town. As dreamy, carefree, lazy, and seemingly idyllic as the town was, the narrator of "Old Times" was discontented. His ambition as well as that of his comrades was to leave the town, take to the river and become steamboatmen. Quite frankly, the river town was dull. The world beyond offered glamour, adventure, and escape.

It was not until 1876 and *The Adventures of Tom Sawyer* that Twain gave the "Hannibal material" its fictionalized place name of St. Petersburg. On the surface of that book, St. Petersburg appears to be the ideal place for any growing kid. During a seemingly endless summer, Tom discovers an abundance of activities to fill both days and nights: hunting for treasure,

Reprinted from the *Arizona Quarterly* 42 (Summer 1986): 157–64, by permission of the publisher.

playing detective, exploring the cave, picnicking, visiting the village cemetery, swimming, whitewashing fences, playing Robin Hood, exploring an
island in the Mississippi, running away from home, to mention only some
of the activities.

What more could a boy ask for? After school had finished and playing
hookey at last had to be stricken as an extracurricular activity, Tom Sawyer,
although still accountable to his Aunt Polly, seemed relatively free. From
the surface existence, then, it's understandable how Bernard De Voto would
cite the idyllic nature of St. Petersburg:

> It has the quality of the phrase from an old song, "Over the hills and far
> away," which he could never think of without tears. This village, though
> violence underlies its tranquillity as it underlies most dreams of beauty, is
> withdrawn from the pettiness, the greed, the cruelty, the spiritual squalor,
> the human worthlessness that Huck Finn was to travel through ten years later,
> that are the fabric of Hadleyburg and Dawson's Landing.[1]

Walter Blair echoes these sentiments: St. Petersburg is a place ". . . of
quiet delight bathed in summer air fragrant with the aroma of meadows,
woodlands, and flowers."[2] In praising the novel, Frank Baldanza speaks
favorably, too, of the town:

> Even though it deals with graverobbers, slow starvation, cruelty, and brutality,
> it ultimately exonerates the values of the small town in which Clemens'
> generation grew up, and, by extension, the small town that each of us carries
> in his memory if only as a kind of historic heritage.[3]

Paradise, indeed! To many, Eden! Even Twain's description of the
village on a Saturday morning continues the idyll:

> Saturday morning was come, and all the summer world was bright and fresh,
> and brimming with life. There was a song in every heart; and if the heart was
> young the music issued at the lips. There was cheer in every face and a spring
> in every step. The locust trees were in bloom and the fragrance of the blossoms
> filled the air.[4]

And yet, dreamlike as the village is, for Tom Sawyer and his gang, village
life is a bore, something to be endured, or, if possible, something to escape.
In fact, as early as the second chapter of the novel and in the sentence
following the ones just quoted, the world beyond St. Petersburg is the one
that beckons the boys. That's where the action is. "Cardiff Hill, beyond the
village and above it, was green with vegetation, and it lay just far enough
away to seem a Delectable Land, dreamy, reposeful, and inviting" (p. 46).

In *Tom Sawyer*, then, it's the satellites around St. Petersburg—Cardiff
Hill, the cemetery, Jackson's Island in the Mississippi, and the cave south

of the village—that provide numerous adventures for the boys and make life *in* the village tolerable for them. In fact, life outside the village isn't essential only for the vitality of the boys; it serves as an energizer for the townspeople as well, for particularly when something happens "beyond" the village, usually to Tom and his friends, does St. Petersburg come alive. When the boys run away to the island, for example, the village bustles with life. The "missing" boys provoke endless topics for conversation as well as numerous activities for the townsfolk. Culmination of the community vitality occurs when the boys return in the midst of their eulogy, and mourning turns to jubilation as the congregation nearly bursts the church rafters with its rendition of "Praise God." And Tom becomes the hero and the talk of the town for days afterward.

> What a hero Tom was become, now! He did not go skipping and prancing, but moved with a dignified swagger as became a pirate who felt that the public eye was on him. And indeed it was; he tried not to seem to see the looks or hear the remarks as he passed along, but they were food and drink to him. (p. 145)

As the weeks pass and the village sinks once again into lethargy, Becky and Tom's failure to return from the cave plunges the community into despair—but life as well. Again, the community buzzes with talk and action. And again at the point when St. Petersburg nearly surrenders to despair, Tom and Becky discover an opening in the cave and despite the lateness of the hour make their grand entrance back to the village and a heroes' welcome.

> Away in the middle of the night a wild peal burst from the village bells, and in a moment the streets were swarming with frantic half-clad people, who shouted "Turn out! turn out! they're found! they're found!" Tin pans and horns were added to the din, the population massed itself and moved toward the river, met the children coming in an open carriage drawn by shouting citizens, thronged around it, joined its homeward march, and swept magnificently up the main street roaring huzzah after huzzah! (p. 217).

St. Petersburg an idyllic place? Paradise? Scarcely! To avoid the blahs, escape from St. Petersburg was essential for the boys, and their life and activities beyond the village "nourished" the community as well. Dullness is certainly a problem of the river town in *Tom Sawyer*. It's a problem festering, though, at the surface of the community; external excitements and sensational developments infrequently bring relief to a rather dreary place. The surface problem, however, is only a symptom of a greater, more serious problem lurking beneath the texture of St. Petersburg, for underneath the blahs, the ennui, and the dullness lie the smugness, hypocrisy, the cruelty, and lies that come to dominate Twain's view of St. Petersburg in 1876 and his later literature as well.

If it's integrity you're looking for, don't look hard for it in St. Petersburg. True, the traditional pillars of society—the lawyer, the doctor, the teacher, and the minister—call St. Petersburg home. But what kind of people actually are they? The young and promising Doc Robinson clandestinely robs graves. When Judge Thatcher learns that his daughter is responsible for the book-tearing episode in school and that Tom Sawyer has taken the rap, we learn how he regards truth and honesty:

> When Becky told her father, in strict confidence, how Tom had taken her whipping at school, the Judge was visibly moved; and when she pleaded grace for the mighty lie which Tom had told in order to shift that whipping from her shoulders to his own, the Judge said with a fine outburst that it was a noble, a generous, a magnanimous lie—a lie that was worthy to hold up its head and march down through history breast to breast with George Washington's lauded Truth about the hatchet! (pp. 232–33)

Perhaps it's too much to expect from a father in this situation, but should a man of law be condoning lies? Shouldn't there, in fact, be a reprimand for his daughter? And what about the teacher in St. Petersburg? Is he really a voyeur or are we to believe that he keeps questionable reading material off limits from his students because of his long-standing and genuine interest in human anatomy? Doesn't his typical style in the classroom (wrath and quick violence toward the students and then a false charm and warmth toward them when visitors are present) unmask his true identity? Isn't his pretentious dress and toupee symbolic of his phony nature? Finally, even the minister is victim and perpetrator of deception in St. Petersburg as we learn from the funeral eulogy.

> As the service proceeded, the clergyman drew such pictures of the graces, the winning ways and the rare promise of the lost lads, that every soul there, thinking he recognized these pictures, felt a pang in remembering that he had persistently blinded himself to them, always before, and had as persistently seen only faults and flaws in the poor boys. The minister related many a touching incident in the lives of the departed, too, which illustrated their sweet, generous natures, and the people could easily see, now, how noble and beautiful those episodes were, and remembered with grief that at the time they occurred they had seemed rank rascalities, well deserving of the cowhide. (pp. 140–41)

If public figures betray our trust, as they appear to do in *Tom Sawyer*, should we be surprised if the community as a whole lets us down? On the surface, the citizens of St. Petersburg look like decent, caring people. But what happens when Muff Potter is charged with the murder of Doc Robinson? For one thing, the excitement of the deed and the prospects of a public trial disrupt the routine and doldrums for the community. How often does a community have the opportunity to talk about a murder, much less the murder of a leading citizen who robs graves at night? Even the children benefit from the tragedy by their afternoon holiday from school. The event seems more important than the victim, for few show sympathy or emotion toward either Robinson or Potter. Even the boys, who supposedly have been shocked by what they've seen, have short memories. Within two chapters, they've "run away" to the island, and the enterprising Tom is soon caught up in engineering the boys' triumphant return to the village on the day of their funeral.

And the cornerstone of American justice—innocent until proven guilty—fares poorly in St. Petersburg. On the basis of a weapon belonging to Potter and a "belated citizen" who came upon Potter washing in the "branch" at one or two o'clock, the community reaches a verdict and begins its pursuit of the murderer:

> It was also said that the town had been ransacked for this "murderer" (the public are not slow in the matter of sifting evidence and arriving at a verdict), but that he could not be found. Horsemen had departed down all the roads in every direction, and the Sheriff "was confident" that he would be captured before night. All the town was drifting toward the graveyard. Tom's heartbreak vanished and he joined the procession, not because he would not a thousand times rather go anywhere else, but because an awful, unaccountable fascination drew him on. (p. 105)

Harmless creature that he is, Muff Potter is the town drunk and vagrant, and in St. Petersburg the latter qualities make him an easy target for the charges of any crime. Although the boys know the truth and Tom does eventually reveal it, they sign a pact in blood not to confess the truth, so Muff Potter suffers in jail as he awaits the trial.

The excitement over the tragedy of Doc Robinson and Muff Potter is, unfortunately, not the only example of the community's true character. Later when Injun Joe, the real murderer of Doc Robinson, is found starved to death at the foot of the locked door to McDougal cave, the village wastes little time in displaying its true colors as well as capitalizing on the tragedy.

> Injun Joe was buried near the mouth of the cave; and people flocked there in boats and wagons from the town and from all the farms and hamlets for seven miles around; they brought their children, and all sorts of provisions, and confessed that they had had almost as satisfactory a time at the funeral as they could have had at the hanging. (p. 221)

In *Tom Sawyer*, even the family lets us down. Instead of being honest, open, and genuine with the children in her household, Aunt Polly, too, reflects the values of her culture. Fluctuating between punishment (raps on his head with her thimble) and praise toward Tom, she never honestly expresses her love for him. Only when she thinks he is dead is she honest in her feelings. In that same scene, we learn that Aunt Polly's failure to be honest with her emotions is probably the norm in St. Petersburg, for only in what she thinks is her loss is Joe Harper's mother able to speak openly with Tom's Aunt Polly:

> "But as I was saying," said aunt Polly, "he warn't *bad*, so to say—only mischeevous. Only just giddy, and harum-scarum, you know. He warn't any more responsible than a colt. He never meant any harm, and he was the best-hearted boy that ever was"—and she began to cry. "It was just so with my Joe—always full of his devilment, and up to every kind of mischief, but he was just as unselfish and kind as he could be—and laws bless me, to think I went and whipped him for taking that cream, never once recollecting that I throwed it out myself because it was sour, and I never to see him again in this world, never, never, never, poor abused boy!" And Mrs. Harper sobbed as if her heart would break. (p. 128)

Being surrounded by smugness and hypocrisy, no wonder, then, even the child's world is subject to corruption. In St. Petersburg, the children learn quickly and easily to emulate the values of the adults around them. Tom Sawyer is the main example of hypocrisy at the child's level. He fights the new boy in town to establish his prowess, cons his friends into whitewashing the fence, and is constantly dealing with others on the barter system to gain wealth and recognition. The loot he garners by hoodwinking his friends to whitewash the fence for him he exchanges for tickets in the Bible contest. In the process, he wins the envy of his peers and the admiration of the adults. With these initial successes, Tom quickly learns the importance of physical force and money in gaining prominence. Transition from the child's world to the adult is complete for Tom when he and Huck discover the treasure and then make their quest to possess it central to the remainder of the book. Although they face dangers and threatened punishment in their quest, they persevere, obtain the treasure, escape punishment by displaying the booty, and become heroes in the process:

> The reader may rest satisfied that Tom's and Huck's windfall made a mighty stir in the poor little village of St. Petersburg. So vast a sum, all in actual cash, seemed next to incredible. It was talked about, gloated over, glorified, until the reason of many of the citizens tottered under the strain of the unhealthy excitement. Every "haunted" house in St. Petersburg and the neighboring villages was dissected, plank by plank, and its foundations dug up and ransacked for the hidden treasure—and not by boys, but men—pretty grave, unromantic men, too, some of them. Wherever Tom and Huck appeared they were courted, admired, stared at. The boys were not able to remember that

their remarks had possessed weight before; but now their sayings were treasured and repeated. . . . (p. 232)

Thus, on the note of greed, *Tom Sawyer* ends. In that novel and in St. Petersburg, all strata of society are infected with the same kinds of vices that plague the citizens of the towns in Twain's later fiction. From the prominent citizens at the top to the drunk and destitute at the bottom, St. Petersburg festers with lies, smugness, hypocrisy, human cruelty, murder, and greed. Indeed, Twain's portrait of the town is anything but flattering. The idyll is only at the surface. Smugness, pretense, deception, and greed permeate the village and strip away the mythology of Eden.

Notes

1.   Bernard De Voto, *Mark Twain at Work* (Cambridge, MA: Harvard University Press, 1942), p. 23.

2.   Walter Blair, *Mark Twain & Huck Finn* (Berkeley: University of California Press, 1960), p. 53.

3.   Frank Baldanza, *Mark Twain: An Introduction and Interpretation* (New York: Barnes & Noble, Inc., 1961), p. 103.

4.   Samuel L. Clemens, *The Adventures of Tom Sawyer*, Vol. IV of *The Works of Mark Twain* (Berkeley: University of California Press, 1980), p. 46. All further references are to this edition and are cited in the text.

Tom Sawyer: Character in Search
of an Audience

Elizabeth G. Peck

The rediscovery of *The Adventures of Tom Sawyer* as a novel worthy of serious critical attention has led to the reversal of a number of long-standing critical opinions. Once almost universally acclaimed a romantic idyll, a nostalgic hymn of praise, and a comic tale suitable for the young and young at heart, the novel has more recently been described as a work that anticipates much of the darkness and bitterness that characterizes Twain's later works.[1] The horror, violence, cruelty, and sadism, earlier dismissed as humorous gothic embellishments, are now viewed as powerful fictional motifs that create a nightmarish vision of reality. Likewise, while early critics chuckled at the innocuous boredom of the sleepy little village of St. Petersburg and the foolish pretensions of its inhabitants, more recent critics have blanched at the spiritual poverty of the community and its peeling veneer of respectability. Whereas foolishness, pettiness, and gullibility were once scoffed at as the villagers' worst failings, the adults of St. Petersburg are now charged with vanity, hypocrisy, false posturing, dishonesty, deception, hysteria, childishness, self-indulgence, sensation-seeking, and self-aggrandizement.[2]

The vices attributed to St. Petersburg adults are seldom imputed to the village children, however. The children show off, tell lies, play pranks, boast, " 'spread' " themselves and tattle on each other; but while their actions are often acknowledged to be parodies of adult behavior, most readers refuse to take them seriously because the children are, after all, just children. Consequently, while Tom Sawyer is widely recognized as a self-centered schemer, an accomplished strategist, and an egotistical sensation-seeker, his character is seldom viewed negatively.[3] In fact, only readers who persist in seeing Tom as a romantic hero, a clever individualist in the midst of dull-witted conformity, or a dedicated rebel who refuses to abide by the inhibiting strictures of his society, feel betrayed by their final view of him.[4] Yet it is perhaps not unfair to suggest that in condemning Tom's actions in the latter part of this novel, readers may be responding not so much to the behavior that might logically be expected of Tom, but to the hopes they have projected

Originally published in *ATQ*, n.s. 2 (September 1988): 223–36. Reprinted by permission of the University of Rhode Island.

onto him. For despite the relentlessness of Tom's naughtiness and the mock-heroic tone Twain uses to describe his adventures, Tom is from first to last not only an integral and well integrated member of the community, but a character who is "in revolt against nothing" (Cox 140). Indeed, the final self Tom exhibits while routing Huck Finn from an empty hogshead and ex-horting him to return to the widow and respectability—because " 'everybody does that way' "—has been well prepared for during the entire course of the novel.

Twain seems to have anticipated reader dissatisfaction, however. In the conclusion to *The Adventures of Tom Sawyer*, he suggested that he might, at a later date, take up his story again to "see what sort of men and women" his young characters "turned out to be" (237).[5] But while Tom continues to appear in a number of Twain's later works, he is never much older than he is at the end of his first novel. Twain never fully explained why he departed from his original plan, but in a letter to William Dean Howells he claimed that taking Tom beyond boyhood would be "fatal" because "the reader would conceive a hearty contempt for him" (5 July 1875). And that contempt has already been registered in critical reactions to Tom's histrionics in the final chapters of *Adventures of Huckleberry Finn*. Most readers would agree that Twain's sequel, as Judith Fetterley observes, "is quite a different book and in it Tom Sawyer is quite a different character" ("Sanctioned" 303), but a closer look at Twain's development of the prankster in *The Adventures of Tom Sawyer* suggests that his characterization thematically foreshadows not only the thoughtless hedonism Tom displays in *Huckleberry Finn*, but Hank Morgan's overpowering narcissism of *A Connecticut Yankee in King Arthur's Court* and the environmental determinism of *The Tragedy of Pudd'nhead Wilson*. Indeed by demonstrating how Tom learns to assimilate himself into the life and society of St. Petersburg, Twain may have written a primer for initiating the young into the "paltry human race."

The fact that Tom is ultimately a product of his environment does not mean that he is a static character, however. His actions, during the course of the novel, do, as Walter Blair suggests, demonstrate that he is undergoing a process of maturation; he is gradually becoming more adult-like. And the process of Tom's development, like that of any other child, is based upon the totality of his experiences, upon the cumulative effect of his perceptions, and upon the types of reinforcement he receives for certain modes of behavior. Consequently, he acquires those qualities Blair contends will "make him a normal adult" (42), not through a series of leaps and bounds of mature insight, but through a gradual process of accumulating, internalizing, and evaluating all the information he receives about himself and his surroundings. This knowledge then serves as the basis of his understanding of the world and his place in it, and functions as the means by which he continually modifies his actions and defines himself according to the responses he elicits from others. Blair views Tom's maturation as mainly positive primarily because he overlooks the negative implications of what it means to be an adult in St. Petersburg. But, as Fetterley points out, since "the adults are hypocrites, ... it hardly makes sense to assume that they provide the yardstick which charts a growth from something negative to something positive" ("Sanctioned" 301). It does make sense, however, to try to redefine what normality and maturity mean in St. Petersburg, for Tom's initiation into adulthood is not only dependent upon his ability to assimilate information, but upon the character of the community from which he derives his concepts of conscience, respectability, and morality.

Thus the relationship between adult dissimulation and juvenile emulation demands closer examination. For as the action of the novel moves Tom from the domestic realm into the larger community, Twain parallels Tom's development with a gradual unfolding of community values. And this process reveals not only that respectability, as Tom ultimately discovers, merely means that " 'everybody does that way,' " but that what everybody does is prompted by a single motive: the desire to " 'spread' " themselves, to create even a momentary sensation that will catapult them onto the community's center stage. In this light, the villagers' superficial pretensions to style— Aunt Polly's "state pair" of glasses (40), Mr. Walter's "Sunday-school voice" (61), Judge Thatcher's "majestic judicial smile" (63), the Rev. Mr. Sprague's "peculiar" vocal style (67), and Mr. Dobbin's wig—hint at the darker motives that govern public conscience and local morality: primal narcissism and personal pleasure.[6] And the adult "performers" in St. Petersburg have no difficulty satisfying their own egos and the demands of the local audience, because the two are wholly interdependent. By showing off, the individual members of the community, like the lawyer in Melville's "Bartleby the Scrivener," "cheaply purchase a delicious self-approval," and by applauding their efforts, the community as a whole demonstrates its appreciation of dramatic style. Neither the performers nor the audience draw moral distinctions among the types of entertainment they approve. Any spectacle, as Injun Joe's burial reveals, is well attended and universally enjoyed:

> people flocked there in boats and wagons from the town and from all the farms and hamlets for seven miles around; they brought their children and all sorts of provisions, and confessed that they had had almost as satisfactory a time at the funeral as they could have had at the hanging. (221)

The indiscriminate satisfaction St. Petersburg audiences derive from feats of accomplishment or acts of perversity—from Prize Day presentations or Prize Day humiliations, from picnics or holidays for murder—clearly indicates not only that the village's besetting sin is boredom, but that attempts to relieve it have resulted in moral vacuity. By applauding any entertainment that promises excitement, the residents of St. Petersburg have come to prefer gaudy acting to true expressions of conscience, theatrical pretense to genuine respectability, and dramatic technique to moral action. And it is against the backdrop of this essentially valueless society that Twain shows Tom coming of age. Consequently, it is not surprising that we see Tom gradually being molded into an actor constantly in search of an audience.

Even as the novel opens, Twain provides us with a psychological yardstick by which we can measure Tom's awareness of the consequences of his mischievous actions and his perception of the mechanics of domestic authority. In spite of Aunt Polly's threats and the switch that hovers in the air above him, Tom shows no hesitation in tricking his aunt into letting him escape punishment; and her response proves that that is just what she had expected, if not hoped for. Aunt Polly's "gentle laugh" and the text of her soliloquy clearly outline the ground rules Tom has learned to follow in his dealings with her: " 'He 'pears to know just how long he can torment me before I get my dander up, and he knows if he can make out to put me off for a minute or make me laugh, it's all down again and I can't hit him a lick' "(40). Though Aunt Polly pretends (even to herself) that she fears she will be the " 'ruination of the child' "(41), it is clear that their relationship of loving antagonism provides the basis for mutual support and definition. By breaking rules, Tom gains his aunt's appreciation of his cleverness and proves his need for her guidance; by enforcing rules, Aunt Polly expresses her belief in conventional morality and shows her concern for Tom. In this way, Tom, who loathes model boys, can happily see himself as a Bad Boy; and Aunt Polly, who has pretensions to "style," can comfortably place herself in the role of guardian of morality. Actually, Tom's behavior makes him what Leslie Fiedler calls a "Good Bad Boy"; he does what a boy's mother or, in this case, Aunt Polly *"really* wants him to do: deceive, break her heart a little, so that she can forgive him, smother him in the embrace that seals him back into her world forever" (*No! in Thunder* 260). What Tom has learned from his relationship with Aunt Polly is revealed when he tries to talk Jim into whitewashing for him. Jim declines because Aunt Polly has warned him against it, but Tom explains, " 'Oh, never you mind what she said, Jim. That's the way she always talks' "(47). Obviously, Tom knows that the edicts of Aunt Polly and the forbidding threats that often accompany them are but empty forms of authority, for her threats are seldom enforced, and when they are she has no expectation that her punishments will be carried out.

Tom has also learned another important lesson from Aunt Polly: the value of the pretense of respectability. He turns the unwanted task of whitewashing into a profitable enterprise by assuming an officious air and exuding a sense of industriousness and responsibility. The other boys are so anxious to experience the same sense of self-importance that they readily hand over their treasures for a chance to take Tom's place. While achieving this slaughter of the innocents, Tom learns yet another lesson, "namely, that in order to make a man or a boy covet a thing, it is only necessary to make the thing difficult to attain" (50).

Whether or not Tom comprehends the meaning of this lesson is uncertain, but he proves that he is far too clever to fall for such a ruse himself. Others might apply themselves to the arduous task of learning two thousand verses to earn a Bible, but he sets about getting one by trading for the necessary number of tickets instead. In this endeavor he is aided not only by the same boys he had earlier taken in, but by the contagion of "showing off" that sweeps through the Sunday school because of its visitors. The epidemic is so wide-spread that it not only rages among the students, but infects the superintendent, the librarian, the young lady teachers, the young gentlemen teachers, and even the august visitor, Judge Thatcher, who sits warming "himself in the sun of his own grandeur" (63). In this atmosphere Tom's play for the Bible is merely the high point of the morning's entertainment, for he offers himself as the sought-for "prodigy" who will make the superintendent's "ecstasy complete" (233). And, true to his expectations, before the source of his ticket supply is discovered, the Bible, the reward for his nefarious dealings, is delivered into his hands. The question and answer session following the presentation reveals that Tom has little acquaintance with scripture; nevertheless, he has gained his prize, the envy of his peers, and the applause of the visiting eminents.

That Tom's success in outwitting authorities is based upon his growing understanding of the rules governing adult behavior is further demonstrated by the bravado he displays in manipulating the schoolmaster. Knowing full well that creating an outrage in the school will result not only in a beating, but in being sent to take the only empty seat on the girls' side, the one right next to Becky Thatcher, Tom enlarges upon the reprehensibility of his tardiness by freely admitting that he stopped to talk to Huckleberry Finn. His ploy is doubly successful; he astonishes his classmates and thereby earns their wondering respect, and he enrages the schoolmaster and in that way gains the seat next to Becky.

Up to this point in the novel, Tom's underhanded dealings have always been prompted by the same motives: satisfying Aunt Polly or promoting his standing among the other boys or in the eyes of Becky Thatcher. He made the work of whitewashing attractive primarily to avoid taunts from his friends, because he knew "they would make a world of fun of him for having to work—and the very thought of it burnt him like fire" (47). Likewise, his desire to own a Bible—if it existed at all—was certainly secondary to gaining the chance to " 'spread himself' " that he knew would come with its acquisition (60). That the Bible was presented in the presence of Becky Thatcher, and that Tom was congratulated by "her parent" made the event even more rewarding than it might otherwise have been (64). Tom's failure in answering the Judge's questions in no way interfered with his real success, for he surpassed everybody in "showing off"—and that, ultimately, was the prize he was after.

The mundane dreams of glory that prompted Tom to undertake these relatively minor acts of deception prove so materially rewarding and personally beneficial that they soon spur him on to even greater heights of daring and intrigue and encourage him to broaden the base of his recognition. Though he never relinquishes his desire to impress the other boys with his feats of daring and imagination, his schemes of self-aggrandizement are increasingly directed at those beyond that limited circle. And in Tom's ever-expanding quest for fame, the methods he employs gradually reveal not only how much he "matures" during the course of the novel, but how the values of the community cultivate and inform the kind of individual he becomes. It is obvious at this point, even before the major episodes of the novel, that for Tom gaining recognition and achieving a dramatic effect are, practically speaking, one and the same. The first time he feels himself poorly treated, unloved, and abused because Becky Thatcher has rejected him, he is so miserable he wishes he could die, if only *"temporarily!"* (87). But he cheers himself up by revelling in daydreams of future diabolical splendor. However, the romantic visions he conjures up—of himself as a soldier, a great Indian chief, and finally the Black Avenger of the Spanish Main—all have one curiously similar element in common: they all end with his glorious and triumphant return to the village. Clearly, running away, even in Tom Sawyer's daydreams, is not a means of escape; it is a way of providing a place to return from. And that return is, for Tom, an absolute necessity, for he himself is growing aware of the fact that he desperately needs an audience.

Tom never loses his appreciation of the gaudiness that fills his daydreams, but increasingly he begins to trade the solace of private fantasy for the necessity of public action. On the same day that he envisions his triumphal returns, he and Joe Harper join in a game of Robin Hood, one that is played by the book, complete with memorized dialogue. This scene emphasizes Tom's love of theatrics and also sets the stage for the beginning of his later development. When Tom and Joe end their game, they do so very significantly; they bury Robin Hood and go off "grieving that there are no outlaws any more, and wondering what modern civilization could claim to have done to compensate for their loss" (91).

Tom soon finds out what his own society has to offer in the way of outlaws, for shortly thereafter he and Huck Finn are the sole witnesses to the murder of Dr. Robinson. This incident serves as Tom's final introduction to the real world and the community and marks the onset of his withdrawal from the world of fantasy. From this time forward neither vengeful daydreams nor playing at being a heroic blackguard can be savored with the same degree of satisfaction they once had. Once Tom is introduced to the reality of violence, he can never wholly immerse himself in the safe world of imagination for a sustained period of time.

As the intensity of the narrative action increases following Dr. Robinson's murder, Tom's actions not only begin to take place within the larger sphere of the community, but begin to accord to the dictates of what he has begun to perceive as social conscience. Thus, in the episodes that follow, as his actions become increasingly public, they also become more calculated, indicating that he is becoming progressively better suited to fit the image of a "normal" adult in his society. Twain emphasizes the development of Tom's increasing sense of village morality and the simultaneous growth of his respectability by contrasting his actions to those of Huck Finn, the "juvenile pariah of the village" (73). In his implicit comparison of these two characters, Twain shows that the distinction between them lies not so much in their ways of being "bad" as it does in their ways of being "good." Both act in response to inner promptings, but the motives behind their actions and the results they hope to achieve are very different.

Despite the fact that Tom and Huck have sworn to keep their knowledge of Dr. Robinson's murder a secret, they both experience a "wavering impulse" to reveal the truth when the murder is discovered the next day (106). But while Huck is satisfied with the wisdom of his action and the inviolability of his pact with Tom (because Injun Joe is not struck dead in spite of his false testimony), Tom continues to suffer pangs of conscience for his failure to speak out against the criminal. His failure, however, is mirrored by that of the community, for though the villagers are anxious to tar and feather Injun Joe for body-snatching, he is viewed as such a formidable character "that nobody could be found who was willing to take the lead in the matter, so it was dropped" (108).

Somewhat relieved by the inadequacy of the public conscience, Tom's anxiety over the murder begins to dissipate, and he is soon caught up in problems of a more personal nature. He is again rejected by Becky Thatcher. With this second rejection, Tom runs through the same course of emotions he experienced the first time, but on this occasion he does not settle for fantasizing—he acts. Tom plans to run away with Joe Harper and Huck Finn, but it is quite evident, even before the boys' departure, that Tom is organizing this expedition with the idea of returning always in mind. The boys make no preparations to leave before they have a chance to "enjoy the sweet glory of spreading the fact that pretty soon the town would 'hear something' " (115). And it is soon apparent that they are taking a good deal more of St. Petersburg with them than that contained in their provisions. Not only is Tom's bookish romantic language employed to provide the proper "style," but most of their actions are carried out to the refrain of "what would the boys say" (118). Even on their first night away from civilization, Tom and Joe say their prayers to appease their consciences; only Finn the Red-Handed sleeps conscience-free.

Without the weight of their accustomed restrictions, and with only themselves to impress, the boys find much "to be delighted with but nothing to be astonished at" (123). They soon lapse into homesickness that, ironically, is relieved by the intrusion of civilization, by the booming of the ferryboat cannon that informs them that they are drowned. Once the boys realize that they have succeeded in causing the "public distress" they half counted on, there is no reason for them to remain on Jackson's Island. But while it is Joe who sends out the first "feeler" about returning to civilization, it is Tom who is so anxious to learn of the village's response to their deaths that he slips away from his companions as soon as they are asleep. Tom is well rewarded for his surreptitious visit, since he not only overhears the information that permits him to arrange the boys' attendance at their own funerals, but he learns that the misdeeds he and Joe had been reprimanded for are retrospectively viewed as endearing mischiefs. As a result, he gains "a nobler opinion of himself than ever before" (129).

The hypocrisy expressed by Aunt Polly and Mrs. Harper during their scene of mourning is mirrored by the sermon delivered at the boys' funeral. While the minister recalls "noble and beautiful episodes" that "had seemed rank rascalities," the entire congregation, including the minister himself, dissolves in a chorus of sobs (140–141). It is at this dramatic moment that Tom Sawyer leads his pirates down the center aisle of the church, and it is in this scene that Twain draws attention to the direction Tom's development is headed and how he and the community are working together to prepare a place for him—he, by creating sensations, and, they, by faithfully responding to them with a display of awe and astonishment. Through this reciprocal process Tom and the community establish a relationship very like the one that exists between him and Aunt Polly. By creating diversions for the bored inhabitants of his shabby village, Tom provides them with the illusion of living lives of vitality and importance; and by applauding Tom for his diversions, the villagers feed his ever-increasing need for recognition. Put succinctly, "they need him and he needs them and every-body gets to be Robin Hood or at least have a nice part in the play" (Fetterley, "Mark Twain" 385).

Once Tom has secured his position under the central spotlight of the community, his main concern is maintaining it. But for him that is not difficult, for he has an uncanny sense of dramatic timing and he knows now how and when to employ it for the most profitable effect. Consequently, he finally wins Becky's admiration by taking her whipping for her, but he doesn't make his false confession until Becky, under examination, "white with terror," begins to raise her hands in appeal. Tom's timing is so perfect, and his sacrifice so noble, that even he is "[i]nspired by the splendor of his own act" (156). And Judge Thatcher later claims that Tom's lie "was worthy to hold up its head and march down through history breast to breast with George Washington's lauded Truth about the hatchet!" (165).

Tom achieves a similar victory at Muff Potter's trial, but not until after he has spent five full weeks of his vacation confined to his bed with a rather curious illness. Twain ostensibly attributes the first two weeks to measles and the latter three to a relapse, but he subtlely hints that Tom's susceptibility to disease may be prompted by mental disturbance, because "[t]he dreadful secret of the murder was a chronic misery. It was a very cancer for permanency and pain" (63). And though the torment Tom suffers is usually explained as a consequence of the terror of the graveyard, his lethargy and vulnerability may well spring from another source of anxiety: the frustration of possessing a great secret—one sure to bring him acclaim—that he cannot reveal.[7] The pathological turn Tom's personality is taking becomes quite evident, for Tom does not fully recover until he unburdens himself by making arrangements the night before the trial to appear as a surprise witness.

When Tom is called to testify, he begins hesitantly, but as his testimony begins to flow, his is soon the only voice in the courtroom and he is once again in his favorite place—center stage—where "every eye fixed itself upon him" (172). Though Tom's performance at the trial makes him a "glittering hero once more," the recognition he is granted is at best a mixed blessing, for "his nights were seasons of horror" (173). Tom's suffering seems unjust in view of the fact that his testimony probably saved Muff Potter's life, but in this seemingly high-minded action, Tom is once again so impressed by his own nobility that he has completely neglected the welfare of his fellow witness. Tom has thoughtlessly placed Huck in jeopardy too. By reneging on their solemn agreement, Tom has gained recognition at the expense of his own integrity and at the price of his friend's safety. Consequently, though Huck ordinarily has no quarrel with Tom's grandstanding techniques, in this instance, as a result of Tom's civic-mindedness, "Huck's confidence in the human race was well nigh obliterated" (173).

In his total disregard of Huck, Tom's development can be seen to be moving in two directions at the same time. As he ascends toward presumed respectability through community involvement, he descends morally as he exhibits an increasingly callous attitude toward his disreputable friend. During the treasure hunt, when the boys are tracking Injun Joe, Twain reveals that Tom, who once bravely announced the forbidden name of Huckleberry Finn in school, now does "not care to have Huck's company in public places" (169). Twain further increases the moral distance between these two characters by dividing the narrative into two separate strains of action.[8] When Tom sets off for the picnic, Huck is left to deal with Injun Joe; consequently, while Tom is lost in the cave, down in the bowels of the earth, Huck is up on Cardiff Hill, saving the Widow Douglas.

Though Twain's tone during the McDougal's cave episode is sympathetic toward Tom, the irony of Tom's position functions as a constantly recurring motif. Tom enters the cave when he has fallen to his lowest moral level, when, after assuring Huck of his reliability by promising, " 'Don't you ever weaken, Huck, and I won't' " (190), he almost immediately finds he cannot "bear to give up the fun at widow Douglas's" (195) and so takes a holiday when Huck might really need him. Tom is lured into the depths of the cave, appropriately enough, by ambition—"the ambition to be a discoverer" (209). But once he and Becky become hopelessly lost, not only is his immediate ambition proved foolish, but also the motivation behind all his ambitions—his dreams of fame, glory, and recognition—is reduced to meaninglessness. The boy who increasingly sought the applause of all those around him now finds only "[p]rofound silence" (211). Unlike the ready response always afforded him by the community, the cave returns his call with only "a faint sound that resembled a ripple of mocking laughter" (211). Instead of the spotlight Tom so thoroughly enjoys and desperately needs, the cave offers "the horror of utter darkness" (214). Tom's hopes are momentarily raised by the light from a candle held by a human hand, but when he responds with "a glorious shout," he finds his spirits were lifted by none other than Injun Joe, the one his self-aggrandizement has most offended (215). Finally, even Becky, Tom's adoring audience of one, deserts him.

The irony of Tom's predicament is heightened by the fact that neither he nor Becky is missed until the day after their disappearance, and he himself is responsible for engineering the deception that delays the search for them. That they might die undiscovered is both a harsh reality and a perversely nightmarish possibility, for all of Tom's earlier "funerals" ended in public lamentation and personal triumph. Now, as Becky sinks into a dreadful apathy, prepared to wait where she is to die, Tom's earlier death-wishes loom ghost-like against the background of the cave's "jeering laughter" (211). The pathos of his dreams, the visions of tearful repentant mourners pleading for his forgiveness, and the dramatic effect of being a martyr are all swallowed up by the emptiness of the cave. The "agony of pleasurable suffering" (55) has been transformed in the cave into "bodings of coming doom" (216). Bereft of human companionship, with no one to reflect and thereby define his image of himself, Tom reaches the lowest point in his development. He is "willing to risk Injun Joe and all other terrors" (216) to find his way out of the abyss and back to the community.

With what remains of his ingenuity, and perhaps motivated by his fear of dying unannounced, Tom continues his search for an escape route and finally sees the light that will lead him back to the world of applause. Tom's emergence into the daylight world is the culmination of his boyish inquisitiveness; his juvenile explorations are at an end. His ambitions from now on will be wholly shaped by the village's expectations; he will continue to astonish and outrage, but only in order to turn and return to the audience that allows him to call himself a hero within its limited sphere. Tom has learned his last lesson in the cave: in the absence of spectators, in the absence of his community, he is but a hollow echo in the midst of darkness.

What kind of man Tom will turn out to be in the future can now be defined in terms of what he has become. Initially a mischievous, but inoffensive, Good Bad Boy, Tom has been transformed, in the process of attempting to adapt himself to the nebulous values of the community, not only into a full-fledged participant in respectability, but into a mirror of its shifting expectations and designs. In the absence of fixed standards of behavior and communally defined and instituted values, the process of Tom's personality development is shown to reflect the instability of his environment. He now conforms admirably to Christopher Lasch's description of a narcissist:

> Notwithstanding his occasional illusions of omnipotence, the narcissist depends on others to validate his self-esteem. He cannot live without an admiring audience. His apparent freedom from family ties and institutional constraints does not free him to stand alone or to glory in his individuality. On the contrary, it contributes to his insecurity, which he can overcome only by seeing his "grandiose self" reflected in the attentions of others, or by attaching himself to those who radiate celebrity, power, and charisma. For the narcissist, the world is a mirror, whereas the rugged individualist saw it as an empty wilderness to be shaped to his own design. (10)

In the final chapters of *Tom Sawyer*, Tom settles comfortably into his role as a respectable community member with "an abounding sense of relief and security" (220), because Injun Joe, the one individual who threatened his sensation-seeking, is now dead, and Huck, the outcast he preferred not to be seen with in public, is now, because of his wealth, also respectable. Readers may be dissatisfied with this ending, with Twain's resolution, and with Tom's invitation to Huck to do what " 'everybody does' " (234), to come and join the gang, if not the whole community. In light of the course of Tom's development, it is clear that Twain cannot be blamed for their disappointment. For those who pin their hopes to Tom Sawyer are not being "sold" by Twain, they are "selling" themselves.

Given the narcissistic character of the community and the egotistical values that govern its notions of morality, it is not surprising that Twain was reluctant to take his favorite character into the "fatal" territory of adulthood where he might ultimately have been viewed with the same horror as Hank Morgan or with the same contempt as Tom Driscoll—as just another faulty product of the "paltry human race."

Notes

1. De Voto's characterization of *Tom Sawyer* as "the supreme American idyll" (304) and Marx's reference to it as a "comic idyll of boyhood" (319) were somewhat tempered by Fiedler's observation that "violence is omnipresent" in the novel. However, Fiedler further claimed that the *"violence doesn't count,"* and he concluded "it is possible to say that *Tom Sawyer* is a fable of lost boyhood" ("Duplicitous" 243, 248). Similarly, though Marks pointed out that St. Petersburg is "dull, sterile, inhuman," he claimed that the story became "a hymn" and "a joyful affirmation as the total composition takes shape" (443). More recent critics who

note the direct relationship between *Tom Sawyer* and Twain's later works include: Towers, Feeney, and Wolff.

2.   For full discussions of the villagers' failings, see Fetterley ("Sanctioned"), Robinson, and Maik.

3.   Cox admits that Tom is a "show-off" who can't "resist the temptation to perform to an audience," but he absolves Tom of moral responsibility by claiming that Tom's reality "lies in his commitment to play" (137, 140). Blues calls Tom a "victimizer" whose "depredations are potentially destructive," but he finds no fault with Tom because "no permanent harm ever comes to those who bear the burden of his imagination" (24). Robinson concludes that Tom is "St. Petersburg's preeminent gamesman"; however, while he recognizes Tom's "intuitive mastery of the arts of deception," he relieves him of personal responsibility because Tom lacks "full self-awareness" (24). Likewise, although Fetterley refers to Tom as a "master entertainer," she concludes that "[i]n spite of the negative undercurrents of the action and structure . . . the tone of the novel is essentially genial and the character of Tom Sawyer emerges as essentially positive" ("Sanctioned" 294, 302).

4.   Wolff, who adamantly claims that Tom has "earned the right to be 'somebody,' " contends that Tom's final " 'self' " is not only a tragic capitulation "to the oddities of his environment," but a contortion into compliance of a character whose author's "vision has faltered" (651–652). Blair, who sees Tom's entrance into the adult community as a necessary accommodation to maturity, reluctantly admits that Tom has ultimately "gone over to the side of the enemy" (45).

5.   For a complete discussion of Twain's original purposes and his debate about whether to launch Tom into manhood and "the Battle of Life in many lands" or confine him to the boundaries of St. Petersburg, see Hill and Gerber.

6.   Johnson applies the Freudian term "primal narcissism" to Tom because he views him as a character whose ego is inseparably connected with the external world. It seems equally applicable here since the reciprocal relationship between village performers and village entertainers forms a bond of emotional dependence that virtually nullifies the distinction between the individual and the community.

7.   Fetterley notes that "the impulse to entertain is, not surprisingly, associated with anxiety"; however, she sees Twain's portrayal of Tom as an entertainer to be "remarkably free from anxiety" ("Mark Twain" 384, 385).

8.   Leary also observes that the story "forks into parallel lines of action," but he sees Tom's emergence from the cave as an ascension to "a more decently mature person" (422, 423).

Works Cited

Blair, Walter. "On the Structure of *Tom Sawyer*." *Modern Philology* 37 (1939): 75–88.

Blues, Thomas. "The Strategies of Compromise in Mark Twain's 'Boy Books.' " *Modern Fiction Studies* 14 (1968): 21–31.

Cox, James M. *Mark Twain: The Fate of Humor*. Princeton: Princeton University Press, 1966.

De Voto, Bernard. *Mark Twain's America*. Cambridge: Houghton, 1932.

Feeney, Joseph J., S. J. "Darkness at Morning: the Bitterness in Mark Twain's Early Novel, *Tom Sawyer*." *Mark Twain Journal* 19.3 (1979): 4–5.

Fetterley, Judith. "Mark Twain and the Anxiety of Entertainment." *The Georgia Review* 33 (1979): 382–91.

———. "The Sanctioned Rebel." *Studies in the Novel* 3 (1971): 293–304.

————. "The Sanctioned Rebel." *Studies in the Novel* 3 (1971): 293–304.

Fiedler, Leslie. "Duplicitous Mark Twain." *Commentary* 29 (1960): 239–248.

————. *No! in Thunder: Essays on Myth and Literature*. Boston: Beacon, 1960.

Gerber, John C. Introduction. *The Adventures of Tom Sawyer*. By Mark Twain. Vol. IV of *The Works of Mark Twain*. Eds. John C. Gerber, Paul Baender, and Terry Firkins. Berkeley: University of California Press, 1980.

Hill, Hamlin. "The Composition and Structure of *Tom Sawyer*." *American Literature* 32 (1961): 379–392.

Johnson, James L. *Mark Twain and the Limits of Power: Emerson's God in Ruins*. Knoxville: University of Tennessee Press, 1982.

Lasch, Christopher. *The Culture of Narcissism*. New York: Norton, 1978.

Leary, Lewis. "Tom and Huck: Innocence on Trial." *Virginia Quarterly Review* 30 (1954): 417–430.

Maik, Thomas A. "The Village in Tom Sawyer: Myth and Reality." *The Arizona Quarterly* 42 (1986): 157–164.

Marks, Barry A. "Mark Twain's Hymn of Praise." *English Journal* 48 (1959): 443–448.

Marx, Leo. *The Machine in the Garden: Technology and the Pastoral Ideal in America*. New York: Oxford, 1967.

Robinson, Forrest G. "Social Play and Bad Faith in *The Adventures of Tom Sawyer*." *Nineteenth-Century Fiction* 39 (1984): 1–24.

Towers, Tom H. " 'I Never Thought We Might Want to Come Back': Strategies of Transcendence in *Tom Sawyer*." *Modern Fiction Studies* 21 (1975–1976): 509–520.

Twain, Mark. *The Adventures of Tom Sawyer*. Berkeley: University of California Press, 1980. Vol. IV of *The Works of Mark Twain*. Eds. John C. Gerber, Paul Baender, and Terry Firkins.

————. "To William Dean Howells." 5 July 1875. Letter 82 in *Mark Twain-Howells Letters*. Eds. Henry Nash Smith and William M. Gibson. Cambridge: Harvard University Press, 1960.

Wolff, Cynthia Griffin. "*The Adventures of Tom Sawyer*: A Nightmare Vision of American Boyhood." *Massachusetts Review* 21 (1980): 637–652.

The Adventures of Tom Sawyer, Play Theory, and the Critic's Job of Work

SANFORD PINSKER

Critics shy away from belabored readings of *The Adventures of Tom Sawyer* for several understandable reasons: the denser, richer textures of *Adventures of Huckleberry Finn* loom ahead; scholarship about Twain's sources has dominated discussion of the novel; and perhaps most important of all, there is a legitimate fear that a work celebrating Play will be forever spoiled by too much heavy-handed critical "work."

Skeptical students are not the only ones who worry about these matters more than they should, who wonder if critics are not creeping up on this innocent text like net-wielders after a lovely butterfly. Perhaps it is time to admit freely that important questions lie just behind these resistances. Can deep reading and an idyll co-exist? How might the circumstances of its composition help us read the novel? What can—and should—a literary critic say about *The Adventures of Tom Sawyer*?

One tack has at least the virtue of making its appeal to what strikes most readers as lying at the very center of Twain's vision—namely, an extended investigation into, and celebration of, *play*. All one need do is add the word "theory" to the proceedings and if that "one" is a critic, he or she is in business. *Play theory* has, after all, a very with-it ring and while there are those who might object that an oxymoron has been slipped into the discussion, those who might argue that talk about "play"—especially as Twain conceived of the phenomenon—requires a dab of horse sense rather than a gob of theory, the fact is that play theory has claims on our attention that, say, theories blowing around New Haven do not.

That much said, however, several *caveats* are in order. Nothing degenerates into the meaningless more quickly than the notion that "play" is omnipresent, unless, of course, one has had some innings with those who insist that every event, from a white, middle-class male professor assigning *The Adventures of Tom Sawyer* to a sparrow's unfortunate fall, is, by definition, political. As Bruce Michelson shrewdly points out, "There are some theorists on play who claim that virtually every human act, or for that matter every

Originally published in the *Midwest Quarterly* 29 (Spring 1988): 357–65. Reprinted by permission of the publisher and the author.

cosmic event, is a gesture in some sort of grand game" (108). Such broad definitions are so broad as to be meaningless. If it is true that *everything* is a game, then it is equally true that "nothing" is a game. As Huck Finn might say, "It's enough to give you the fan-tods." It is also how the next generation of deconstructions—if there is one—will be born.

Moreover, play theory will become an exercise in the obvious if it is merely applied to those scenes that, in *The Adventures of Tom Sawyer*, come equipped with Twain's narrative commentary. For better or worse, the fence-painting episode has moved from the pages of Twain's novel to our collective unconscious. Long before we heard the term "reverse psychology" in a lecture hall, we knew how the game worked and many of us had tried our hand at substituting younger siblings for Tom's gang and dinner dishes for a fence needing whitewash. To be sure, Twain had help—from Norman Rockwell, from versions of Tom on stage and screen, from the culture at large. Readers and non-readers alike *know* about Tom and his playful scam in the same mythopoeic way that they know about Little Eva crossing the ice or about Huck and Jim floating down the Mississippi on a raft. The image is as indelible as its "moral" is self-evident. Twain, who could no more resist the itch to play Philosopher than he could the itch to engineer a Tom Sawyer-like effect, put it this way:

> [Tom Sawyer] had discovered a great law of human action, without knowing it—namely, that in order to make a man or boy covet a thing, it is only necessary to make the thing difficult to attain. If he had been a great and wise philosopher, like the writer of this book, he could now have comprehended that Work consists of whatever a body is *obliged* to do, and that Play consists of whatever a body is not obliged to do. And this would help him to understand why constructing artificial flowers or performing on a treadmill is work, while rolling tenpins or climbing Mont Blanc is only amusement. (*Tom Sawyer*, 22)

Homo Ludens (1950), Johan Huizinga's seminal study in the play element of culture, says much the same thing: "Play to order is no longer play . . . By this quality of freedom alone, play marks itself off from the natural process" (7). In this regard, Judith Fetterley makes a telling point when she compares the respective adventures of Tom Sawyer and Huckleberry Finn this way:

> One of Tom's defining characteristics in *Tom Sawyer*, succinctly dramatized in the whitewashing episode, is his capacity to convert all work into play. In *Huckleberry Finn* the process is reversed: what should be play becomes work. (72)

I shall return to other reversals in a moment, ones that speak to the shape and ring of Twain's canon, but for the moment let me concentrate on the difference between play that reigns supreme, that neither threatens nor is threatening, and play that turns cruel, turns nightmarish and, in adult hands, turns deadly. I am speaking, of course, about what makes *The Adventures of Tom Sawyer* a boy's book, one that, in George P. Elliott's wonderful phrase, turns everything—school, work, money, even sex—into a "kind of vacationing" and the darker rhythms of moral consequence that *Adventures of Huckleberry Finn* investigates. It is not so much that the Tom Sawyer of *his* book is a lovable scamp, a boy so full of life, and of devilment, that *all* of us—even the beleagured Aunt Polly—finally prefer him to the bloodless goody three shoes called Sid, but, rather, that Tom's itch for "adventure," his abiding sense of play, transmogrifies a dull St. Petersburg into a world more attractive.

In short, Tom is precisely the sort of rapscallion adults love, and secretly wish *they* could be. Today, it is the ritual of "Tom Sawyer's Gang"— complete with bone-chilling oaths, bloodcurdling screams and forbidden pleasures of smoking; tomorrow, the Moose Lodge! Put another way, Tom Sawyer livens up his sleepy Missouri town by superimposing the best, and the worst, of the Romantic tradition into its pedestrian, workaday landscape. Cervantes, Alexander Dumas, the Arabian Nights' Entertainments . . . these are the fragments Tom Sawyer has shored against his boredom.

For Tom, going by the Romantic book—what Huizinga calls the "play concept"—is an actively essentially unrelated to the getting-and-spending that comprises an adult day. Indeed, it is this boyish imagination that Twain both celebrates and allows to circumscribe the dreamy world we enter when we read *The Adventures of Tom Sawyer*. As Huizinga suggests:

> All play has its rules. They determine what "holds" in the temporary world circumscribed by play. The rules of a game are absolutely binding and allow no doubt . . . as soon as the rules are transgressed the whole play world collapses. The game is over. The umpire's whistle breaks the spell and sets "real" life going again. (11)

Adventures of Huckleberry Finn is, among other things, the umpire's whistle blown, the spell of play broken. Real life—in this case, a world where people tote guns rather than lath swords; where going by the romantic book means shooting down a defenseless drunk; where, as Huck rightly says, "People can be mighty cruel to one another"—reasserts itself in deadly earnest.

To be sure, Twain's attitudes about romance's power were as divided as his pseudonym. He could blame Walter Scott for the Civil War and take Fenimore Cooper to humorous task, but it is also true that Romanticism had an attraction he could never entirely shake. Tom Sawyer's penchant for *style*, for gathering up steam toward some grand effect, found similar expression in the public face Twain wore as lecturer, humorist, writer, world-class celebrity. Like any artist, he made what he did look easy—in his case, by yoking the playful with the preachy. The discipline, the sweat, in a word, the *work* was less obvious.

Which brings me to reversals of a different order. The arc of Twain's canon—from *The Innocents Abroad* to *Roughing It*, from *Life on the Mississippi* to *The Adventures of Tom Sawyer*—moves steadily backwards, not only in chronology, but also in a need to recapture his childhood by reimagining it. One could argue, of course, that there is playfulness aplenty in Twain's debunking of travel book pieties in *The Innocents Abroad* or in his construction of a tenderfoot-as-schlemiel persona in *Roughing It*, but the "playful" is not synonymous with *Play*. Twain is one of American literature's great counter-punchers, which is to say, he took a great delight in letting artificial, high-falutin' language swing away at airy nothingness and then in knocking it flat with a well-aimed American lick. Romantic expectations were especially good candidates for Twain's playful deflations. The Scotty Briggs of "Buck Fanshaw's Funeral" who says: "Why, pard, he's *dead*!" is but one example; there are countless others, stretching from an apprentice piece like "The Dandy Frightening the Squatter" to final ones like "Captain Stormfield's Visit to Heaven."

Play, I would argue, was another matter altogether. Huizinga argues that the nineteenth century "lost many of the play-elements so characteristic of former ages." Always the cultural anthropologist, he attributes this fact to by-products of the Industrial Revolution:

> The 19th century [Huizinga insists] seems to leave little room for play. Tendencies running directly counter to all that we mean by play have become increasingly dominant. Even in the 18th century utilitarianism, prosaic efficiency and the bourgeois ideal of social welfare—all fatal to the Baroque—had bitten deep into society. These tendencies were exacerbated by the Industrial Revolution and its conquests in the field of technology. Work and production became the ideal, and then the idol, of the age. All Europe donned the boiler-suit. (191–92)

However many "faults" Twain had—and the list of crimes, both real and imagined, was very long—being a Luddite is not among them. Like Franklin, Twain was a tinkerer, a believer in the proposition that gadgets of all kinds could make life better. Unlike Franklin, however, Twain was largely a flop—sometimes spectacularly, as in the case of the ill-fated Paige typesetting machine; sometimes modestly, as in his self-pasting scrap book (which actually turned a small profit) or the Mark Twain History Game (which did not).

In Twain's case, such dreams were fueled by the prospect of becoming rich, a condition that would allow him to pay his evermounting bills without the need either to lecture or to write. It is no small paradox, then, that lecturing and writing—both difficult, both draining, both products of dog-ged work on Twain's part—were the only activities he could finally depend on. His alternative careers—as a printer, a silver miner, a steamboat pilot, a journalist—provided material for the platform lecture and the blank page.

And with virtually each lecture, each book, Twain moved steadily backwards to Hannibal. "Old Times on the Mississippi," a series of articles that appeared originally in the *Atlantic Monthly* of 1875, is, in this sense, inextricably linked to *The Adventures of Tom Sawyer* published in the following year. Here, memory and desire mingle with History and technological advance—and always in ways that deeply divided and only settled, if indeed they are, in the making of fiction.

Not only was the prospect of becoming a steamboatman the "one permanent ambition" among Twain's boyhood friends, but it was also the one profession Twain presumably valued above all others:

> If I have seemed to love my subject [Twain remarks in *Life on the Mississippi*], it is no surprising thing, for I loved the profession far better than any I have followed since, and I took a measureless pride in it. The reason is plain; a pilot, in those days, was the only unfettered and entirely independent human being that ever lived in the earth. (37)

To be sure, the Civil War and the locomotive scotched that career long before Twain's "glory story" of how a wide-eyed cub became a sharp-eyed pilot could sink into the tedium, the *work*, if you will, of trip after trip along the same stretches of the Mississippi.

For Twain, the issue is complicated and inextricably tied to his notion of *power*. For all of Twain's relentless attacks on Romanticism—whether it comes dressed in the costumes of Walter Scott's historical romances or it stalks through imaginary forests wearing the mocassins of Fenimore Cooper—it was the grip of Romance, its sheer *power*—that held him spellbound. Bixby's hard lessons make piloting itself possible, but they come with a price tag. And we are hardly surprised when Twain, being Twain, wonders if the assets outweigh the liabilities:

> Now when I had mastered the language of this water and had come to know every trifling feature that bordered the great river as familiarly as I knew the letters of the alphabet, I had made a valuable acquisition. But I had lost something which could never be restored to me while I lived. All the grace, the beauty, the poetry had gone out of the majestic river! (*Life on the Mississippi*, 67)

Unlike the world of Tom Sawyer, where "swaps" are restricted to dead cats and hoop sticks, "acquisitions" in the adult world are fraught with compromise. Twain found it easy to wax romantically elegaic about piloting and, later, to turn downright "philosophical" about Life with a very large L, but playfulness had a way of eluding him, except as a matter of will and childhood memory.

There is more to be said about this aspect of "play" in Twain because one could argue that a "willed playfulness" is also a desperate playfulness, that behind the dream of Tom Sawyer's fantastic play lies the nightmare of Huck Finn's death-haunted life. Henri Bergson argues that "the comic comes into being just when society and the individual, freed from the worry of self-preservation, begin to regard themselves as works of art" (73). Bergson's savvy remark tells us much about, say, the Benjamin Franklin who set about the task of constructing [inventing?] his *Autobiography* and by oblique angles, about the Mark Twain who could only free himself from the worries of "self-preservation" in the guise of Tom Sawyer, and in the mode of Play. Unlike Franklin, Twain is so busy settling old scores, so consumed with self-serving, that his *Autobiography* strikes us as more "ledger" than legerdemain.

The image of unfettered freedom, of a radical independence, however, remained. One of its faces belongs to the Tom Sawyer who tests out the possibilities of Play in a sleepy, altogether conventional Protestant culture; another, of course, belongs to the Huck Finn Twain himself described as modeled on Tom Blankenship: "the only really independent person—boy or man—in the community." In a nineteenth-century world that equated progress with the boiler suit and an efficiency expert's watch, *Adventures of Tom Sawyer* is, I would submit, an extended counter-argument on behalf of liberation-as-Play. Twain, who made the cause of freedom his life's work, alternately hoped and despaired about the role that technology, that "gadgets," might play in the pursuit of that happiness he called Progress. In *A Connecticut Yankee in King Arthur's Court*, Twain tests out the possibility of armor-as-boiler suit and discovers that it will, sadly enough, not suffice. In his case, the dynamo destroys not only the Virgin—that is, the established Church, with its legacy of superstition and its abuses of power—but also the very notion of human betterment. We are left with mountains of charred bodies and bitter laughter.

By contrast, *The Adventures of Tom Sawyer* insists that play can thwart figures of adult authority—parents, preachers, teachers—and certified villains like Injun Joe. The novel not only brought Twain back to the locale, and the source, of his greatest achievements, but it also reminds us—critics and common readers alike—of what Play can be, and how important that commodity still is.

Bibliography

Bergson, Henri. "Laughter." Wylie Sypher, ed. *Comedy*, New York, 1956.
Fetterley, Judith. "Disenchantment: Tom Sawyer in *Huckleberry Finn*." PLMA, 87 (1972).
Huizinga, Johan. *Homo Ludens: A Study of the Play Element in Culture*. Boston, 1950.

Michelson, Bruce. "Huck and the Games of the World." *American Literary Realism*, XIII (1980).

Twain, Mark. *The Adventures of Tom Sawyer*. With an Afterword by George P. Elliott. New York, 1959.

———. *Life on the Mississippi*. New York, 1961.

Undoing Romance: The Contest for Narrative Authority in *The Adventures of Tom Sawyer*

HENRY B. WONHAM

While Mark Twain relished the image of an imaginative "tank" that only time could refill, his decision to pigeonhole *Tom Sawyer* repeatedly during its composition owed as much to generic confusion as to a shortage of material or inspiration.[1] Even during the productive spring of 1875, during which he rapidly brought the manuscript to a conclusion, Twain remained unsure about what kind of book he was writing, a parody of romantic expectations in the manner of "Old Times on the Mississippi" (1875) and *Roughing It* (1872), or a boyhood romance containing elements of parody.[2] When he sent a completed draft to William Dean Howells in July of that summer, he seemed convinced that the book was definitely a satire rather than a romance, for he explained that "it is *not* a boy's book, at all. It will only be read by adults. It is only written for adults."[3] Two sentences from his friend, however, were enough to effect a complete reversal of opinion. Howells considered the book an outstanding romance of boyhood adventure, and he advised Twain to temper the satirical tone in order to attract an adolescent rather than strictly an adult audience: "I think you should treat it explicitly *as* a boy's story. Grown-ups will enjoy it just as much if you do; and if you should put it forth as a study of boy character from the grown-up point of view, you'd give the wrong key to it" (*Letters*, 1:110–11).

Despite Howells's suggestions for revision, or perhaps in part because of them, Twain's indecision on the question of an audience is audible throughout the finished manuscript. Like the novel's author, the narrator of *Tom Sawyer* seems trapped between two attitudes toward his material, one detached and ironic, the other engaged and romantic, and he remains peculiarly undecided about which attitude he prefers. He is reluctant to invite suspension of disbelief from his readers, yet he remains attuned to what Twain much later in his career described as "the exigencies of romantic literature."[4] Those exigencies called for a dose of

This essay was written especially for this volumn.

heightened pathos in the aftermath of Injun Joe's death by starvation, which the narrator presents straightforwardly in language that seems ripe for a deflating rejoinder.

> The poor unfortunate had starved to death. In one place near at hand, a stalagmite had been slowly growing up from the ground for ages, builded by the water-drip from a stalactite overhead. The captive had broken off the stalagmite . . . to catch the precious drop that fell once in every three minutes with the dreary regularity of a clock-tick. . . . That drop was falling when the pyramids were new; when Troy fell; when the foundations of Rome were laid. . . . It is falling now; it will still be falling when all things shall have sunk down the afternoon of history, and the twilight of tradition, and been swallowed up in the thick night of oblivion. . . . To this day the tourist stares longest at the pathetic stone and that slow dropping water when he comes to see the wonders of McDougal's cave.[5]

There is no Mr. Brown present to interrupt the narrator's reverie with a horse sense comment, but Twain can't resist the temptation to poke fun at his own inflated rhetoric. His attempt at pathos is sincere, and the overstated images of antiquity betray no hint of irony; yet just as sincere is the ensuing satire of precisely the same brand of tear-soaked sentimentalism that the narrator has just finished expressing. Having established Injun Joe's demise within a historical context that reaches from ancient Egypt to the present, the narrator turns to the subject of a petition for Joe's pardon, and his extraordinary sympathy turns suddenly into parody:

> The petition had been largely signed; many tearful and eloquent meetings had been held, and a committee of sappy women been appointed to go into deep mourning and wail around the governor and implore him to be a merciful ass and trample his duty underfoot. Injun Joe was believed to have killed five citizens of the village, but what of that? If he had been Satan himself there would have been plenty of weaklings ready to scribble their names to a pardon-petition and drip a tear on it from their permanently impaired and leaky water-works. (240–41)

After twenty years of exploiting credulity in fools, Twain found it difficult in *Tom Sawyer* to sustain a romantic attitude without occasional lapses, and critics have traditionally focused on this apparent confusion of the narrator's attitude as the novel's principal shortcoming. Bernard De Voto's important introduction to the 1939 edition persuasively identified the generic vacillation between boyhood romance and adult parody as the book's "gravest limitation," though similar opinions had been appearing in reviews of the novel since its publication in 1876.[6] Forrest G. Robinson is the most recent critic to approach *Tom Sawyer* in terms of what he deems its author's "bad faith" in the project of romance:

Mark Twain's ironic indignation is more the product of his own self-indulgence than of superior self-knowledge or integrity. . . . As narrator of the tale Mark Twain has demonstrated a more urgent itch for melodrama than the one he condemns in the crowd. Perhaps it began to dawn on him that his scorn, if fully unleashed, would inevitably find its way back to its source. If we grant him the intimation that the angry exposure of others threatened to reveal the same fault in himself, we can begin to make sense of his hasty retreat to higher ground. For then Mark Twain's apparent return to superior detachment from village hypocrisy appears in its true colors as an uneasy truce with his own bad faith.[7]

While Robinson's verdict on the novel is harsher than most, it departs only in intensity from the traditional assumption that Twain was either unconscious of his narrator's conflicting attitudes or simply unable to control them. Yet these two narrative faces—one expressing romantic indulgence, the other common sense parody—had been providing the raw material for Mark Twain's comedy since the 1850s, and it seems unlikely that in writing *Tom Sawyer* the veteran humorist suddenly forgot how to manipulate his favorite postures. In fact, a large part of the novel's charm and complexity lies precisely in its author's ability to juxtapose the attitude of the romancer against that of the straight-faced yarn spinner in a subtle competition for narrative authority. That competition is reflected in part through the narrator's tendency to undercut his own inflated sentimentalism, though an even fiercer contest of attitudes occurs between the narrator and the novel's other principal spokesman, Tom Sawyer. In his role as an amateur storyteller and showman, Tom indirectly deflates the narrator's purple prose with a subtler brand of the same poison that Mr. Brown employs with his verbal jibes at the romantic "Mr. Twain" in the author's Sandwich Island letters. It is certain, as Robinson and others have objected, that Tom's knack for undermining the narrator's style effectively prevents Twain from arriving at the kind of consistency of perspective that might constitute "good faith," yet it is largely this lack of consistency and symmetry that makes *The Adventures of Tom Sawyer* the challenging novel that it is.[8]

Because the narrator frequently sneers at the excessive sentimentalism of his characters—often immediately after having indulged in a soppy reverie of his own—his attitude toward the story remains difficult to pin down. One constant feature of his performance, however, is the perfect omniscience with which he observes the life of St. Petersburg. His descriptions appear to be drawn from a great distance, and the terrific scope of his perspective is constantly reflected in a diction that smacks of the picturesque mode Twain had parodied effectively in *The Innocents Abroad* (1869) and many other writings. In the narrator's vision, Jackson's Island becomes a self-contained fictional world whose remoteness from the limiting conditions of reality suggests a parallel with Cooper's Lake Otsego and other classic settings of

American romance. "It was the cool gray dawn, and there was a delicious sense of repose and peace in the deep pervading calm and silence of the woods. Not a leaf stirred; not a sound protruded upon great Nature's meditation. Beaded dew-drops stood upon the leaves and grasses. A white layer of ashes covered the fire, and a thin blue breath of smoke rose straight into the air" (106). Twain's already fabulous reputation as a humorist in 1876 rested largely upon his ability to construct such picturesque scenes by impersonating a naively romantic perspective. The punchline usually arrived with a sudden interruption or re-vision by some more experienced character, an "old timer," whose understated realism chastens the deluded romantic and explodes the illusion.[9] But the corrective explosion that might alter the narrator's image of Jackson's Island never occurs in *Tom Sawyer*. There is significantly no interruption when the narrator indulges in the sort of scene-painting that Twain knew so effectively how to ridicule. Instead, the novel's official narrator invites his reader to enter an imaginary world by conforming to its laws, ignoring for the time being, as A. C. Bradley puts it, "the beliefs, aims, and particular conditions which belong to you in the other world of reality."[10]

Within the self-contained fictional world created by the narrator, however, there exist other voices, one of which constantly challenges the narrator's creative endeavor by describing the same scenes and adventures according to very different narrative principles. The reader learns in chapter 1—where Tom returns from a day of hooky "in time to tell his adventures to Jim"— that Tom Sawyer's love of play is inseparably linked to his gift for narration (3). He and Joe Harper obtain "glittering notoriety" in St. Petersburg, for example, not by performing feats of heroism on Jackson's Island, but by narrating exaggerated heroics to the credulous folks at home: "They began to tell their adventures to hungry listeners—but they only began; it was not a thing likely to have an end, with imaginations like theirs to furnish material" (138). Tom's hungry listeners are the citizens of St. Petersburg, and their eagerness to suspend disbelief encourages Tom to stretch the facts every time he describes his escapades. Hence, while the reader experiences the adventure in McDougal's cave as an adolescent love story, reported from the narrator's omniscient perspective, the novel's inside audience receives a very different version of the same events, one for which perfect suspension of disbelief is a dangerous enterprise: "Tom lay upon a sofa with an eager auditory about him and told the history of the wonderful adventure, putting in many striking additions to adorn it withal . . ." (234). Even among friends Tom can't resist embellishing the facts. After his midnight visit to town from the hideout on Jackson's Island, Tom "recounted (and adorned) his adventures" for his comrades, Huck and Joe (118). Virtually every adventure in the novel receives such double treatment, being first presented as romance by the narrator to the reader, and second narrated as an oral tale by Tom, "with striking additions to adorn it withal," to a living audience.

Tom's propensity for storytelling is really the narrative extension of what James M. Cox has called his "commitment to play," and, like Tom's games, his stories embellish and transform the narrator's world.[11] Thus the woods surrounding St. Petersburg alternately become Sherwood Forest or the Spanish Main according to Tom's, not the narrator's, intentions, and while those imaginary settings are borrowed from literary romance, under Tom's creative authority they never masquerade as anything but play. Whereas the narrator depends upon the illusion generated by his fictional setting, Tom's imaginary landscapes invite suspension of disbelief only from his naive victims, whose mistaken credulity ironically mirrors the reader's own imaginative investment in the project of romance. Tom's pirate and Indian games are romances tinged with enough consciousness of their own fictionality that the boys can shift instantaneously from one game to another when boredom threatens to destroy the fun (127). When members of the gang shout elaborate nautical orders at one another in order to enhance the sense that their raft is actually an oceangoing pirate vessel, the narrator comments that "it was no doubt understood that these orders were given only for 'style,' and were not intended to mean anything in particular" (101).[12]

Similarly, Tom's embellished retelling of events in the novel is a form of game-playing, and his stories, like his games, are a conscious transformation of the narrator's romance rather than a rival romance. In effect, Tom's stories are tall tales that he performs within the narrator's fictional context, not for the reader's entertainment exactly, but for the benefit of *his* audience, the population of St. Petersburg. And while a portion of that audience consists of wide-eyed "innocents" whose fate is to be "slaughtered" by Tom's fabrications, most of its members recognize his role as a yarn spinner and expect him to perform it well (15). Aunt Polly, for example, frequently plays the victim, admitting at one point that "old fools is the biggest fools," yet even in that capacity she is an enthusiastic participant in the interpretive game that surrounds each of Tom's narrative performances (2). She expects him to embellish the truth and does her best to "trap him into damaging revealments" whenever she can (3). When Tom passes up the opportunity to gild the facts, as in his first encounter with the school master, St. Petersburg is confused and disappointed (53).

Tom Sawyer's peculiar brand of creativity provided Twain with a tentative solution to a problem he had been writing about without attempting to solve for many years. His extensive training in burlesque during the 1850s and 1860s had taught him the useful lesson that romance and the tall tale are irreconcilable forms, better suited for humorous contrast than for compromise. The two genres presuppose in their respective audiences such entirely different attitudes toward the enterprise of storytelling that combinations of tall tale and romance, like the ill-fated *Occidental* novel in chapter 51 of *Roughing It*, are bound to create confusion, and Twain was an expert at exploiting the humor of such confusion without risking it himself.[13] He gave the dilemma its most articulate expression in "Old Times on the Mississippi," where the cub laments his loss of romantic appreciation once he has acquired a pilot's ability to discern danger beneath the surface appearance of the river. The same knowledge that qualifies the cub as a cultural insider and member of the yarn-spinning pilot house community disqualifies him from enjoying romantic illusions about the river. One can either appreciate the reality—and with it the tale that mocks reality—or one can appreciate the illusion in all its picturesque splendor, but never both at the same time, for one perspective cancels out the other.

In *Tom Sawyer* Twain manages to sustain both perspectives at once by establishing two separate audiences, each of which approaches the story with very different expectations, and Twain is careful to ensure that the interpretive efforts of one group reflect ironically upon those of the other. Thus while the narrator seems perfectly reasonable in soliciting his reader's confidence in a romantic picture of the river—that "vast vague sweep of the star-gemmed water" (102), which in daylight becomes "the shallow limpid water of the white sand-bar" (107)—Tom is simultaneously engaged in "slaughtering" those members of *his* audience, the citizens of St. Petersburg, who buy into his tales with the reader's degree of romantic indulgence. The demands made upon the two audiences—the narrator's readers and Tom's listeners—are completely different, so that interpretive success in one case amounts to failure in the other, and vice versa. In essence, Tom and the narrator are one more formulation of the Mr. Brown/Mr.Twain character axis, with the crucial difference that here the two antagonists never confront one another directly.[15] Tom's creative adorning of the story's "facts" is more a subtle jibe than a direct rebuke of the narrator's creative endeavor, yet the persistent struggle for narrative authority suggests a stark, if unstable, contrast of approaches to storytelling. Even the most romantically inclined reader is aware that Tom mercilessly exploits precisely the kind of voluntary credulity that the narrator expects from *his* audience.

This is not to suggest that the novel's readers are victimized for their willingness to experience the novel on the narrator's terms, as a romance. On the contrary, it is the subtlety with which Twain sustains the conflict of styles and interpretive assumptions that signals an important departure from the narrative method of "Old Times" and *Roughing It*. The narrator of *Tom Sawyer* begs for the reader's suspension of disbelief, but Tom's counter-performance constantly reflects upon the narrator's creative project by warning against a response that even approaches total anesthetization. Moreover, the effect of Tom's exaggerated retelling of the narrator's story is to make the novel less a romantic tale than what might be called a conditional romance, for through Tom the novel relentlessly parodies its own demands for imaginative investment from the reader. Unlike the *Occidental* episode in *Roughing It*, in which the tall tale's deflating wit utterly confounds the authors of a popular romance, here Tom's habit of elaborate storytelling provides an ironic counterbalance to the narrator's performance without explicitly discrediting or burlesquing that performance. In effect the tall tale, as Tom Sawyer's natural idiom, becomes a means of engaging the debate over narrative authority in a novel that manages to be a romantic adventure without committing itself to the assumptions endorsed and defended by its romantically inclined narrator.

While Tom never explicitly critiques the narrator's performance, his "spectacles" repeatedly serve to expose the sham of quality of the narrator's brand of inflated rhetoric.[16] He frequently subverts the performances of rival speakers whose eloquence or affected passion commands the respect, but not the interest, of the St. Petersburg audience. Mr. Walters, the Sunday school superintendent, is only the first of several pious and upright orators in the novel to adopt an artificially elevated style for official occasions: "Mr. Walters was very earnest of mien, and very sincere and honest of heart; and he held sacred things and places in such reverence, and so separated them from worldly matters, that unconsciously to himself his Sunday-school voice had acquired a peculiar intonation which was wholly absent on week-days" (32). Mr. Walters's style of Sunday dress, like the "peculiar intonation" of his speech, "unconsciously" confuses reverence and respectability with affectation: "His boot toes were turned sharply up, in the fashion of the day, like runners—an effect patiently and laboriously produced by the young men by sitting with their toes pressed against a wall for hours together" (32).

When Tom trades his fish hooks for Sunday school tickets, he is of course expressing a similar concern about style and "effects," for it is "the glory and eclat" associated with earning a Bible, rather than the Bible itself, that he covets (31). Unlike Mr. Walters, however, Tom deludes neither himself nor his audience with false pretenses toward humility, and when he takes center stage to receive his prize he is entirely conscious of the sensation he hopes to produce. Judge Thatcher's insistence that Tom should name Christ's first two disciples places the hero in a difficult predicament, but it also gives him the opportunity to disrupt Mr. Walters's laboriously choreographed performance with a climax that is more appropriate to Tom's style. If he answers correctly or names the wrong two apostles, Tom will have contributed to the Superintendent's sham spectacle by further falsifying the game without exposing its hypocrisy. When he finally shouts "DAVID AND GOLIAH!" to the expectant audience, however, he reveals that not only his own performance but the entire event is inspired by vanity and sustained through careful affectation. Just as Tom frequently challenges the narrator's authority by retelling the story of his adventures according to a yarn spinner's rather than a romancer's method, here he has stolen the stage from Walters by pushing an unacknowledged fiction to the limit of absurdity. Tom's pride and naughtiness are finally no different from Walters's artificial piety except in that, like a yarn spinner, Tom plays to an inside audience, one that tastes before it swallows, and he therefore makes no effort to conceal the nature of his performance from those who can appreciate it.

The narrator draws "the curtain of charity over the rest of the scene" before it becomes clear how Tom's audience will react to his absurd rejoinder, but in general St. Petersburg is relieved and appreciative when he interrupts the course of conventional oratory (36). Judith Fetterley has called Tom a "sanctioned rebel," noting that the community actually demands his irreverence "because it provides excitement and release, and because the ultimate assimilation of the rebellion constitutes a powerful affirmation of their values."[17] St. Petersburg is indeed a captive audience for the novel's official windbags, and while its citizens sneer at behavior not sanctioned by officialdom's platitudes, they are starved for diversion and regard Tom, without admitting it, as their deliverer. At the church service that follows Sunday school, Tom's boredom extends to the entire St. Petersburg audience, and his antidote to ennui simultaneously cripples the sermon and inspires a communal spirit of laughter among the congregation. The narrator pays special attention to the minister's "peculiar style" of oratory, which, like Mr. Walters's "Sunday-school voice," exhibits its own studied affectation:

> His voice began on a medium key and climbed steadily up till it reached a certain point, where it bore with strong emphasis upon the topmost word and then plunged down as if from a spring-board. . . . The minister gave out his text and droned along so monotonously through an argument that was so prosy that many a head by and by began to nod—and yet it was an argument that dealt in limitless fire and brimstone and thinned the predestined elect down to a company so small as to be hardly worth saving. (39–40)

When Tom releases his pinch-bug and disrupts Mr. Sprague's sermon, he creates a spectacle that draws the sleepy and fragmented audience together into a true congregation. The victim in this episode is neither religion, nor piety, nor even Sprague himself, but an unnatural style of speaking that has earned the minister a great reputation while adding nothing to the spiritual life of the community. The minister's ornate and seemingly passionate style, like Mr. Walters's "peculiar intonation," is part of a grand cultural delusion against which, according to Satan in "The Chronicle of Young Satan," the human race possesses "unquestionably one really effective weapon—laughter."[18] Tom's counter-performance, like his retelling of the narrator's story, undermines Sprague's affected fire and brimstone by unleashing an "unholy mirth" of which Satan himself would have approved (43).

In his address at the funeral service for Tom, Huck, and Joe, the minister relies more on sentimental than apocalyptic hyperbole, and this time his presentation more successfully exploits the congregation's hunger for sensationalism. The eulogy is fraught with fictions that the audience willingly accepts because they enhance the entertainment value of the performance. The episode functions almost like a commentary on the reader's own interpretive endeavor, for what is at stake is the validity of suspension of disbelief as response to narrative invention.

> As the service proceeded, the clergyman drew such pictures of the graces, the winning ways and the rare promise of the lost lads, that every soul there, thinking he recognized these pictures, felt a pang in remembering that he had persistently blinded himself to them, always before, and had as persistently seen only faults and flaws in the poor boys. . . . The congregation became more and more moved, as the pathetic tale went on, till at last the whole company broke down and joined the weeping mourners in a chorus of anguished sobs, the preacher himself giving way to his feelings, and crying in the pulpit. (131)

The minister fails to realize until too late that his "pathetic tale" is predicated upon a larger fiction, one that invites suspension of disbelief only in order to mock those credulous enough to offer it. Despite the persuasiveness of Sprague's embellished "pictures," Tom again steals center stage—and again in the manner of a yarn spinner—by exposing the congregation's inflated sentimentality for what it really is. As the boys make their triumphant entrance into the church, the " 'sold' congregation" unites in appreciation of the joke, admitting that "they would almost be willing to be made ridiculous again to hear Old Hundred sung like that once more" (131–32). Tom's performance at the funeral does not involve an actual tall tale (only later does he embellish the story of his adventures on the island), yet he successfully orchestrates a tall tale situation by playing upon the credulous expectations of his audience. Two kinds of fiction—the minister's sentimental hyperbole and Tom's pretended death—come directly into conflict, and the game triumphs by exposing the sham.

Tom's most successful subversion of the novel's several official rhetorics occurs at the "Examination Evening" ceremony, where the village school-children are enlisted to entertain their parents and friends with literary and oratorical performances. Tom has been selected to deliver "the unquenchable, indestructible 'Give me liberty or give me death' speech," and he approaches the stage full of his usual vanity and confidence (155). But Tom's rhetoric of adornment and exaggeration, the rhetoric of the tall tale, is useless on this stage, and he is seized with a fit of anxiety that leaves him uncharacteristically speechless. Members of the audience offer a "weak attempt at applause" but quickly forget their disappointment when the next several orators deliver a series of "declamatory gems" (156). The evening's star performers are the young ladies who read from "original 'compositions' " on such subjects as "Memories of Other Days," "Religion in History," and "Dream Land," always applying an appropriately "laboured attention to 'expression' and 'punctuation.' " The narrator comments that: "A prevalent feature in these compositions was a nursed and petted melancholy; another was a wasteful and opulent gush of "fine language"; another was a tendency to lug in by the ears particularly prized words and phrases until they were worn entirely out; and a peculiarity that conspicuously marked and marred them was the inveterate and intolerable sermon that wagged its crippled tail at the end of each and every one of them" (156).

The narrator's opinion of "the glaring insincerity of these sermons" is explicit enough, though it is difficult finally to see in what way his own "fine language," which he never hesitates to invoke, differs from that of the young ladies. His eulogy for Injun Joe—"Did this drop fall patiently during five thousand years to be ready for this flitting human insect's need?"—might easily bear one of the saccharine titles that he satirizes above (240). Despite his condescension toward the fluffy poetics of the "Examination Evening," the narrator is responsible for having transformed the Mississippi River into "the vast vague sweep of the star-gemmed water," and Tom's miserable failure to imitate passion during his recital therefore signals an important difference between his own and the narrator's creative abilities and intentions. The narrator practices a different art from that of his hero, and the contrast between their two approaches to language and narrative emerges in large part through the narrator's frequent, though apparently inadvertent, commentary on his own style.

Having suffered humiliation on what might be called the narrator's stage of conventional literary performance, Tom fares more gallantly in his own element. The boys stage a performance of their own when they contrive to remove the teacher's wig and expose his gilded pate to the delighted audience (160). Just as in an earlier scene Tom's mischief "crippled" Mr. Sprague's fire and brimstone sermon, he and his friends successfully deflate the evening's "fine language" through an act of interruption and exposure, the two principal gestures that define Tom's relation to the rest of St. Petersburg. The prank functions like a tall tale in its insistence that illusions, both linguistic and cosmetic, are to be laughed at rather than soberly revered as substitutes for truth; and, as in church, laughter proves more effective than either the teacher's or the narrator's loftiest eloquence at uniting the community behind a common sentiment. The yarn spinner—unlike the romancer, the pedant, the Sunday school superintendent, or the minister— invites suspension of disbelief only from his naive victims, and his triumph occurs through a humorous affirmation of reality that takes place, to the delight of all St. Petersburg, upon the teacher's embarrassed face and across his blazing skull.

Tom's performance resembles the teacher's own ostentatious display in that it is motivated by vanity, but the two performers differ significantly in their choice of tactics. Forrest Robinson has suggested that "St. Petersburg society is a complex fabric of lies," in which "Tom is exceptional only in the sheer quantity of his showing off" (Robinson, 26). Indeed, Tom encounters formidable competition in his bid to remain the town's center of attention, not least from Aunt Polly, who reveals on page 1 that Tom's obsession with "effects" may have a genetic explanation: "The old lady pulled her spectacles down and looked over them . . . they were her state pair, the pride of her heart, and were built for 'style,' not service" (1). As Robinson suggests, the rest of adult St. Petersburg seems equally driven by a desire to occupy the spotlight. Judge Thatcher's presence at the Sunday school presentation inspires such excitement that the preening becomes virtually epidemic:

> Mr. Walters fell to "showing off," with all sorts of official bustlings and activities. . . . The librarian "showed off"—running hither and thither with his arms full of books. . . . The young lady teachers "showed off"—bending sweetly over pupils that were lately being boxed. . . . The young gentlemen teachers "showed off" with small scoldings. . . . The little girls "showed off" in various ways, and the little boys "showed off" with such diligence that the air was thick with paper wads and the murmur of scufflings. And above it all the great man sat and beamed a majestic judicial smile . . . for he was "showing off" too. (33–34)

Despite such stiff competition, Tom consistently distinguishes himself as the town's leading attention-getter, *not* because he shows off more but because he shows off differently from the rest of St. Petersburg.[19] Tom has a yarn spinner's gift of self-consciousness, and when he creates an "effect," he does so without losing sight of the reality from which his performance departs. Unlike Mr. Walters, who mistakes his Sabbath day affectations for sincere piety, Tom refuses to be sold by his own or his society's fictions. Aboard the raft with Huck and Joe Harper, he knows that his piratical orders are "not intended to mean anything in particular" (101). Similarly, his public "spectacles" are staged to produce a sensation, but they invariably do so by exposing rather than perpetuating the town's pet hypocrisies. As Fetterley suggests, Tom's frequent adornment of the truth, his "rebellion" from the behavior sanctioned by society's platitudes, finally constitutes "a powerful affirmation" of the community's underlying commitment to unpretentious common sense (Fetterley, 301). St. Petersburg rallies around Tom not because he is a more persistent or effective master of affectation than either Walters or Sprague, but because he is a gamesman and yarn spinner who is capable of entertaining the community with a self-conscious fiction, a fiction that reaffirms rather than obscures reality through the process of narrative embellishment.

The unstable discrepancy between Tom's self-conscious style of performance and the narrator's brand of literary romance undoubtedly complicates the reader's task in reconstructing the novel's meaning, yet it is only in terms of this reconstructive endeavor that Twain's dexterity can be fully appreciated. There persists throughout the novel a "tension," to use Wolfgang Iser's term, between the role the narrator asks us to play and the role we naturally wish to adopt as culturally attuned members of Tom's, as opposed to the narrator's, audience.[20] As so many critics have noticed, this tension becomes a source of confusion in the novel, yet by placing different interpretive demands upon Tom's as opposed to the narrator's readers, Twain manages to coordinate an ingenious compromise between literary romance and the tall tale. In effect, he indulges in the narration of a romantic story that begs for the reader's unqualified suspension of belief while at the same time mocking his narrator's request. The novel is a romance with an escape hatch, an engaging story of courtship and adventure whose yarn-spinning hero continually laughs at the very interpretive conventions its narrator appears to take for granted.[21]

Twain remained susceptible throughout his career to what Henry Nash Smith has called "infection from 'wildcat literature,' " though he found it difficult to commit himself entirely to a form of storytelling that makes facile demands upon the reader's confidence (Smith, 82). What Twain primarily rejected, as his essays on Cooper's literary offenses much later made clear, was not romantic fiction itself, but the excesses of certain romancers, namely those like Emerson Bennett—a favorite target—who regarded the reader's suspension of disbelief as an automatic response, something given rather than something earned. In *The Adventures of Tom Sawyer*, the tall tale provided Twain with a counter-fiction that operates as a corrective to romantic indulgence without entirely invalidating the project of romantic narration itself. James M. Cox has called Tom Sawyer's character "an index to Mark Twain's inability to 'believe' in conventional fiction," and indeed one of the hero's primary tasks in the novel is to subvert the sham language and behavior that both he and Twain associate with insipid romantic indulgence (Cox, 148). The yarn-spinning hero's explicit targets are easily identified and defeated, though his most formidable challenge comes indirectly from the narrator himself. Tom's subversive tactics—his knack for timely interruption and ability to adorn the narrator's story according to his own creative impulse— allow Twain to question the method of his novel as he writes it.

Notes

1. Samuel Clemens, *Mark Twain in Eruption*, ed. Bernard De Voto (New York: Harper, 1922), 197. Walter Blair's chapter on *The Adventures of Tom Sawyer* in *Mark Twain and Huck Finn* (Berkeley: University of California Press, 1960) thoroughly examines the chronology of the novel's composition, though some minor points of Blair's analysis have been challenged by Charles A. Norton, *Writing Tom Sawyer: The Adventures of a Classic* (Jefferson, N. C.: McFarland, 1983), 8.

2. I use the term "romance" less as a strict generic category than as a general tag for the large body of "wildcat" adventure fiction that Twain often derisively labeled "romantic." When he used the term to attack writers like Emerson Bennett, Twain had in mind the kind

of narrative that makes unreasonably excessive demands upon the reader's willingness to suspend disbelief. Celebrated definitions of the American "romance" novel by such authorities as Henry James, Nathaniel Hawthorne, and Richard Chase, therefore, are not directly relevant to the term as it is being used in the context of this essay.

3. Henry Nash Smith, William M. Gibson, eds., *Mark Twain–Howells Letters: The Correspondence of Samuel L. Clemens and William D. Howells, 1872–1910*, 2 vols. (Cambridge: Harvard University Press, 1960), 1:91; hereafter cited as *Letters*.

4. Samuel Clemens, *The Autobiography of Mark Twain*, ed. Charles Neider (New York: Harper, 1959), 74. M. H. Abrams argues very reasonably that no author expects or even desires total suspension of disbelief from his or her audience. My point in this article is not to contradict Abrams but to show that Twain's profound ambivalence toward the interpretive demands that characterize literary romance caused him to modify his narrative strategy in *Tom Sawyer* in several interesting ways. See M. H. Abrams, "Belief and Suspension of Disbelief," *Belief in Literature*, ed. M. H. Abrams (New York: Columbia University Press, 1958), 17; hereafter cited as Abrams.

5. Samuel Clemens, *The Adventures of Tom Sawyer*, eds. Paul Baender, John C. Gerber (1876; Berkeley: University of California Press, 1980), 239; hereafter referred to parenthetically within the text.

6. Bernard De Voto, *Mark Twain at Work* (Cambridge, Mass.: Harvard University Press, 1942), 18–19.

7. Forrest G. Robinson, *In Bad Faith: The Dynamics of Deception in Mark Twain's America* (Cambridge, Mass.: Harvard University Press, 1986), 50; hereafter cited as Robinson.

8. Walter Slatoff has argued that a narrator's struggle for consistency, even when it ultimately fails, ought not to be counted automatically as a strike against the work. The confusion that besets the narrator's performance in a poem like *Paradise Lost* or in a novel like *The Trial* can enhance the reader's experience, according to Slatoff, by suggesting that a human consciousness is actually struggling with deeply conflicting feelings. He explains that "the contradictory emphases and vague or ambiguous rhetorical fumblings seem not so much flaws as evidences of the severity of the struggle." *With Respect to Readers* (Ithaca, N.Y.: Cornell University Press, 1970), 129–31. I find Slatoff's comment particularly relevant to the incessant discussion of "flaws" in *Tom Sawyer*.

9. See Henry Nash Smith, *Mark Twain: The Development of a Writer* (Cambridge, Mass.: Harvard University Press, 1962), especially chs. 1, 3, and 4; hereafter cited as Smith.

10. A. C. Bradley, quoted in Abrams, 8.

11. James M. Cox, *Mark Twain: The Fate of Humor* (Princeton, N.J.: Princeton University Press, 1966), 140; hereafter cited as Cox.

12. Alan Gribben argues persuasively for Tom's ability to manipulate the materials he extracts from literary romance in "How Tom Sawyer Played Robin Hood 'by the Book,' " *English Language Notes* 13 (March 1976): 201–204.

13. Samuel Clemens, *Roughing It*, eds. Paul Baender, Franklin R. Rogers (1872; Berkeley: University of California Press, 1972), 325–36.

14. Samuel Clemens, "Old Times on the Mississippi," *The Atlantic Monthly* 35 (Jan.–July 1875): 288–89. Perhaps the best discussion of this famous passage is by Leo Marx, "The Pilot and the Passenger: Landscape Conventions and the Style of *Huckleberry Finn*," *American Literature* 28 (May 1956): 129–46.

15. Everett Emerson's *The Authentic Mark Twain* (Philadelphia: University of Pennsylvania Press, 1984) is the most recent major study of the "voice" that links Twain's early writings, including his Twain/Brown newspaper correspondence, to his later work as a novelist.

16. It is interesting that the sequel to *Tom Sawyer* begins with Huckleberry Finn's explicit critique of the earlier narrator's performance. See *Adventures of Huckleberry Finn*, eds. Walter Blair, Victor Fischer (1885; Berkeley: University of California Press, 1985), 1.

17.   Judith Fetterley, "The Sanctioned Rebel," *Studies in the Novel* 3 (1971): 293–304; hereafter cited as Fetterley.

18.   Samuel Clemens, *Mark Twain's Mysterious Stranger Manuscripts*, ed. William M. Gibson (Berkeley: University of California Press, 1969) 165.

19.   For a more extensive consideration of Tom's role as a showman, see Sargent Bush, Jr., "The Showman as Hero in Mark Twain's Fiction," in *American Humor: Essays Presented to John C. Gerber*, ed. O. M. Brack (Scottsdale, Ariz.: Arete, 1977), 79–98.

20.   Wolfgang Iser, *The Act of Reading* (Baltimore: Johns Hopkins University Press, 1980), 37. Iser discusses this phenomenon in his section on "Readers and the Concept of the Implied Reader," 27–38.

21.   A New Critical obsession with organic unity in literary works has dominated Mark Twain criticism generally during the last forty years, and its legacy survives in repeated attempts to explain Twain's "failure" to achieve coherent form in any of his novels. George Toles, for example, identifies essentially the same formal confusion in *Pudd'nhead Wilson* that De Voto and Robinson describe in *Tom Sawyer*. Toles argues of the latter novel that "the form of closure Twain adopted could not resolve the many 'voices' that are intermittently heard in *Pudd'nhead Wilson* into one, unified voice" (56). Only recently have certain critics begun to appreciate that much of Mark Twain's power as a novelist lies precisely in this "failure" to "resolve the many 'voices' " of his fiction into a unified and authoritative voice. Twain achieves some of his greatest effects, in *Tom Sawyer* and elsewhere, by dramatizing the interplay of competing discourses, often destabilizing a dominant voice in order to renegotiate its claims to authority. See George E. Toles, "Mark Twain and *Pudd'nhead Wilson*: A House Divided," *Novel* 16 (Fall 1982): 55–75; M. M. Bakhtin, *The Dialogic Imagination*, ed. Michael Holquist, trans. Caryl Emerson and Michael Holquist (Austin: University of Texas Press, 1981); for recent approaches to Twain's fiction that agree with my own outlook on this question of unity, or lack thereof, see David R. Sewell, *Mark Twain's Languages: Discourse, Dialogue, and Linguistic Variety* (Berkeley: University of California Press, 1987); Maria Ornella Marotti, *The Duplicating Imagination: Twain and the Twain Papers* (University Park, Penn.: Pennsylvania State University Press, 1990).

Index